SANDS OF SORROW

November 1991

To Fran — (Herb Jacobs)

with best wishes, & hopes for peace.

[signature]

Sands of Sorrow

ISRAEL'S JOURNEY FROM INDEPENDENCE

Milton Viorst

1817

HARPER & ROW, PUBLISHERS, New York
Cambridge, Philadelphia, San Francisco, Washington
London, Mexico City, São Paulo, Singapore, Sydney

To Simcha Flapan, Tahsin Bashir, the late Emil Grunzweig, the late Fawd Kawasmeh, and to the others in Israel and the Arab world who have given of themselves, some with their lives, for peace

Copyright acknowledgments follow the index.

SANDS OF SORROW. Copyright © 1987 by Milton Viorst. All rights reserved. Printed in the United States of America. No part of this book may be used or reproduced in any manner whatsoever without written permission except in the case of brief quotations embodied in critical articles and reviews. For information address Harper & Row, Publishers, Inc., 10 East 53rd Street, New York, N.Y. 10022. Published simultaneously in Canada by Fitzhenry & Whiteside Limited, Toronto.

FIRST EDITION

Designer: Sidney Feinberg
Copyeditor: Marjorie Horvitz
Indexer: Auralie Logan
Maps by George Colbert

Library of Congress Cataloging-in-Publication Data

Viorst, Milton.
  Sands of sorrow.

  Bibliography: p.
  Includes index.
  1. Israel—History. 2. Jewish-Arab relations—1949– . 3. United States—Foreign relations—Israel. 4. Israel—Foreign relations—United States. 5. United States—Foreign relations— 1945– . I. Title.
DS126.5.V54 1987   956.94'05   86-45705
ISBN 0-06-015707-0

87 88 89 90 91 HC 10 9 8 7 6 5 4 3 2 1

Contents

MAPS

Acknowledgments

It is not easy to remember all the people who generously contributed their time and wisdom over the years to help me understand the Arab-Israeli conflict. In addition to those from whose interviews I have quoted, I would thank particularly Aharon Amir, Tamar Avidar, Shlomo Avineri, Nahum Barnea, Liora Barash, Shaul Ben-Haim, Meron Benvenisti, Ido Dissentshik, Hagai Eshed, Amos Ettinger, Simcha Flapan, Willi Gafni, Ora Namir, Meir Pail, Dan Pattir, Avi Pazner, Matti Peled, Anan Safadi, Israel Stockman and Mordechai Virshubski. Israelis, they are my friends, though they may not subscribe to all I have written. I recall also the agreeable hours spent in Israel learning from fellow American journalists William Claiborne, the late William Farrell, Lawrence Meyer, Jonathan Randal, Trudy Rubin and Douglas Watson, and from American diplomats, especially Irwin Rubenstein and Daniel Kurtzer. I want to thank the Alicia Patterson Foundation for the grant that enabled me to begin this study and Danielle Hunebelle for assignments that permitted me to continue it. I feel special gratitude to the good friends who read and criticized the manuscript: Leonard Beerman, Jack Heller, Sharon Russell, Merle Thorpe, Patrick Quinlan, Michael Zigmond, and my editor at Harper & Row, Ted Solotaroff. I thank my wife, Judy, and my sons, Anthony, Nicholas and Alexander, for cheerfully tolerating my long journeys abroad. If you have noticed the absence of Arab names from this list, it is because I plan to pursue this study and to write a companion volume on the Arab world in the context of the Middle East conflict. In it, I will express the deep appreciation I feel. I have learned much from Arabs too.

1

Entering Zion Gate

THIS BOOK IS PART JOURNALISM, part historical and political commentary, part personal odyssey. Journalism has been my craft, history and politics have been my field throughout most of my adult life. The odyssey began even earlier, and it is not over yet.

It began more than a half century ago, in an American Jewish home, which was not particularly religious but where, as a matter of course, I was taught to drop pennies into a *pushka* to help the Jews returning to Palestine. It was, in that sense, like all the other Jewish homes I knew. I was then only vaguely aware of Hitler as the incarnation of evil, and the Holocaust had not yet happened. But being only a generation away from Poland, and constantly reminded of my good fortune to be in America, I naturally acquired a sense of solidarity with those Jews seeking to escape to a better life. It never occurred to me that I might *not* be a Zionist, committed to the return of the Jews to the land of their forefathers, to make a country of their own.

I believed then that Zionism would do no one harm, and in looking back at the statements of the early Zionists, it is clear that is what they, too, believed. Zionist doctrine at the time held that Palestine was "a land without people for a people without land." I was surely not among those who challenged that assertion. Of course, I rejoiced in being part of the people who made the desert bloom, who built hospitals and universities in the wilderness, who created and defended free institutions, and who in 1948 founded the state of Israel.

So it is a source of dismay to me that Zionism, whose justice I considered self-evident, has in many circles become a term of opprobrium. Zionism has become identified with territorial expansion, with religious zealotry, with military oppression, with political intolerance. I resist those definitions. Having held stubbornly to the rightness of the ingathering of the Jews and of their living in peace and freedom in a place of their own, I believe as strongly as ever that Zionism is a noble concept. Within the framework of that conviction, I call myself a Zionist today.

Like every Jew in my circle of friends, like every member of the worldwide community of Jews, I exulted in Israel's victory in 1967. It was a triumph that made us all feel better about ourselves. We stopped having to apologize for being weak, for being dependent, for being Jews. We were winners at last, after two thousand years of losing, and whatever concerns about Israel I have since acquired, that feeling of joy has remained.

Yet, in retrospect, it is clear the Six-Day War transformed Israel in ways that went far beyond the military consequences. I was not alone in sensing, within a few years, that something had gone amiss. Zionism, having been rescued from prospective annihilation, appeared to have wandered into a moral desert, the practical result of which was to leave Israel not safer but more imperiled. I perceived that a basic political change was taking place, one I wanted to understand. These were days when I was raising three sons, and thinking more about my Jewish heritage. Since my work of many years was to examine the dynamics of politics, I was drawn professionally as well as personally to the study of what was happening in the Middle East.

I make this point because many Jews in our time believe that on issues relating to Israel there must be no study, that the Jewish people must speak in one voice, that no virtue supersedes solidarity. Jews whom I respect, Jews whom I love, Jews with power and

Jews without, Jews who regard free speech and critical inquiry as among mankind's highest values, have tacitly taken an oath to waive the right of dissent from the policies of the state of Israel. By temperament and training, I could not adopt that attitude. It seemed to me more appropriate—more loyal, if I may say so—not to remain silent at all but to shout for everyone to hear, if I had a foreboding that Israel was embarked on a perilous journey.

In the course of preparing this work, I have reflected much on the attitude of American Jews to Israel, and on my place among them. I understand better than I did before how their aversion to internal dissent is largely the reflex of a people that has so long felt itself besieged by the outside world. Though, among ourselves, we Jews have historically been a contentious lot, our instinct in facing the outside world is to stick together. To understand that response, however, is not to accept it as being in Israel's best interests. Silence, in my judgment, does a greater disservice to Israel's future than dissent. I note, neither defensively nor defiantly, that my message largely departs from the Jewish consensus. This book is where my odyssey has taken me.

This book is an inquiry into the Arab-Israeli struggle. It is as truthful as I know how to make it, but I do not pretend that it is detached from ideological bias. The bias holds that peace is good for the Jews, good for the Arabs, a contention that recent history has shown to be strangely controversial. Indeed, there are certain segments of Jewry that thrive on the conflict, just as there are those who take satisfaction in the belief that the distance between the two sides is unbridgeable. The premise of this book is that the Arab-Israeli conflict, passionate though it may be, is not irresolvable at all, and that reasonable men and women can close the differences between the parties. Unfortunately, reasonable men and women remain in short supply.

Arabs and Jews both have interests that are to them eminently legitimate. It is these interests—and not a confrontation of good and evil, as partisans would have us believe—that define the Middle East conflict. Both sides would quite willingly make peace, each on its own terms. I am reminded that during the 1960s, anti-Vietnam activists liked to quote Tacitus—"Where they make a desert, they call it peace"—to describe one way to end a war. Were we to ask history's most committed warmongers—even a Hitler or a Genghis Khan—they would no doubt answer that they would forgo war, on the condition that they could attain their goals without it. The question facing the Middle East is not which side wants peace and which does not, but what compromises both will make to attain it.

Observers, partisan or detached, have probably not appreciated enough how difficult it is for Israel and the Arab world, both of them societies still groping for identity, to build a framework of peace. Centuries of colonialism, during which neither Arabs nor Jews controlled their destiny, were just coming to an end when the battles between them began. As they grappled with each other, they were simultaneously transforming the Middle East from a collection of colonies into a region of sovereign nations, for the building of which they had no blueprints. It would be historically unprecedented for a transformation so profound to take place without severe disruption. If this book stops to examine the transformation at a moment in an evolving process, let us remember that the disruptions are part of the search for an equilibrium in the new political era.

By now, some forty years after the departure of the colonial powers, it is apparent that neither Israel nor the Arab world is strong enough to impose peace alone. Neither can "make a desert," much less a stable society of nations. Not alone. The late Israeli soldier-politician Moshe Dayan, speaking of the Egyptian fortress seized by Israel in 1967, used to say he would rather have "Sharm el Sheikh without peace than peace without Sharm el Sheikh," but he later changed his mind. Dominant as its army is in the region, Israel cannot force peace on one hundred million Arabs. Numerous as they are, the Arabs have failed repeatedly to crush Israel. What peace requires is that each give up something it considers important, without demanding in return something that the other cannot live without.

In the two decades after Israel's War of Independence, the two sides had few concessions to offer each other in the interest of peace. The 1948 war had left an asymmetry, in which Israel wanted Arab recognition of its sovereignty but had nothing to offer that the Arabs would take in return. The position of the Arabs was that they would have no Israel at all.

The Six-Day War gave a new balance to the relationship. Israel, in capturing the West Bank from Jordan and the Gaza Strip from Egypt, not only extended its borders to the entirety of historical Palestine but went on to seize Egypt's Sinai Desert and Syria's Golan Heights. Its acquisition of a commodity that the Arabs wanted gave birth to the principle of "territory for peace" as the basis for a political settlement. Each now had something the other coveted. But, at the same time, Israel's victory was so enormous that it created asymmetries of its own, providing an avenue to peace but, at the same time, erecting huge barriers which, to this day, stand in peace's way.

I was not among those who recognized early that the victory, by its overwhelming nature, contained seeds of sorrow. Indeed, the euphoria I shared with other Jews seemed vindicated in the half-dozen years that followed, which in retrospect could be called Israel's Golden Age. At home, there was prosperity. On the borders, the enemy's armies were at bay. Terrorism was in retreat. Immigration and financial contributions from abroad were at record levels. Moreover, the United States, the greatest of the superpowers, had become Israel's patron, providing a plentiful supply of modern weapons for its armed forces. By any available measure, Israel's place in the world seemed secure.

In those years, the goal proclaimed by the early Zionists—a Jewish state that was "normal" like other states—appeared at hand. Relieved of the burden of national jeopardy, of the rigors which for so long had been intrinsic to Zionism, Israelis turned inward, to private concerns. The proud motto of the early immigrants—"The way of a pioneer is hard; if it isn't hard, make it hard"—suddenly sounded naive. Though some Israelis lamented the decline of challenge, and many were made uneasy by the pervasive quest for wealth, it was hard to quarrel with the society's feeling of well-being. This feeling produced a consensus that Israel had no better course to follow in dealing with its neighbors than to preserve the status quo.

In that period of my life, I wrote chiefly about American politics, both domestic and international. As a columnist for the *Washington Star,* I traveled more or less where I liked, and at least once a year I visited Israel. Being there recalled to me the years I had spent growing up in my Jewish enclave in America, but this was a whole Jewish world run by Jews. I felt at home in it.

At that time, the other world—the world of the Arabs—remained foreign and forbidding. I had yet to see any part of it. When Nasser, Egypt's demagogic president, died in 1970 he was replaced by a less menacing leader named Sadat, but otherwise nothing had changed. At least, that was what the Israelis told me, and I deferred to their understanding of the region. I also endorsed the conventional American position that the Israeli army, the most powerful military force in the region, was watching out for American interests in the struggle against the Communists. My view of the politics of the Middle East was not much more sophisticated, or well informed, than that.

Still, by the early 1970s, I was troubled by what I was beginning to observe in my visits to Israel. The sense of well-being that had made life so pleasant had evolved into insularity, and few Israelis had noticed the change. Israelis had become so condescending about the Arabs' war-making capacity that they did not bother examining whether the Arabs might be preparing to win back what they had lost. It was considered certain they could not. In retrospect, I surely saw only the top of the dune when, in February of 1972, I wrote about Israel's complacency in the *Star.* The report, I think, conveys my apprehension that something in the Jewish state was not right.

KIBBUTZ GENNOSAR, Israel—"Right after the Six-Day War in 1967," our driver said, when en route to this beautiful settlement on the Sea of Galilee, "Israelis crowded the West Bank every weekend. The traffic jams were terrible.

"They were rushing to see the Jewish shrines from which the Jordan government had kept them since 1948. I remember one lady who visited Hebron eight times in the first few months, and the Old City of Jerusalem even more often. They said they were rushing to visit before we gave them back.

"Well, they don't go there so much any more. They come up here to the Galilee, where it's quiet and lovely. None of them think any longer that we're going to give those places back to the Arabs."

Indeed, a feeling of permanence has settled over Israel—and the country seems more relaxed than I have ever seen it. People still talk about negotiations, because they want peace. But any settlement likely to be negotiated—if a negotiated settlement is imaginable at all—cannot possibly be as good as what Israelis have now.

For the peace they have now is more peaceful than anything they have had in the brief quarter-century of Israel's history—and they're not disposed to return to anything like the more precarious one which existed before June 1967.

Take, for instance, the situation here in Gennosar, one of the dozens of kibbutzim in the Galilee. Here is the heart of the kibbutz movement, where young Jews from Europe first began cultivating the land. All of the Galilee, until the Six-Day War, lay within easy range of Syrian guns on the neighboring Golan Heights. . . .

Today, the only threat to life comes from the Al-Fatah terrorists—and it seems almost theoretical. The guerilla movement has largely disintegrated in the Arab countries and the remaining bands have been stymied by Israeli security measures on the borders.

Now the children of Gennosar sleep above ground and play on the shore of the lake. The kibbutzniks till their fields in relative security and, every weekend, tourists from Tel-Aviv and Haifa come to swim or to picnic in the woods.

They all know, at night, that the lights which flicker on the sides of the Golan and at its summit are not Syrian artillerymen. The lights are from the new settlements which Israelis have founded since the war. . . .

Indeed, there is peace in Israel—and, as never before, security seems part of the Israeli psyche, inherent to the Israeli way of life, a comfort to the Israeli soul.

To be sure, security is a delusion—as it has always been in the Middle East. Just over the horizon in Cairo, President Sadat continues to make menacing speeches. To say that Israelis dismiss his words would not be quite true.

But security is also relative and, thanks to the victories of 1967, the enemy's armies are not at the doorstep of Israel but beyond the Sinai Desert, the Jordan River and the Golan Heights.

Four years ago, the lady who visited Hebron again and again was— like Israelis generally—reconciled to the return of most of the territories won in the war. Today she is not.

The years that have passed without a peace agreement have been too peaceful. There is little inclination in Israel to change that now.

I recall a tiny incident that occurred in 1971, when my wife joined me for her first visit to Israel. As we left the Church of the Holy Sepulchre in Jerusalem's Old City, she looked around at the throng of tourists, mostly Christian, and asked our guide, a keenly intelligent Israeli who spoke English with a slight East European accent, whether she was expected to leave a donation for a candle. "Darling," he answered, in the familiar manner Israeli guides tend to adopt, "you're not expected to do anything you don't want. This is Israel. We don't care here what the *goyim* think." The remark conveyed the fierce pride Israelis felt in the new Jewish state, and in the liberation it embodied from centuries of subservience to the Gentiles.

Yet, looking back, I believe it also conveyed a loss of perspective common to Israelis. In their celebration of Jewish emancipation, Israelis have tended to dismiss Jefferson's admonition to maintain a decent respect for the opinions of mankind. Jews, who take pride in no longer having to be fearful and servile in dealing with anyone, have created a social structure which demands that Arabs be fearful and servile in dealing with them. They often sneer at criticism of this arrangement, maintaining that they need take reproaches from no one. No longer distressed at the slurs of their enemies, they have not learned to value the well-meaning judgment of their friends. Quite apart from whether this reaction is good for the Arabs, I do not think it is good for the Jews.

Similarly, in creating a powerful army, Israel has freed the Jews of the age-old torment of impotence, imparting to them a sense of mastery over their future. But in doing so, it has failed to grasp the limits of what armed might can achieve. It behaves as if it need not deal with the West Bank and the Gaza Strip as political problems. It relies on guns, so unfamiliar in the Jewish past and so suddenly acquired, to solve problems that are only peripherally military, or not military at all.

After the Six-Day War, Israel persuaded itself that, given the shift in the strategic balance in the Middle East, there was advantage only to the Arabs in reaching an overall peace settlement. It looked upon victory as a substitute for rather than an avenue to peace. Defense Minister Dayan, Israel's chief strategist, summed up the official attitude after the war with the taunt that Israel was "waiting for the phone to ring." Israelis misled themselves by taking the victory to mean that the basic issues of the conflict, if not resolved, had somehow been permanently buried. Meanwhile, the Arabs, too stunned to grasp the significance of their defeat, were also too humiliated to accept it. Israel was convinced the spoils of victory had made the state secure, while the Arabs were sure they could avoid the price of defeat by rejecting the give-and-take of a negotiated settlement.

From every perspective, the temptations to Israel of the status quo were irresistible. Having won decisively on the battlefield, Israelis regarded themselves as morally justified in making the enemy come to them. Politically, it was the path of least resistance for them to sit tight rather than provoke the outrage of powerful forces opposed to giving up any of the captured territory. Strategically, Israelis felt safer than they had ever been, with their armies in control of the Sinai, the West Bank and the Golan Heights. And yet they were nervous.

The paradox of Israel's victory in the Six-Day War is that the territories that were occupied became more a burden than a bulwark of the nation's security. Extending and defending borders is a conventional way for states to safeguard their people. But since 1967, Israel has fought three costly wars—the War of Attrition in 1970, the Yom Kippur War in 1973, and the Lebanon war in 1982 —to defend its distant borders, and none of these wars was a response to a threat to the state itself or to the people.

A look at some figures raises serious questions about whether a better way than permanent military occupation of Arab territories could not have been found to provide Israel with the protection it needs.

- Within a decade of the Six-Day War, Israel had more than two and a half times as many men permanently under arms as it did in 1966 (65,000 in 1966; 178,000 in 1976).

- Within the same time span, Israel's ratio of defense spending to gross national product grew from about the same as that of the United States to a level six times higher (in 1966, U.S. 8.4 percent, Israel 8.7 percent; in 1976, U.S. 5.4 percent, Israel 30.7 percent).

- In dollar terms, during this period, Israel's defense budget grew sixfold and, by 1980, more than sevenfold ($616 million in 1966; $3.7 billion in 1976; $4.5 billion in 1980).

- The length of conscripted service for Israeli men rose after the Six-Day War from 26 to 36 months, and for Israeli women from 20 to 24 months. In addition to conscripted service, Israeli men can now expect by age 54 to have served 28 months on reserve duty. In economic terms, it is estimated that the military's use of manpower diminishes Israel's gross national product by 13 percent annually.

The number of lives lost in the wars fought since the victory has been even more painful for Israel. Some 500 died in the ruinous War of Attrition, sometimes called Israel's forgotten war, waged from 1967 intermittently until 1970 from stationary emplacements along the Suez Canal. In the Yom Kippur War, fought against Egypt in the Sinai and Syria on the Golan Heights, an estimated 2,250 Israelis died. It was the sobering experience of this war, conveying the lesson of vulnerability, that brought Israel's Golden Age to an abrupt end.

All the losses that Israel has endured since 1967, furthermore, are not measurable in terms of lives and money. Militarization, social schism, foreign occupation and international dependency have incalculably damaged the values on which Israel was founded, if they have not altogether shattered the Zionist dream.

• Over the course of two decades, Jews have ruled over a foreign people for the first time in modern history. Assuming a burden both unfamiliar and uncomfortable in the context of the Jewish experience, Israel has not done it well. Governing the West Bank and the Gaza Strip has not only brought constant conflict with 1.2 million Arabs but provoked bitter ideological quarrels within Israel itself, badly shredding the nation's social fabric. It has led inexorably to Israel's being seen abroad, by friends as well as enemies, as an oppressor state.

• Israel's huge financial obligations for arms, notwithstanding generous American subsidies, have sapped the country's economic system. They have depressed the standard of living, discouraged immigration and encouraged emigration, and forced deep reductions in educational and social programs. They have also made Israel a permanent client of the United States. To finance its occupation of the territories, Israel has placed a heavy mortgage on the Zionist vision of Jewish self-reliance and independence.

Israel's invasion of Lebanon in 1982 must also be regarded as a fruit of the occupation. It was the product of a mistaken theory that military dominance could make political difficulties disappear. Its planners contended that Palestinian resistance to Israeli rule in the West Bank and the Gaza Strip could be brought to an end by eliminating the structure of the Palestine Liberation Organization in Lebanon. The invasion was a surrender to the temptations of military power.

Ironically, the passive role of occupiers had taken the edge off the fighting efficiency of Israel's army. Three years of low-level combat in Lebanon, furthermore, shifted the attitude of the average Israeli soldier from saving the state to getting out alive. The Israeli army had never performed more poorly. The outcome of the war was widely recognized as a military disaster.

The war's human costs were horrendous. It imposed a huge toll in blood (650 dead, 3,800 wounded) and resources (nearly $4 billion, according to standard estimates). It accelerated the erosion of Israel's reputation in the international community. It undermined the confidence of Israelis in their army. It added an array of new enemies in Lebanon, while leaving intact the old ones in the West Bank and the Gaza Strip. Though it succeeded in wrecking the PLO's political organization in Lebanon, the invasion had no impact on the Palestinians' political power. The Lebanese war, if anything, encouraged a new wave of anti-Israeli terrorism, both inside and outside the occupied lands.

David Ben-Gurion, father of Israeli independence, took a strong position on what to do about the occupied territories. Visionary though he was, Ben-Gurion was also tough-minded and practical, with little patience for fanaticism. If he had a motto, it was "Don't overreach." Ben-Gurion did not reject compromise by mistaking it for sellout, or wear ideology as a straitjacket. He knew when to stand firm and when to retreat. Though he cherished the concept of Jewish borders that touched the Mediterranean and the Jordan River, he foresaw the dangers of occupation. Shortly before he died in 1973, Ben-Gurion said:

> Never forget that *historically* this country belongs to two races—the Arabs of Palestine and the Jews of the world. . . . The logic of all this is that to get peace, we must return in principle to the pre-1967 borders. . . . So when I consider the future of Israel, I only consider the country before the Six-Day War. We should return all gains except . . . East Jerusalem for history and the Golan for security—and considering the strength of Arab sentiment, some degree of accommodation will be necessary even here. As for Sinai, Gaza, the West Bank—let them go. Peace is more important than real estate.

In looking back on the two decades that have passed since the Six-Day War, it is evident that Israel, having won all the battles, has lost the peace. The victory of 1967 set off a chain reaction which transformed the nation's character. Ignoring Ben-Gurion's admonition to remember that the land belonged to two peoples, Israel shifted its preoccupation from construction of the Jewish state to preservation of its conquests. Zionism, a humane set of values which for nearly a century had inspired the dream of a Jewish homeland, itself took on a new flavor, which was more aggressive, less generous, increasingly nationalistic. If the recompense for these losses was greater security, one might perhaps defend the transaction. But as the end of the 1980s approached, with the Middle East still in ferment, Israel's state never appeared more precarious.

Yet, for all that was negative, I would argue that there was also much that was positive among the consequences of the Six-Day War. I am not philosophically a pacifist, and I recognize, though perhaps reluctantly, that wars sometimes resolve problems on which peaceful deliberations founder. There were issues in the conflict between Israel and the Arabs which were so severe that the battlefield may have been the only place where they could have been put to a test. I would scarcely argue that the war settled them all. It even aggravated some. But, in my judgment, it also narrowed the gap in at least one vital area of contention. The effect was to enhance the *prospect*—though the realization has been much slower in coming—of Middle East stability.

The war was the last concerted effort of the Arab nations to destroy the Jewish state. When the battle was over, the Arabs looked at the debris of their military might lying in the sand and understood that it meant the conclusion of an era. Slow as they may have been to seize upon the lesson, they did not deceive themselves into a denial of their defeat. The war had confirmed a major shift in the equilibrium of power between Arabs and Jews. Less obvious but no less important, it transformed the collective Arab psyche.

I have no doubt the Arabs were convinced prior to 1967 that the imminent destruction of Israel was foreordained. Some Arab apologists would have us believe otherwise, that the Arab aim was somehow more innocent. They are rewriting history, to correspond with post-1967 realities. The Arab dogma that the Jewish state was a passing phenomenon was left tottering in 1948; it was transformed by defeat in the Six-Day War. The succeeding wars —the War of Attrition and the Yom Kippur War—were, however bloody, fought for limited political gains. Whatever the Arabs' dreams, I do not believe that, as a practical matter, they have entertained the notion of eliminating Israel since their armies were swept from the battlefield two decades ago.

I recognize, of course, that Israel's military power has been a barrier to Arab ambitions, but it is only part of the explanation for the change since 1967. I would not for a moment contend that the Arabs became more favorably disposed toward Israel. If anything, the continued occupation of the territory lost in the war exacerbated Arab grievances. Yet, in decisive fashion, the war ended one era and began another in the political evolution of the Middle East. The consequence, in my judgment, is that the Arabs will not, at least in our time, try to destroy Israel again.

In explaining why I think that is so, let me begin with an observation that what is loosely referred to as the "Middle East conflict" is, in reality, three conflicts wrapped into one.

First, there is a *Zionist-Palestinian* component, which started early in the current century as a struggle within Palestine over the possession of the land, between Jews imbued with the doctrine of return and the native Arab inhabitants.

The next component, consisting of *Israel versus the Arab states,* began in 1948, when the Zionist-Palestinian conflict was subsumed by a classic war among nations. This component matched Israel, the newly founded Jewish state, against the Arab nations, themselves freshly liberated from colonialism. The issue was not a Jewish presence in the Middle East, since Jews had always lived among Arabs. At stake was the establishment of a Jewish *sovereignty* in a region the Arabs considered theirs.

The third component, the last to join, was the *superpower rivalry* that has raged around the globe since the end of World War II. Conventionally designated "the cold war," it did not reach the Middle East, however, until the mid-1950s. Since then, the superpowers have manipulated and been manipulated by Arab and Jewish interests, with each of the participants promoting its own goals. Among friends as well as enemies, tangles of relationships have emerged, often indecipherable, though on close examination these tangles usually reveal a peculiar organization of their own.

The Six-Day War did nothing to settle the first of these conflicts, known in diplomatic circles since 1948 as the "Palestinian problem." In fact, in installing Israeli rule over areas highly populated by Arabs, the outcome of the war aggravated matters. Partition had kept Jews and Arabs apart, eliminating friction, in the decades that followed Israeli independence. But after 1967, occupation exposed Palestinians to Israelis relentlessly, shortening tempers, inflaming nationalism. Israel's military occupation carried the Zionist-Palestinian struggle to the marketplaces, the schools, the roads, where it became more pedestrian, bloodier, more personal.

Nor did the war have a significant impact on the third component of the conflict, the superpower rivalry. Without doubt, the outcome sharpened the confrontation, by eliciting from both the United States and the Soviet Union a strong commitment to impose a new shape on Arab-Israeli relations, more congenial to their own global interests. Still, the superpowers were engaged in confrontation in so many regions of the world that, by itself, the Six-Day War probably made little difference in the cold war.

Where the Six-Day War produced a transformation was in the second of the three contests, the struggle between Middle East nations. War is the means by which peoples have throughout history established their right to territory, and in modern times, to nationhood. I suspect that making war for this purpose may be a brutal law of nature, no less applicable to the current age, however civilized we think it is. A people's nationhood may be conceived by its philosophers, popularized by its journalists, structured by its academicians, proclaimed by its statesmen, but the pattern of evidence suggests that a nation must be forged in battle. History's sad lesson, I believe, is that a people affirms its right to live as a nation only by sending its sons to die to defend the ground it claims as its patrimony.

In this sense, Israel's *declaration* of independence in 1948—the climax of two millennia of messianic dreaming, a century of Zionist organizing, a decade of preparation by the Jewish settlers in Palestine—was no more than a scrap of paper. When a majority of delegates at the United Nations voted to found the Jewish state, most Jews were indignant that the Arabs rejected it coldly. But the Arabs were indignant too, at the United Nations' audacity in giving away *their* land. They saw the U.N. at that moment as a conspiracy of the old colonial powers, remaking the map of the Middle East by proclamation. Examined calmly in retrospect, theirs was a quite understandable response—we might even call it "normal"—to what they saw as outright theft.

The Arabs, who had themselves waited so long for their freedom, were not prepared to give up Palestine, either in part or in whole. They saw the Israeli claim as, indisputably, a *casus belli.* As the laws of nature go, the Arabs were challenging the Jews to show on the battlefield just how committed they were to their new nation. The Jews met the challenge, affirming in war the claim to independence asserted in their declaration.

The Arabs repeated the challenge in 1967, and in the Six-Day War Israel completed its response. Its victory made it a full participant in the *reality* of the Middle East. Respectfully, grudgingly, the Arabs acknowledged the ferocity with which Israel fought. They had blamed their defeat in 1948 on their disarray, and in the Sinai campaign of 1956 they persuaded themselves it was not Israel but their old colonial masters, Britain and France, who had returned to the Middle East, seeking to reenslave them. In 1967, however, they had themselves picked the fight and were as ready for battle as they ever were likely to be. Nonetheless, their armies were devastated. In winning, Israel established its legitimacy in the Middle East region.

I choose the word "legitimacy" deliberately, conscious that it is a crucial concept in the life of nations. It is not an easy term to define. Diplomatic recognition is not enough to convey legitimacy, any more than is membership in the United Nations. Although legal elements are involved, legitimacy is a concept with qualities that are near-mystical. It has to do with people, with their ties to the land and with the sacrifices they are willing to make to live together as a nation. The Six-Day War provided the evidence that the Jews who had chosen Palestine were deadly serious about their choice.

The war required the Arabs to face the fact, once and for all, that Israel was not a paper nation. It made clear that the Arabs were deceiving only themselves in dismissing it as an artificial creation of retreating empires, the fantasy of geopoliticians or geographers. Israel's citizens, having drawn on the history, religion and social tradition they shared to make a nation, had now established decisively that they could and would do whatever was needed to be done to defend it. The diplomatic elements of legitimation could come later, as an embellishment. Defeat in the war forced the Arab spirit to come to terms with Israel. In creating a new reality in the Middle East, Israel's victory established its legitimacy.

The Arabs acknowledged as much, though sullenly. Before, they had talked confidently of Israel's destruction, as if it were simply a matter of finding the right occasion. In 1967, having found the occasion, they watched their forces being decimated. After the war was over, the talk shifted to the negotiation of boundaries. The shift, to be sure, originated as a diplomatic tactic within the framework of the bargaining to undo the consequences of defeat. But gradually, the concept of boundaries was absorbed into the Arab mentality, along with the sense of the existence of Israel itself.

Among the tragedies of the Six-Day War for both sides was Israel's choice not to offer, or even to explore, incentives to hasten the transformation of the Middle East. The eye it kept on the Arabs focused on retribution, not reconciliation. I am not suggesting that an equitable settlement was available to Israel for the taking, especially at the start. But while the Arabs were far from generous in what they offered, Israelis—as we shall see in greater detail later in this book—showed no disposition to negotiate at all. They declared they would not submit to an "imposed" peace, which was understandable enough, but they had no peace program of their own. Guided by decades of Arab intransigence, loaded with the baggage of persecution, Israel rejected accommodation with its former enemies. One can acknowledge that its attitude was human, and still lament the heavy cost.

I made my first visit to Egypt early in 1974, shortly after the cease-fire that halted the Yom Kippur War. Egypt and Israel were involved in "disengagement talks" to separate two armies still locked in disarray on the battlefields flanking the Suez Canal. In the air was an unfamiliar scent of hope, faint but exciting, for an end to warfare. I would return many times to the Arab world, but never again would I experience quite so much excitement of discovery, or perceive quite the same buoyant sense of promise, as during those first days I spent in Cairo.

My mentor in Egypt was a warm, round-faced intellectual named Tahsin Bashir, an assistant to President Sadat, who was assigned to introduce unschooled correspondents like me to the complexities of the Arabs. Bashir educated a generation of Western journalists who passed through Cairo. If he should properly be called a PR man, he gave a special dignity to the term. Indulgent of my ignorance, generous with his insights, Bashir told me much about the Arabs over cups of half-sweet Turkish coffee that he and I drank together, sometimes late into the night. In looking back on what has since happened in the Middle East, I do not think he misled me.

During my visit to Egypt, I filed the following report to the *Star:*

CAIRO—If we applied to Egypt the cynical French adage that "the more things change, the more they remain the same," we would dismiss Anwar Sadat as unimportant, his de-Nasserization program as a hoax—and peace as an illusion.

Indeed, everyone asks, "Is Sadat for real?" The Israelis, conditioned by four wars and 25 years of bellicose Arab bombast, find it hard to believe that Egypt is now governed by a man who genuinely wants to change the course of affairs in the Middle East.

I, too, came to Egypt very skeptical. I've now talked to dozens of people—officials giving me the government line, non-officials echoing the ideas in the air. The conclusion I've reached, correctly or not, is that Sadat *is* trying to turn aside the spirit of war which Arab propagandists inflamed for so long—and that his desire for peace is real.

"Sadat has broken the cycle," Tahsin Bashir said to me in his ornate but shabby office in the presidential palace. Bashir, a man of wide-ranging and supple intellect, is the authorized interpreter of Sadat's thought.

"He has broken with the absolutist mentality of the Arab world. He understands that, as a practical matter, the Arabs cannot destroy Israel, any more than Israel can destroy the Arabs. I believe the mainstream of Arab thought is now groping for something like this.

"Sadat is a very different man from Nasser. Nasser was a dreamer, who had within him both greatness and its own undoing. When he ruled, Egypt was half-asleep, half-awake, like an early morning reverie.

"In the minds of the people, the Nassers never fail. Rather, they are betrayed, while the dream lingers on. Nasser succeeded, as long as the dream remained intact. Now Sadat has taken the Arabs from dream to reality."

Bashir makes no claim that Sadat will be able to stir the masses with appeals to reason and moderation, the way Nasser did with appeals to emotion. On the contrary, a leader who demands realistic thinking of his people must himself come forth with real attainments.

Prior to Egypt's crossing of the Suez Canal last October, Sadat was in serious political trouble. Unwilling to intoxicate Egyptians with dreams, he was unable to satisfy them with discernible achievement.

"Sadat put his neck on the line in October," Bashir said. "First he gambled on crossing the canal, and won. Then he announced he wanted to talk peace with Israel. He knows there are ultra-bellicose Arabs who would have him fail, just as there are Israelis who would have him fail, too.

"But Sadat wants to persuade the moderates—both in Israel and in the Arab countries—that now is the time to abandon old myths and clichés. His problem is that he does not have Nasser's capacity to evoke sympathy in defeat. He must continually succeed, or he's finished."

Israelis who read Sadat carefully will find in his message a hint of extortion. "Cooperate with me," Sadat is saying, "because if I fail, those who step over me will be much tougher for you to deal with." Extortion it may be, but nonetheless true.

Bashir pointed out to me that Egypt's cadre of trained professionals, in both the liberal and the technical arts, are a significant political asset. "The other Arabs may have limitless amounts of money," he said, "but they need Egypt. We have the training, the culture and the stability. We are recognized for the leadership we can provide."

But, he warned, if the momentum Sadat acquired in the October war is arrested, then old-fashioned Arab absolutism is likely to regain its pre-eminence.

"If the Arabs progress along practical lines," Bashir said, "in twenty years Israel will be a forgotten problem. If Sadat fails, we may lose ten or twenty or who-knows-how-many years before someone will try such a course again.

"We are now at a turning point. Sadat would like green fields, creative schools, productive factories—instead of shifting sands."

The danger is that if Israelis continue to act as if nothing has changed in Egypt, their conviction will become a self-fulfilling prophecy.

In rereading what I wrote from Cairo more than a decade ago, I find Bashir to have been remarkably prescient. I also see, in retrospect, that he was signaling a change which was not limited to Egypt. Sadat was blazing a trail for the Arab world. He was saying that Egypt had had enough of war with Israel, and wanted to get on with the challenges of economic and social development. Vilified as Sadat was during his later years, I believe that most of the Arab world has since adopted his priorities. On Israel's part, there was surely no duty to be gullible about Sadat's message, but there was a duty—if only to itself—to *explore* whether it held out new prospects for peace.

I remember, on my return to Washington, trying to convey some of the excitement of the visit to an Israeli friend who occupied a high post in the diplomatic corps. When I said I thought

Sadat's terms deserved attention, he scoffed, and the response I received from acquaintances within the American-Jewish "establishment" was much the same. It troubled me to find that the ideas circulating in the enemy camp which were to me a fresh and promising revelation were proof to them that I had been duped.

The Cairo trip was an important stop in my personal odyssey. After that, I often visited each of the states on Israel's periphery —Egypt, Syria, Jordan, Lebanon—and nearly all of the more distant Arab countries too. I talked in palaces and apartments, in newsrooms and government offices and college classrooms, in restaurants and taxis and markets, in military posts and refugee camps. In none of them did I make a secret of the fact that I was Jewish, or that I fully endorsed Israel's sovereign status. For a journalist, it is easier, of course, to work in Israel, where institutions are free and access is available to mountains of information. Nonetheless, I was always received courteously among the Arabs, and invited to ask whatever questions I liked.

I did not believe all the answers I heard, but that is hardly a caveat, for its application goes well beyond Arabs. The journalist's task is to weigh answers and try to distill from them a measure of truth. I am certain one of the factors prolonging the Arab-Israeli struggle is the inability of journalists on both sides to cross the barrier to arrive at their own truths. The consequence of isolation is that each side lives with stereotypes frozen in time, perpetuating mutual antagonisms, inflating mistrust. I will not claim that familiarity would breed affection between Arabs and Jews. But I think it is important, nonetheless, for them to hear for themselves some of the things that I have heard, and draw their own conclusions. The answers I received became my raw material. I believe it gives me an advantage over those who have had to reach judgments about the Middle East without addressing any questions to the other side at all.

I am speaking particularly of those Israelis—and they may be a majority—who are convinced that Arabs reject totally the idea of living at peace with a sovereign Jewish state. I stipulate that, twenty years ago, this view of the Arabs was true. But to hold the view today, *without reexamination,* is to assume that history stands still. It takes for granted that Arabs, faithful to old fantasies, have no regard for self-interest. It assumes an immunity to the influence of time, of suffering and war, of economics and education and technology, of the passing of generations. In fact, among some Arabs such immunity exists. But I am persuaded that Arabs collectively—including Palestinians—have decided to live with Israel, not because they want to but because they understand they have no other practical alternative.

I am reminded of an interview I had in 1986 in a Gulf state with an Arab fundamentalist leader, who told me that Islam could never make peace with Israel. "The Jewish people can live among us as they always have," he said, "but we are against a Zionist state." Then he stopped and sat quietly for several minutes. "Can I speak off the record?" he said finally. I replied that he could, which is why I cannot identify him. "That's my public position. But the Arab people needs peace and stability to develop, and we cannot make war with Israel anymore. My private position is that we ought to make peace at once."

I tell the story as an interesting variation on a persistent theme. Most Israelis, while proclaiming their own dedication to peace, seem determined to believe the Arabs will have none of it. I am reminded of a 1986 cartoon by Ya'acov Kirschen ("Dry Bones") in the *Jerusalem Post,* in which an everyday Israeli, abandoning himself to the dream of peace, muses, "Somehow the skies have turned blue overnight. . . . Somehow we're on a yellow brick road again. . . . I feel like the weight of pessimism has been lifted from my heart. . . . Sigh! . . . And somehow it makes me feel a little nervous." The prospect of peace makes many Israelis so nervous, in fact, that they dismiss as disloyal all assertions that the Arabs have any interest in peace at all.

How do we account for that? One explanation is that societies normally prefer the status quo, even when it is painful, to leaping into the unknown. Israelis long ago made an adjustment to permanent tension. But is it more than that? Another explanation is that by blaming the Arabs, Israelis relieve themselves of responsibility for the absence of peace. But the dread seems to go beyond even these explanations. At some level of consciousness, Israelis know peace will require them to contemplate tough questions that the state of war has enabled them to avoid. The questions have to do with defining Israel itself.

The aspirations of the early Zionists appeared modest. They wanted a homeland, where Jews could live together and in peace. Though they took for granted their right to settle in Palestine, they talked little of a state, in part out of fear of upsetting the Arabs. Too moral to do evil deliberately, the Zionist pioneers wanted to believe the two peoples could inhabit the land in harmony. They confronted the prospect of having to fight for the land only after the Turks left in 1918, when title appeared to be up for grabs. It was then that Jewish and Arab claims assumed a stridency which has characterized them ever since.

In the War of Independence in 1948, Ben-Gurion chose not to send Israel's victorious army as far as the Jordan River, in the hope that the Palestinians would be content to share a partitioned state. They were not, and the struggle continued. Then, in 1967, Jewish stridency surged forward, as Ben-Gurion's rather measured conception of Zionism came under assault by more extravagant notions. Some Jews found evidence in history, others in religion, both declaring it was Jewish destiny to create a state throughout all of Biblical Israel. If historical imperative was not enough, there was God's commandment to justify taking over the land. This goal erased all distinction between Israel as a modern nation-state and Eretz Yisrael as a historical-religious ideal. It shrugged off Ben-Gurion's assertion that Palestine belonged to two peoples to share. The concept of the state as identical to the Judaic ideal implied that giving back as much as a stone to the Arabs, even for the sake of peace, would delegitimize the title.

I am reminded of the painful story of the Palestinian Arab who journeyed from the West Bank to pay a nostalgic visit to his former home in Haifa, from which his family had fled during Israel's War of Independence. The story is a common one, repeated with minor variations since 1967, when the government abolished the barriers that separated Israel from the occupied territories, enabling Arabs to cross the old border freely. The house was now occupied by an Israeli who had immigrated from Poland, to whom the Arab presented himself with some embarrassment. The Israeli's impulse was to extend a gesture of hospitality, while recognizing that fairness required even more. But instead, he responded by slamming the door, fearful that any kindness would be a confession of the Arab's right to take the house back.

Within the current generation of Israelis, the belief in Zionism's right to the land, while proclaimed more stridently, seems weaker than before. The early Zionists were surer of their title to the homeland than are those who today insist upon exercising sovereignty over every dunam from the Mediterranean to the Jordan River. The screaming voices of the current generation suggest uncertainty, at the very moment when Arabs seem increasingly willing to deed title to land that Israel held in 1948 in return for territory that Israel had chosen not to claim. Rather than explore the offer, alarming numbers of Israelis are drawn to shrill extremist movements, as if spurning compromise will somehow validate their claims.

That there is a crisis of conviction in Zionism should not be surprising. The Zionism to which Jews historically gave their loyalty was nationalism with a human face. It contained no provision for the Jews to become the oppressors, much less the uprooters, of the Arabs. Many Jews, acknowledging their distress, assert that Israel today has no choice but to be oppressive. Others dismiss humane Zionism as intrinsically naive, even hypocritical, claiming that the term itself is inherently contradictory. Indeed, many Jews respond to the moral dilemma created by Israel's occupation of conquered territory by dismissing earlier Zionist values as anachronistic. To others, the lesson is precisely the opposite: Get out of the territories.

Currently, there are 1.2 million Arabs living in the West Bank and the Gaza Strip, in addition to 500,000 living in Israel. On one issue the Arabs and Jews of Palestine are in agreement: Neither favors integration into a "binational" state. Each insists on retaining its separate cultural identity. Indeed, the very basis of Zionism is the creation of a Jewish community, living its own life, unassimilated into a Gentile world.

Israel is currently debating three possible courses for dealing with the problem of the Arabs under its rule. Each of them might be measured by three objectives important to Israel's future: (1) whether it protects the "Jewishness" of the state, (2) whether it meets reasonable standards of decency as set by world opinion, and (3) whether it holds out a promise of peace.

One course is Kahanism, the virulent new ideology that has captured the allegiance of an alarming number of Israelis. Named for American-born Rabbi Meir Kahane, its leader, it proposes that the Jews, having declared their sovereignty over all of Palestine, solve the problem of the Arabs by forcing them across the borders, out of the country. Kahanism would relieve the Jews of all burden of moral concern by driving the Arabs out of sight.

Kahanism would certainly guarantee Israel's Jewishness, but it would also guarantee Israel's alienation from world opinion, as well as the permanence of conflict. Even if one forgives Kahane for the resemblance which his ideas bear to Hitler's Nuremberg Laws—his followers do—there remains the troublesome difference between the Jews' relation to Germany and the Arabs' to Israel. Being few, the Jews had no recourse for what was done to them by the Nazis, and so they have made peace with Germany. In contrast, Kahane's program for resolving the Palestinian issue guarantees that one hundred million Arabs, backed by worldwide indignation, will pursue retribution against Israel far into the future.

Less harsh than Kahanism are a series of intermediate options on the agenda of Israel's Likud Party and its allies in the parliament's right wing. These options begin with the premise of Israel's annexation of the occupied territories. One proposal would give the Arabs "autonomy"—authority over such communal matters as education, marriage and divorce, personal disputes—powers exercised by the Jews in the shtetls of Eastern Europe. Another would offer Arabs a choice between Jordanian and Israeli citizenship, although it is unclear how in practice that would work. A third would perpetuate the existing system in the territories, which simply ignores the question of political rights.

The flaw in these proposals is that none resolves the dilemma that a large Arab minority presents to the preservation of Israel's Jewishness. They are designed to fit the Arabs into the state with second-class citizenship and limited political influence. Yet, in accommodating to a permanent Arab presence, all create the binationalism that neither side wants. Were Israel to resolve the dilemma by denying all political power to the Arabs within its border, it would be creating outright apartheid. Some Israelis defend such a solution, but it is surely not what Zionism was meant to be.

On a practical level, all of the intermediate options provide the assurance of permanent unrest. As half measures, they will fail to satisfy Arab political aspirations, while at the same time welcoming the permanent presence of an Arab fifth column. Some Israelis, acknowledging the threat, dismiss it by contending simply that the army will take care of it. But each of these options is an invitation to terrorism, and all would institutionalize in the heart of Israel a permanent, deadly risk.

Partition, more or less along the pre-1967 lines, is the third possible course. Alone among the three, it would permit the Jews to cultivate their own values in their own communities, while allowing the Arabs to live their lives as *they* choose in theirs. As fair a solution as is possible in a land that two peoples claim, it will win Israel important support from international public opinion. By offering the Arabs a stake in their own homeland, furthermore, it is the only one of the three that promises to put an end to permanent war.

To be sure, there is some justice to the strategists' complaint that partition will complicate Israel's security problems, though, after a period of adjustment, it is likely to make the Israeli army leaner, more mobile, better motivated, able to concentrate on dealing with real enemies rather than a dissident civilian population. Partition will no doubt invite Israeli fanatics who claim a holy mandate to promote political disruption, as they have done for the last decade. But I believe Israel's leadership must face these prospects. Only by returning to Arab rule the land on which Arabs live can a *Jewish* state hope to survive within a framework of stability in the Middle East.

In saying this, I am trying not to be victimized by my own positions, dismissing rebuttals out of hand. Many practical-minded Israelis insist that since traditional Zionist values will never flourish with the Arabs' *consent*, Israel must retain the territories as the outer walls of a Jewish fortress. They contend that the interest some Arabs have shown in reaching a settlement—including Egypt, which has signed a treaty of peace—is an expedient, at best deferring the goal of Israel's destruction to a more propitious moment.

I cannot state categorically that these contentions are false. But, for argument's sake, let us assume the Arab consensus, concealed beneath conciliatory phrases, is still to destroy Israel at the earliest possible moment. Would that disqualify the pursuit of Middle East peace? I do not think it would.

We might remind ourselves that few are the countries of the world that do not have territorial disputes with some other nation. Most of these disputes, however, are "historical," and rarely do they provoke war. I recall learning that after France lost Alsace-Lorraine in 1870, the patriot Gambetta said, "Let us think of it always, talk of it never." A half century later, France regained Alsace, though other aggrieved nations have been less fortunate. After three hundred years, Spain still nurses a grudge over Gibraltar. Mexico mourns for Texas, Greece for Cyprus. As for the Jews, they long dreamed of returning to their forefathers' land. "Next year in Jerusalem" was their slogan, but it took them two millennia to realize it. During all but the last years of that period, however, they waged no wars.

If Arabs and Israelis reached a settlement based on the partition of Palestine, grievances would indeed remain in the hearts of both. History makes no permanent territorial commitments, and Israelis would be prudent to assume that, at some future time, the Arabs might seize an opportunity to take all of Palestine back. Arabs would be equally prudent in making that assumption about Israel.

But historical grievances are not the same as war. Though the Old Testament promised their ultimate triumph, the Jews had to wait two thousand years to make their bid for Palestine. Arabs like to point to the Crusaders, who in the Middle Ages established a kingdom in Palestine of a century's duration, as evidence that they inevitably will prevail. If the Arabs of today are willing to show a century of patience—or better still, show the same patience as the Jews—they will bequeath to the Middle East a long era without war. And wars deferred are peace.

A conviction that war is always imminent, however, generates policies that tend to make of themselves a self-fulfilling prophecy. Every country has its own list of national priorities, on which destruction of an enemy might somewhere appear. But whatever the level of hostility of Israel's neighbors, it surely distorts available information to conclude that the *highest* national priority is necessarily Israel's immediate defeat.

I am convinced that war with Israel is currently resting comfortably in the lower reaches of the agenda of most of the Arab world. Sadat stunned Israel by showing that Arabs have widespread domestic concerns to which they would prefer to shift their attention. Most Arab governments now share these priorities. The obsession with the war against Israel has faded. For a decade, at least, I believe the Arabs have been ready to live with Israel in peace.

But there is a condition, which is the return of the occupied territories. The Palestinian-Israeli question remains the thorn in the side of Middle East peace. It is the issue on which the superpower rivalry in the region thrives. Alone among the Arabs, the Palestinians were deprived of nationhood when the colonial era ended. More than that, they lost their homes. The Palestinian problem, while not the only concern of the Arab world, is surely one that all Arabs share. Unresolved, it will remain the lowest common denominator of militant Arabism. I am convinced that the means for resolving the issue are at hand in the return of the West Bank and the Gaza Strip to Arab rule.

This is not to say that, even in peace, Israel would be freed of the need to maintain armed forces in readiness. Few are the countries whose security does not require them to keep the price of foreign conquest prohibitive. Nor does it suggest that Israel should quit the territories without a wide range of security guarantees. The pattern of such guarantees was established in the negotiations with Egypt over withdrawal from the Sinai. But even acknowledged that it is unlikely to be perfect, peace would serve Israeli security better than the permanent threat of war.

Admittedly, in arguing that an Arab consensus in behalf of peace exists, I recognize that there is substantial dissent in the ranks. As my mentor Bashir pointed out in my first trip to Cairo, peace—unlike demagoguery—has to produce results. A wry Palestinian said once that Arab leaders have been busy in recent years negotiating conditions among themselves, precisely because Israel will not negotiate with them. They know that once the motion stops, conveying the admission that the negotiating process is dead, the hard-liners will take over. The intransigents are in the wings, anxious to reshape the Arab consensus to correspond to their own passions. Palestinian and non-Palestinian, their calling is Israel's destruction. Unlike those who want to negotiate, they will be satisfied not in getting back the land captured in 1967 but only in getting Israel itself. As long as Israel occupies the territories, they will have a living issue, which no Arab can ignore.

The cause of the hard-liners thrives on the rejection of a compromise peace. In contrast, the Arab consensus in behalf of peace can survive only with a promise of success. The dead end of peace efforts will not bring reversion to a tranquil status quo. It will only invite more Middle East war.

Israel continues the course on which it is currently engaged—the perpetuation of the status quo in the Middle East—only with the active collaboration of the United States. This collaboration began in the immediate aftermath of the Six-Day War, when American forces were mired in battle in Vietnam. At that time, Washington made a public vow to promote Israel's economic development and military security. In return, it exacted of Israel a tacit promise to serve as a friendly outpost in its own competition with the Soviet Union. This quid pro quo has been the key to all that has since transpired in the Middle East.

Having frozen the diplomatic process after 1967, Israel had to fight the Arabs twice within the next six years. Washington's position was that these subsequent wars would never have occurred without Soviet partisanship toward the Arabs. This was true, of course, but it discounted the factors indigenous to the region itself. The United States responded to each of the two subsequent wars within the context of its cold war interests, by increasing the already significant margin of military superiority that Israel held over its enemies. Israel, in its willingness to fight America's war against the Russians, was freed of responsibility for resolving the issues of its own war against the Arabs.

Henry Kissinger, celebrated as a peacemaker for his "shuttle diplomacy," is the man who, more than any other, put his stamp on the relationship. Kissinger created the mechanism that hardened the obstacles to real peace. He deployed American resources to institutionalize an Israeli war machine too powerful for all the Arab nations together to resist. In doing so, he weakened Washington's influence over the peace process. But at the same time, he set a trap for Israel, in which there were powerful political forces more than willing to be ensnared. Kissinger guaranteed to Israel a margin of military superiority so wide that it had no incentive to reconcile with its neighbors. Among the victims of this arrangement has been Middle East peace.

Since 1967, politicians in the United States and Israel have referred to the relations between the two countries as an "alliance," though no actual treaty of alliance exists. What does exist is a relationship that politicians in the two countries find expedient to treat as an alliance. As its senior partner, the United States has on several occasions—most notably at Camp David—put its power to the service of peace in the Middle East. But more often, it has attached to the quest for peace a lower priority than the quest for strategic advantage.

Many of the ensuing pages in this book will dwell on the relationship that for two decades has dominated events in the Middle East, and the impact it has had on the prospects for an end to the Arab-Israeli struggle.

2

Two Characters, Two Visions

In ISRAEL, almost everyone's life is a personal drama, shaped by the exotic circumstances of wars, persecution and migration. Israelis, in two or three generations, will perhaps be as humdrum as other peoples, with backgrounds as "normal" as the Zionist pioneers hoped a Jewish state itself would one day be. When that time comes, every Israeli—or at least every Israeli's parents—will not have come from some intriguing other place, have escaped from some terrifying encounter, have arrived over some perilous route. But for now, the unique is ordinary. The *typical* Israeli is someone created by the uncommon.

Yitzhak Rabin and Geula Cohen, ordinary Israelis, represent the "two Israels" which are currently struggling to shape the society of the Jewish state. Though commonly used, the term "two Israels" is actually an oversimplification. Like an apple, Israel can be bisected from many points. Three cuts are crucial to our concerns. There is the Ashkenazi-Sephardi bisection. There is the religious-secular. There is also the Mainstream-Revisionist. Each represents a separate arena of combat, but together the outcome of the three struggles will determine what Israel will be, not just within its borders but in relation to its neighbors. I will introduce these struggles in the present chapter, and return to them at greater length when I examine Israel's transformation after the Six-Day

War. I will also talk often of Rabin and Cohen, who, as nearly as human models can, represent the bisections of the Israeli social order today.

Rabin, with his fair skin, is Ashkenazi, coldly pragmatic, secular. Cohen, with her dark eyes, is Sephardi, hotly ideological and mystical, if not religiously devout. Rabin is often described as dour, distant, cerebral, Cohen as ardent, a trifle coarse, a nature child. Rabin is an "establishment" Israeli, Cohen is an "outsider." Rabin holds ideas consistent with Mainstream Zionism, a body of Jewish redemptionist thought which came out of Central Europe in the last century. Cohen's outlook is Revisionist, emerging from a schismatic school of Zionism founded in Eastern Europe after World War I.

Guided by their sharply different conceptions of what Israel is, and ought to be, Rabin and Cohen each speak of the other's way with some contempt. Yet both have devoted their lives to the service of Israel: Rabin as soldier in the War of Independence, chief of staff, ambassador to Washington, prime minister, minister of defense; Cohen as heroine of the underground in the War of Independence, member of the Knesset, Revisionist gadfly, founder of a new ultranationalist political party. Pushing in different directions, each has had a significant impact on the course that Israel has taken.

Rabin's mother, one of ten children of wealthy Russian parents, emigrated to Palestine in 1919 after falling out with the Communist Revolution. His father, born in the Ukraine, migrated to America and lived in Chicago until World War I, when he volunteered to fight with the Jewish Legion in Palestine. The founder and commander of the Legion was Vladimir Jabotinsky, who would achieve fame as leader of the dissident Revisionist movement. Rabin is quick to point out, however, that both his mother and his father were social democrats, far removed in their politics from the militant nationalism that Jabotinsky espoused.

Born in Jerusalem in 1922, Rabin was raised within the framework of the Zionist labor movement, on the ideals of Mainstream

Zionism. Zionism's responsibility, as the Mainstream saw it, was not simply to bring the Jews back to Palestine but to create a new society, free of the servility and pessimism that perpetual oppression had imbued in the Jews of the ghetto. Like Marxism, from which much of its idealism emerged, the Mainstream cherished a belief that a reconstructed society would produce better men and women. Mainstream Zionism spoke of creating a "new" Jew. Its highest expression was the kibbutz, where Jews lived collectively, sharing selflessly, tilling the soil. Rabin assumed he would one day be a kibbutznik.

In those days, the Mainstream almost never talked of founding a sovereign state. During the early years of pioneering, when the Turks ruled Palestine, sovereignty seemed farfetched. After 1917, when the Balfour Declaration (see Appendix A) promised a Jewish *homeland,* Zionism seemed satisfied by the prospect of a dependency under the British flag. In the back of their minds, the early Zionists surely dreamed of statehood, but to talk of it was certain to alarm not just the British but the Arabs. Zionism chose not to look ahead to whether the Jews, to attain their goals, had to suppress or supplant Palestine's natives. Proud of its morality, Zionism insisted it intended the Arabs no harm. In retrospect, its position appears naive, perhaps even disingenuous. But in those days, the Mainstream asked only for a haven in which Jews could plant their roots and pursue their goals together. Sovereignty seemed a small matter, since Zionism's chief concern was the perfectability of Jewish society and the Jew.

"My parents believed in the Zionist movement as the liberation movement of the Jewish people," Rabin said, "and returning to Zion to them meant helping to establish a society in which Jewish life could reach its full meaning. That meant revival of the Hebrew language and building an educational system based on Jewish values, in the place where our history is rooted. It meant creating a self-sufficient society, with Jewish workers, doctors, bankers and policemen, and a democracy with all the humanistic advantages of the Western world. It meant a 'normal' structure of national life."

Geula Cohen's Jewish background was a dramatic contrast to Rabin's. Her mother was born in Jerusalem's Old City, of parents who had immigrated from Morocco. Her father, having crossed the Arabian desert on foot from Yemen, was committed far less to the dry intellectualism of the Talmud than to the mystical concepts of Judaism embodied in the books of the Cabala. Born in Tel-Aviv in 1925, she described her upbringing as "traditional," which meant religiously Orthodox and family oriented, socially conservative, far removed from a concern with shaping a new Jewish identity. As a girl, she told me with obvious pride, she learned that her grandfather had died during a solitary pilgrimage into the hills of Yemen, praying for the prompt coming of the Messiah.

"The Yemenite Jews first arrived here in 1882," she said, "before the first Zionists. They didn't have a movement. They didn't even have a leader. But all their poems, all their songs, were about coming to Zion, Zion, Zion. My mother always told me stories of her ancestors, who were Jewish vizirs to the kings of Morocco, and my father sang me Yemenite songs about rebuilding the Kingdom of David. She was the practical one, he was the dreamer. I think I am a combination of both of them."

No one was able to say for sure, when Israel was founded after World War II, how the disparate parts of world Jewry would fit together. The early theorists of Zionism had conceived of the homeland they yearned for as an ingathering of the Jews, without asking who "the Jews" might be. They had foreseen the problem of assimilating German and French Jews, shaped by sophisticated Western values, with Polish and Russian Jews, whose communities had been left almost untouched by the influences of the Enlightenment. Zionist leaders worked hard in the early years to narrow the cultural gap between the Jews of Eastern and Western Europe. It never occurred to them to look beyond.

But in two millennia of exile, Jews had scattered well beyond Europe. They lived on every continent and were shaped by an almost infinite range of cultural encounters. They adopted different languages, different religious practices, different social values, and they even acquired different physical features. Whatever the miracle that preserved Jewish identity, it was an identity preserved in many and conflicting varieties.

As Israel approaches a half century of history, it is apparent that the problems of fitting together the disparate segments of the Jewish people to create a nation are far from resolved. It was not until the early 1980s that a majority of Israelis claimed Hebrew, the official language, as their mother tongue. Israel remains a tumultuous place, with diverse communities of Jews ranged against one another in harsh competition. That there should be such competition in a new nation is not surprising. The prelude to a workable social compact is surely an era of stress, during which rival forces struggle for place. Israel, with some winners and some losers, will one day emerge with a cultural and political synthesis. But the day has not yet come.

It never occurred to the early Zionists how much reconciliation a Jewish state would require. They were familiar with the troubles experienced by the Italians, for example, who lived in proximity to one another and spoke the same language, in forming a single nation. They had not understood that bringing together Jews from Europe and the Arab world, whose differences were not only cultural but ethnic, would prove much more formidable. Nor had they contemplated the depth of the conflict between religious and secular Jews, each determined to shape the character of the state. And though they were themselves divided by deep political differences, they never dreamed that conflicts of political ideology might be profound enough to keep a Jewish state at the edge of civil war. The early Zionists relied on an assumption—far too innocent, in retrospect—that the common quality of *Jewishness* would somehow be basis enough for a viable homeland.

Indeed, the common quality of Jewishness, whatever it is, must surely tell us much about the character of Israel today, as a society and as a nation-state. Competent scholars have spent lifetimes grappling to define Jewishness, and what it means to the everyday life of a Jew. I join them with trepidation, to touch on the cultural foundation of the Jewish state, particularly as it affects the operation of the levers that determine the course of war and peace in the Middle East.

Let me start by noting that Jews throughout history have had a sense of themselves as members of a special community, defined only in part by Judaism as a religion. In our own day, in fact, a substantial segment of the community considers itself no less Jewish for living with little or no involvement in religious practice. Yet few Jews are unaware of the special category assigned to the Jewish people in the Bible. More intrinsic than religion is the feeling within Jews of having been singled out from other peoples to be among God's Chosen.

At the same time, Jews sense that there is a reverse side to being Chosen. It is the pervasive hostility, known as anti-Semitism, directed against them by the outside world and most specifically by European Christianity. Since the end of World War II, the manifestations of anti-Semitism have declined in the West from what they once were. But, conditioned to its history, Jews rarely let down their guard against it. Most are convinced it lurks in the shadows of the Christian world, waiting to emerge.

These companion notions—Chosenness and anti-Semitism—may vary enormously in the influence they have on Jews as individuals, and their impact on the body of Jews has varied from region to region and from one period of history to another. Some Jews find strength in their membership in the special community of Jews, while others dislike or even deny it. But the paired sensations of Chosenness and anti-Semitism nourish a tight cohesion and a powerful collective dynamism among Jews as a whole. Without these feelings, there would never have been an Israel.

In our own century, European anti-Semitism struck with unprecedented savagery, killing six million human beings for the crime of being Jews. The Holocaust left a scar on every Jewish soul, though more deeply upon Ashkenazim, for whom it was more immediate and personal, than upon Sephardim.

The personal definition of nearly every Jew who lives today has been shaped by the Holocaust. Its importance in the Jewish soul cannot be overestimated. For non-Jews, the Holocaust is a tragic historical episode. But it is neither posturing nor reproach to say that they cannot feel the Holocaust as deeply, as personally, as Jews do. Friends, no less than enemies, often fail to appreciate the depth of the presence of the Holocaust within the Jewish spirit. Few are the Arabs, preoccupied with their own tragedies, who are able to comprehend its meaning at all. The Holocaust is the seminal Jewish experience of our time.

The Holocaust conveyed to Jews the lesson that, in their Chosenness, they had only themselves to count on for survival. From Nazism they learned that they had to shed the passivity which had for centuries characterized the Jewish response to the menacing world of outsiders. It was a happenstance of history that establishment of a Jewish state was on the international agenda at the moment when Jews resolved to be *active* in their own salvation. Until the death camps made their appearance, many Jews, and a larger proportion of non-Jews, recognized no need for Jewish sovereignty. The Holocaust persuaded all but a few Jewish doubters, and enough non-Jews to make it possible, of the importance of establishing a Jewish state that was independent, self-reliant, strong.

There are few ceremonial occasions when Israeli leaders omit the Holocaust theme. President Ephraim Katzir typically told Israelis, years after the end of World War II, "The hatred that beats in the heart of that devil [Nazism] has not ceased to this very day, and a great part of humanity has not learned the lesson. . . . Woe to us if we remain complacent in the face of this reality. . . . The people in-gathered again in its ancient homeland will preciously guard these eternal values for which a third of our people sacrificed their lives."

The Holocaust shifted Zionism's purpose from simply establishing a homeland for the Jews to creating a nation-state capable of fulfilling for Jewish posterity the much repeated pledge: Never Again.

The duty to fulfill that pledge fell not only to Israelis but to world Jewry. It imparted to Israel's service the Jews' immense cohesion, created by their sense of Chosenness and their reflex to anti-Semitism. It has evoked nobility and selflessness from the Jews as a people. In the name of this pledge, Jews around the world—most notably in America—organize their manpower, give their money, exercise their political power. Few would deny that Jews have risen magnanimously to identify with Israel.

What in fact seems to have happened in the secular atmosphere of our time is that the Jewish nation-state has taken the place of Judaism as the religion of much of worldwide Jewry. The new religion has produced its own dogma, which endorses a militancy toward outsiders, even a pugnacity, that was unknown in centuries of Jewish history. It has also produced its own orthodoxy, from which dissent is considered heresy. This religion of nationalism has kept the Jewish community in the decades since World War II in a state of high mobilization.

But this mobilization has not just a positive side. Referring to the establishment of Israel, the Israeli novelist Amos Oz wrote in *The Hill of Evil Counsel,* "We turn over a new leaf only to smudge it with ancient neuroses." The memory of the Holocaust, arousing atavistic responses to persecution, sometimes forces the judgment of the Jews into channels of unreason.

No Israeli was more obsessed with the Holocaust than former Prime Minister Menachem Begin. In his announcement in 1982 of the invasion of Lebanon, which surely had nothing to do with the annihilation of the Jews in Europe, Begin declared, "It is our fate that in the Land of Israel we have no choice but to fight unflaggingly. Believe me, the alternative is Auschwitz. We have resolved that there will not be another."

Begin was accused during his term of office of debasing the Holocaust, of politicizing it, of exacting from the Arabs penance for the sins of the Nazis, all of which was true. But all Jews—even those profoundly offended by his political ideology and practices —shared with Begin the Holocaust's heavy presence in their consciousness of being Jewish.

So much, in brevity, for the common quality of Jewishness, the bedrock of commitment to Zionism. Let us now return to the divisions of the Jews, for on this bedrock is built Israel, a Tower of Babel. Present-day Babel, its inner framework soldered by Jewish cohesiveness, trembles, nonetheless, for being skewed this way and that by Jewish diversity.

As the first difference, let us take the Ashkenazim and the Sephardim. "Ashkenazi" was a term first applied to German Jews, but over centuries it came to designate all Jews, including the great communities of Russia and Poland, exposed to the main currents of European culture. "Sephard" was the name originally given to the Jews of Spain, where a major Jewish community thrived throughout the Middle Ages, but over the centuries it was applied to all Jews influenced by the culture of Islam. The ways of the two—rites, traditions, costumes, the pronunciation of Hebrew —were different, but both thought of themselves throughout history as branches of the worldwide Jewish family.

The Jews were expelled from Spain at the time of the Inquisition and dispersed around the Mediterranean. Many settled in the south of Europe, particularly in the Balkans, by then under Ottoman rule. In Salonika, they created a great center of culture, which lasted until the Nazis came in World War II. But many also gravitated to the Arab world, establishing important communities along the littoral of North Africa. There they encountered Jews who had migrated from Palestine as early as the Biblical era. Baghdad and Damascus contained ancient Jewish communities, and the Koran, written in the seventh century, speaks of the Jews of Arabia. In Israel today, the term "Sephardim" chiefly designates the Jews whose historical roots are in Arab lands. Sephardim and Ashkenazim, who knew rather little of each other throughout the ages, came together in Israel in the twentieth century.

It was the Ashkenazim who founded modern Israel, for Zionism was an Ashkenazi political movement. The Jews who settled the new land were, for the most part, Eastern Europeans, who brought with them ideas current in the world they left behind. Under the British, Ashkenazim founded Israel's principal institutions, including its major political parties. Though they are no longer a popular majority, and their influence is waning, Ashkenazim remain the preponderant force in the political system. They are the Israeli "establishment." Understandably, they regard Israel as *theirs.*

During the many centuries of Diaspora, however, the idea of a return to Zion may have been more deep-seated among the Sephardim. Though rarely persecuted by their Moslem neighbors, the Jews of Islam were denied full participation in the economy and the society. Then, in the late nineteenth century, with the Ottoman empire in decline and Arab nationalism on the rise, their position became more precarious. For the first time, European doctrines of anti-Semitism circulated in the Arab world. Their Christian neighbors, with whom they had shared the burdens of minority status, began turning against them. Incidents of violence, though still random, occurred more frequently. Insecurity entered the life of the Jews of the Arab world.

It was at that time that a trickle of Arab Jews—including Geula Cohen's father—began the move to Palestine, though until 1948 they remained only a tiny fraction of the Jewish community there. The great wave arrived in the wake of Israel's declaration of independence, when Jews became the targets of wrath throughout the Arab world. Some left in peaceful fashion. Many had to be rescued in semicovert Israeli operations, leaving their possessions behind while bringing with them a deep residue of animosity. By the early 1950s, nearly all had departed, ending more than two thousand years of Jewish presence in the Moslem lands. These Jews came knowing little of Zionism, without political designs, generally impoverished, and poorly educated for modern life. They nonetheless resented any Ashkenazi notion that they were not full partners in the society, or that Israel was any less *theirs.*

It was only after the Six-Day War that the relationship between Ashkenazim and Sephardim exploded into open struggle. In Israel's first two decades, adjustments had been slow, subtle, evolutionary. Observers, while concerned about the gulf between the "two Israels," did not foresee that it would produce social disruption. Then the war, which created a new geographical reality on Israel's borders, established a new psychological reality at home, sharply intensifying the competition among diverse cultural groups. The atmosphere turned increasingly raucous and the old ruling class, with its Mainstream Zionist values, came under heavy assault.

In contrast to the ideas of democracy, secularism, liberalism and socialism that the Ashkenazim had brought with them, the Sephardim brought to Israel the Islamic tradition of patriarchal rule and the Koranic view that religion is inseparable from the political structure. To this day, Sephardim have difficulty adapting not only to the Western theories of democracy under which Israel is governed but to a notion of pluralism which is essential to stability in a heterogeneous state. More disposed than Ashkenazim to a black-and-white vision of politics, they have tended to inject into the everyday contest for power a passion generally associated with the East rather than the West.

At the same time, the Sephardim have drawn the lines more sharply in Israel's struggle with its Arab neighbors. Despite centuries of relative tranquillity in the Arab world, they made clear once they arrived that they nursed deep historic grudges. The Ashkenazim, though hardly fond of Arabs, have tended to regard them chiefly as a security problem, within Israel's power to somehow solve. The Sephardim, in contrast, respond to Arabs with emotions that are often raw, angry, intense. The Six-Day War suddenly presented them with the prospect of evening scores against an old enemy. This opportunity tantalized them as they reached out for more political power in the years that followed.

The Six-Day War, in addition to accelerating a shift in power from Ashkenazim to Sephardim, changed the framework of the rivalry between Israel's religious and nonreligious Jews. This division has created a second construction of the "two Israels."

Throughout most of their history, Jews largely were defined—and defined themselves—in religious terms, as a people dedicated to a particular idea of God, rejecting Christianity in the West and Islam in the East. Not until the Enlightenment did there appear the concept of the secular Jew, asserting an ethnic, even a national, but not necessarily a religious basis of Jewish identity. In the antireligious atmosphere of the nineteenth century, the concept of secular Jewishness spread. Then, out of Enlightenment thought, Europe gave birth to the ideology of Zionism. Though religious in its roots, it was political and social in its objectives, and secular in its character. It did not appeal to Orthodox Jews. It was Jewish, but not Judaic.

In this sense, Zionism might be considered an anomaly in the long scroll of Jewish history. Interestingly, in the mid-nineteenth century, before Zionism began to take root, some twenty to thirty thousand Orthodox Jews left Europe to settle in the Holy Land, particularly in Jerusalem. Their commitment was to waiting for the Messiah, not to establishing a homeland. Religious Jews, generally, found Zionism a heathen doctrine promoted by heretics, a presumptuous usurpation of God's pledge that the Messiah would redeem the land. The Orthodox Jews already in Palestine were cold, if not actively hostile, to the arriving Zionist pioneers.

Nonetheless, Mainstream Zionism took pains to cultivate Orthodox Jewry. However secular, Zionism never became anticlerical, in the European sense. Often at the sacrifice of temporal values, Mainstream Zionists tried to minimize the alienation of the religious Jews. At independence, Israel's new government agreed upon a compact not only to protect their rights but to grant them special privileges. Seizing the opportunities presented by Israeli democracy, Orthodox Jews formed political parties to promote these privileges, and they exercised significant power in the Knesset. Still, the majority of Orthodox Jews remained piously detached from Zionism. Some even worked to undermine the state.

By and large, the detachment ended after the Six-Day War, which Israelis widely hailed as a miracle signaling God's endorsement of Jewish statehood. Though some segments remained un-forgiving, the Orthodox community embraced this view, joined in the celebration, and adopted a new tolerance of the state. A major part, in fact, suddenly became fervently patriotic. It took a military triumph in the second century of Zionism to persuade Orthodox Jews that harmonious relations with a Jewish government did not compromise their religious integrity.

The result has been that since 1967, religion has become an increasingly powerful force in Israel's political arena. Before, the political parties of the Orthodox Jews promoted observance of the Sabbath, aid to religious schools, and rabbinical control over "personal status" issues like marriage and divorce. Then, as they moved from the periphery to the center of political combat, they intensified the campaign to apply their own interpretation to the question "Who is a Jew?" the answer to which defined power of the Orthodox rabbinate in terms of the right of Israeli citizenship. Later, contemplating Israel's huge conquests, they turned territorial, and claimed it to be sacrilege to return the land taken from the Arabs, particularly the West Bank, which they called by the Biblical names Judea and Samaria. Orthodox Jews even initiated debate on construction of a Third Temple—the first having been destroyed by the Babylonians in 586 B.C., the second by the Romans in A.D. 70—on Jerusalem's Temple Mount, an Islamic holy place since the time of Muhammad.

And so Zionism's conquests on the battlefield opened the door to a tumultuous reexamination of the political and religious character of the Jewish state. Though Zionists had quarreled fiercely among themselves, they never seriously disputed the goal of creating a "normal" country—by which they meant a democratic and secular country, like the nations of the West. Their doctrine had emerged out of the vision of Zionism's founder, Theodor Herzl, a secular Viennese who, having failed in his effort to escape anti-Semitism, had concluded reluctantly that the Jewish people had to have a homeland of their own. Though his seminal work was called, in English, *The Jewish State,* his emphasis was less on the state than on the rebirth of the Jewish people in an environment of liberty and security. To his followers, a Jewish homeland meant creating a Western society in Palestine, free of rabbinical controls, exalting economic justice and individual freedom.

Now, while Sephardim were asking, "Why democracy?" Orthodox Jews were saying, "Why secularism?" The debate was a reminder that the values bestowed upon the Jewish state by the Zionist pioneers, far from being revealed truth, were the conventional thinking of Europe in a liberal age. The challengers proclaimed that by definition, a *Jewish* state was different from a *normal* state. The Chosen People, with its responsibilities God-given, could not, they said, establish a country like everybody else's. They placed issues basic to the nature of the society, once thought to be settled, back on Israel's agenda.

With the Sephardim geographically distant and religious Jews uninvolved by choice, debate among Jews over the realization of Zionism was conducted in the quarter-century after Herzl within narrow philosophical bounds. Only in the 1920s did Mainstream Zionism encounter a serious challenge to its values. Then, under the influence of the charismatic thinker and activist Vladimir Jabotinsky, there appeared a doctrine of Jewish supernationalism, designated Revisionist Zionism or, simply, Revisionism. It provoked the third bisection in the "two Israels" of today.

Born in Russia in 1880, Jabotinsky, though an admirer of British liberalism, chose Garibaldi, the free-booting Italian nationalist, as his personal model. In World War I, he founded the Jewish Legion to help Britain supplant the Turks in the Middle East. Though he favored democracy and secularism, he gave a higher priority to exalting a "muscular" Zionism over the "social" or "cultural" Zionism of the Mainstream. Jabotinsky was impatient. He called for prompt steps to establish a strong and militant nation-state as the true expression of the Jews.

By the 1920s, when the British ruled, the Balfour Declaration was ostensibly the guide to Palestine's future. The strategy of

Mainstream Zionism for securing the Jewish presence, under the British as it had been under the Turks, was to purchase land, parcel by parcel, from Arab landowners. Jabotinsky dismissed such a gradualist approach. Nor had he any use for Mainstream Zionism's moral ambiguity in dealing with the Arabs, arguing that it was time to acknowledge that an "iron wall" divided the two peoples. Jabotinsky was contemptuous of socialism, and of the Mainstream's yearning for a "new" Jew. His single interest was a Jewish state, which he proposed to establish with Jewish arms, against any British or Arab attempts to stop it. His imperative was Jewish power, for which he was ready to sacrifice the liberal values that to Mainstream Zionism were fundamental.

Compared with the plodding pragmatism of Mainstream Zionism, Jabotinsky's Revisionism had outsized ambitions. It envisaged a state powerful enough to assert Jewish interests, draw Jewish boundaries and intimidate Jewish enemies, wherever they might be. Jabotinsky, more sensitive than the Mainstream to the rise of anti-Semitism after World War I, instinctively understood the dangers presented by Nazism in Germany and sought to mobilize world opinion for the rescue of European Jewry. Yet Revisionism, even as it organized to oppose Fascism's threat to the Jews, adopted much of Fascism's style and doctrine. Its followers, scoffing at democracy, dressed in military uniforms and trained in the use of arms. By the eve of World War II, Revisionism's aggressive practices had won a substantial following among Jews, both in Palestine and in Europe.

It is in no small part owing to Revisionism that the world has come to think of Israel as a *fighting* country. The early literature of Zionism promoted pacifist positions, which seemed natural enough for a people who since Biblical times had no military tradition. Under Turkish rule, the pioneers had used weapons only reluctantly, to protect their settlements against marauders. Under the Mandate, the Jews of Palestine, content to leave their protection to Britain, rarely took up arms themselves. Early Zionism produced no military treatises, and its major thinkers, if they returned today, would be incredulous to learn that the homeland they conceived was more esteemed for its *military* prowess than its moral virtue. Surely, one great paradox of Zionism is that it gave birth to a culture of arms. Revisionism, in providing the ideology, deserves much of the credit.

Though a dissident movement until the 1970s, Revisionism exercised a huge influence on Israel. Its values, having reshaped many of the beliefs of Mainstream Zionism, were in part absorbed into the institutions of the state. Still, the gap between Mainstream and Revisionist thought remains fundamental to the anger that persists between the "two Israels" today. Revisionism ebbed after the War of Independence, then rose again in 1967, when it injected into Israel's ethnic and religious struggles an ultranationalist doctrine that appealed to Sephardim and to religious Jews, despite its Ashkenazi and secular roots. Since 1967, Revisionism has been the linchpin of a new coalition of forces in Israel, whose common commitment is to retain the occupied territories.

What we have seen then, in the two decades that followed the Six-Day War, is a gravitation of the disparate strains of world Jewry that settled in Israel into two rival camps. The one consists of a heterogeneous coalition of Revisionists, Sephardim and religious Jews. In the other are the Mainstream Zionists, who by definition tend to be the Ashkenazim and the secular Jews. There are many exceptions to that formulation. In a democracy as freewheeling as Israel, there is inevitably an exception to every political generality. But a poll published in an Israeli newspaper in mid-1985 showed, for example, that Sephardim and religious Jews were about twice as likely as Ashkenazim and secular Jews to take extreme positions in favor of suppression of the Arabs of the occupied territories.

It was Revisionism that forged Sephardim and religious Jews into a coalition of extremist forces. Since 1967, and particularly since the Yom Kippur War in 1973, the influence of the Revisionist coalition has grown steadily, and the "two Israels" have moved farther and farther apart. In the coming pages, we will examine further how Revisionist ideology came to dominate the policies and practices of the Jewish state.

Yitzhak Rabin, child of Mainstream Zionism, had a rigorous Zionist education at the austere School for Workers' Children in Tel Aviv. His life at home, as he describes it, was spartan and nonreligious. The lessons he received there were rich in the culture of Europe and the tenets of Zionism. As a young man, Rabin planned to go on to an agricultural school and then help establish a kibbutz, where he would live his life collectively with other sons and daughters of Zionist pioneers.

"It was only natural to go off to an agricultural school," he told me, "because agriculture represented the symbolic change in Jewish life from the big Jewish concentrations in the cities of Eastern Europe. I never visited Eastern Europe. In fact, I never left Palestine during my boyhood. Everything I knew came from my parents and from the books I read. But for me, agriculture was the means of creating the *new* Jew. It represented the *normal* life of a people. It meant the rooting of ourselves in the land of Israel."

Geula Cohen went to regular public school in Tel Aviv, and never thought much about living on a kibbutz or working the land. "First of all, the idea of socialism, I didn't need it," she explained. "Second, I didn't fit. I'm too individualistic. Third, it was enough for me to be a Jew, to sacrifice for the *great* kibbutz, the Jewish people, to bring them back to their homeland." When she was thirteen, on the eve of World War II, she joined Betar, the paramilitary youth organization of Jabotinsky's Revisionist Party, whose foundations of power still lay in the ghettos of Eastern Europe.

"Sure, Betar was very European, very Polish," Cohen said, "and my father was one of the leaders of the Yemenite community here. The leftists, all Europeans, talked about making a new human being, a new Jew, which the Yemenites did not understand. Ben-Gurion talked about socialism, and the Yemenites didn't understand socialism. The leftists were against religion—'no king, no

God, no this, no that'—and the Yemenites were religious. Even now, put Yitzhak Rabin in the middle of the Yemenite quarter of Tel Aviv and no one will understand him.

"Jabotinsky, of course, was also a European, but my father admired him very much and so did I. When I was a little girl, I read his books and sang his songs, and when I went out on the street I was called 'fascist' and 'militarist.' My father liked Jabotinsky because he was very concerned about Jewish honor. He was not a socialist. He talked about bringing all the Jews here, no matter how they are or what they think. He was not religious, but he respected religion. My father understood that Jabotinsky did not consider himself better than another Jew. He talked to us as if we were partners in the same struggle. Jabotinsky spoke from the heart."

While Cohen was training for guerilla warfare in the uniform of Betar, Rabin was learning the use of arms under the wing of the Jewish regulars of the Haganah. He trained first at the agricultural school, then at a kibbutz on the shores of the Sea of Galilee. That both should be getting ready to make war was no surprise. In Europe, war was in the air, and by then there had already been twenty years' violence between Jews and Arabs in Palestine, which showed no signs of abating.

Throughout these twenty years, the Jewish community had proceeded as if Britain, true to the pledge of the Balfour Declaration, was laying the groundwork for a Jewish homeland. Then, in their celebrated White Paper of 1939, the British barred further Jewish immigration to Palestine, forcing even the most trusting Jew to acknowledge that Britain was unlikely to keep its pledge. Once this prospect became apparent, the Jews saw no alternative to lumping the British with the Arabs as enemies of Zionism.

The shift produced a curious polarity. In Betar, Cohen was preparing for combat against the British, while in the Haganah, Rabin was getting ready to do battle against the Arabs. Neither had much use for the other's plans. What this polarity bespoke was the Mainstream's bitter political clash with Revisionism. Ben-Gurion, the

Mainstream's leader, had been slow to give up the belief in a *homeland* under British patronage, a concept that Jabotinsky, committed to absolute sovereignty, had long before rejected. Even after publication of the White Paper, Ben-Gurion was not convinced the Jews would have to fight the British for their objective. The Revisionists, in contrast, had been organizing an underground army for a decade. Cohen was training for a "war of liberation" against the British. Rabin, on the other hand, was getting ready for the war against the Arabs that Mainstream Zionists expected to fight after Britain's departure.

The differences that separated Mainstream Zionists from Revisionists were not hair-splitting abstractions, and even in the face of Hitler's rise, the two sides could not compose them. Their first open break had taken place as far back as 1933, when Chaim Arlosoroff, an important Mainstream leader, was murdered in Tel Aviv. The Mainstream leadership accused the Revisionists of plotting the murder, and a Revisionist follower was subsequently tried for the crime but acquitted. In the atmosphere of mutual recrimination that followed, Jabotinsky withdrew the Revisionists from the world Zionist movement, publicly accusing the Mainstream of timidity in response to swelling anti-Semitism in Europe. Meanwhile, observing the flirtation with Fascist ideas and tactics, the Mainstream grew increasingly concerned about Revisionism's threat to Zionist democratic values.

By the start of World War II, the Jewish community in Palestine had in the field two secret armies, representing the competing ideologies. Ironically, Jabotinsky had founded them both. The Haganah, whose allegiance was to Mainstream Zionism, was descended from a force that Jabotinsky organized during civil strife in Palestine in 1920. After a period of disuse, it was rebuilt by the Jewish Agency, the Jewish community's representative body, with the tacit collaboration of the British, who assumed it might one day be useful in the looming war in Europe. Meanwhile, Jabotinsky had also organized an underground army called the Irgun, faithful to Revisionism and sworn to Britain's expulsion from

Palestine. The Irgun recognized neither the Jewish Agency's authority nor its official dogma of keeping hands off British forces. The British were determined to destroy the Irgun and, to the Revisionists' dismay, the Haganah sometimes helped them.

On the eve of World War II, in fact, it was not clear to Zionism who the principal enemy was. Despite Nazism, few Jews were willing to fight for Britain. Only in 1941, when German forces reached Egypt and Syria to threaten Palestine from two directions, was a Jewish consensus established that Britain was the lesser of evils. David Ben-Gurion, the leader of the Jews in Palestine, coined a formula meant to resolve the dilemma presented by Britain's policies. Jews, he said, were to "help the British in their war against Hitler as if there were no White Paper; [and] resist the White Paper as if there were no war." Some thirty thousand young men accepted the advice and volunteered to fight at Britain's side. But thousands of others held back. Neat as it was, Ben-Gurion's *jeu de mots* did not settle the problem for all the Jews.

Rabin was among those who were not prepared to accept Ben-Gurion's word, though he was loyal to the Jewish Agency and the Jewish institutional structure in Palestine. He was no rebel, and even today he scoffs at the Revisionists for diverting their energies to a "war of liberation" for which he saw no need. But Rabin declined to fight in the British army. He wanted the British to authorize Jews to form their own army to fight Germany, and when they refused, he enlisted in the Palmach, the Haganah's elite corps. Throughout the war, he continued to train in semisecrecy, and once he saw combat at the side of the British, during the short-lived expedition into Syria in June of 1941. Practically speaking, however, Rabin sat out the war at home.

For Cohen, not only was the Mainstream's Haganah too meek; so was Revisionism's Irgun, into which she graduated from Betar when she was sixteen. After a brief stay, she transferred to a rival, more violent secret faction called Lehi, known in the Western press as the Stern Gang, and she was assigned to make underground broadcasts in its name. As early as 1942, Lehi began a campaign of terror against the British. The Irgun, more cautious, did not follow suit until the Nazi forces no longer threatened Palestine. In October 1944, Lehi members assassinated Lord Moyne, Britain's highest official in the Middle East, and for several months the Haganah cooperated openly with Britain in going after the killers. Meanwhile, Cohen's throaty voice had become familiar throughout the land, as she moved from place to place for her clandestine radio transmissions.

As soon as the Germans surrendered in Europe, the Revisionist underground movements abandoned all inhibitions, declaring full-scale clandestine war. The British found it increasingly difficult to curb the violence that ensued. In an attack in 1946, Cohen was captured, then wounded in an unsuccessful attempt at escape. Recaptured, she was put on trial in a British court.

"My mother watched my whole trial," Cohen told me, "nursing my baby brother. I couldn't talk to her. At the end, when the judge said, 'Geula Cohen, nine years in prison,' I heard music from the side where she was sitting among the lawyers and the newspapermen. I turned my face and I saw her standing at attention, singing *Hatikvah* [the Jewish anthem], forcing the British judge and the British soldiers and everyone in the courtroom to stand at attention until she was finished. I remember the face of the judge as if it was yesterday. When my mother was singing the song, I saw the thought written on his face, 'With such mothers, we can't win.' That was my mother."

A year later, Cohen escaped from prison for good, resuming her broadcasts as the underground stepped up the terror. Wanting to see combat herself, she protested indignantly to me at having been overprotected by Lehi's men. She told me proudly of two occasions—once at a British air base, once at a police station—when her commanders allowed her to go into action carrying a machine gun. Unlike Rabin's, Cohen's was no armchair war.

Not until unmistakable information arrived from occupied Europe that the Jewish communities there were being decimated did Mainstream Zionism take a clear stand on statehood. Out of concern for the Holocaust's survivors, and at the urging of Ben-Gurion, Zionism committed itself officially at a conference in New York in 1942. By the end of the war, international public opinion —appalled at what Nazism had wrought—had come to Zionism's support, and only British stubbornness stood in the way. London's decision in 1945 to continue the policy of the White Paper, refusing to open Palestine to the Jewish refugees, hardened Zionist determination. Vanished for good was the benign vision of a Jewish homeland, organized under British protection, flourishing within the comfortable framework of the British empire. Zionism had resolved that the Jewish state would be, and would survive on its own.

Rabin reflected the conventional Mainstream interpretation when, in speaking of the pre-independence era, he told me:

"Even before the knowledge of the Holocaust came to us, we understood what was happening in Europe from the refugees who were arriving. What more could happen to the Jewish people to justify the need for a land, a country, a state of our own? It didn't matter what the boundaries would be. What mattered was that we needed a Jewish state *now*. In my opinion, to push for a state *now* was Ben-Gurion's greatest decision, the greatest decision of a Jewish leader in the last hundred years."

Where Ben-Gurion differed from the Revisionists, at this juncture, was in holding on to the straw of negotiating Britain's departure from Palestine, hoping thereby to conserve precious resources for the impending battles against the Arabs. The Haganah's mission, as the Jewish Agency defined it after the Nazis' defeat, was to make it possible for refugees from Europe to evade the military cordon with which the British had ringed the country. Only rarely did the Haganah go into action against British forces as such. But rarer still were the occasions when it cooperated with the Revisionists in military actions against the British. Until the end, the Jewish Agency's policy was to reach an agreement to avoid outright Jewish-British war. Meanwhile, the Revisionist un-

derground, operating outside the Jewish Agency's authority, made
British life in Palestine miserable.

Geula Cohen provides in her memoirs, *Woman of Violence,* her
sense of the bitterness of the underground war:

> Nights were spent in the radio station. "This is the Voice of the Hebrew
> Underground! This is the radio station of the Freedom Fighters of
> Israel!" . . . Twice a week Lehi radio went on the air to announce a
> growing list of almost daily operations: army bases and police stations
> attacked; military trains blown up; scores of British soldiers and detec-
> tives killed; railroad tracks, bridges, telegraph lines destroyed. . . .
> Gradually, the British were being thrown on the defensive. Their tanks
> and armor were being used less to terrorize the Jewish community than
> to protect themselves. The army bases more and more resembled ghet-
> tos and beleaguered forts. Finally, the situation became unendurable.
> The government of Great Britain took stock, added up the profits and
> the losses, calculated the odds and decided to dump the whole problem
> into the lap of the United Nations.

In 1942, Menachem Begin, barely thirty, became chief of the
Irgun. A militant Revisionist, he had just arrived overland from
Eastern Europe, where he had been a protégé of Jabotinsky, who
had died two years earlier. Begin was as zealous as his mentor,
though he differed from him in being devoutly religious. Less
strategist and fighter than propagandist, he worked for years as
Irgun leader in permanent disguise, moving from house to house,
issuing proclamations which steadily elevated the pitch of the
confrontation, not only with Britain but with Mainstream Zionism.
A staunch ideologue, contemptuous of compromisers, Begin established himself during the underground war as an anathema not
only to the British but to Ben-Gurion as well.

Mainstream Zionists do not like to give credit to Jabotinsky for
leading the way to Jewish statehood, nor to the Revisionist underground for forcing the British to leave. Revisionism, in defying
official Zionist policy, undermined the political institutions that
the Mainstream was trying to create as structure of the forthcom-

ing state. Its brutal terror, furthermore, jeopardized the Mainstream's efforts to rally international support to Zionism's cause. Yet whatever the Mainstream's disapproval, it is hard to imagine that the British would have left, or at least have left so soon, without the underground's relentless attacks.

Mainstream Zionists become livid when Revisionists today insist it is Jabotinsky, not Ben-Gurion, who should properly be called the father of Israel's independence. The Revisionist claim, though exaggerated, is not without substance. Jabotinsky must be credited with imbuing in Revisionism a much clearer vision than the Mainstream had of the impending destruction of European Jewry. His early assertion that the Jews needed not a "homeland" but a state of their own as a means of salvation was, in retrospect, prophetic. He, more than anyone, was the organizing force behind the Jewish armies, both the underground and the Haganah. It was not until after his death that his vision was vindicated, first by the Mainstream's demanding, then by its declaring, finally by its defending a sovereign Jewish state. And yet there is good reason why Jabotinsky and the Revisionist movement are as much denounced as praised in Israel today.

Indeed, if Zionists were united at the end of World War II by the objective of statehood, they remained deeply divided about the nature of the state. Zionism's preoccupation was, by definition, the *Jewish* community, not the Arab, much less other religious and ethnic communities that made their homes in Palestine. The obsession of Zionist leaders with immigration issues in the period before independence was in part the product of their concern for Europe's Jews, but no less so was their conviction that only a Jewish majority could safeguard the interests of the Jews in the Jewish homeland. Zionist thinkers rarely dwelt on the question of how to organize a land in which native Arabs, hostile to their aspirations, equaled or outnumbered Jews.

In the early days of the British mandate, a few Jewish idealists in Palestine, led by Judah Magnes, an American-born Reform rabbi, and Martin Buber, the venerated philosopher, called for brotherhood with the Arabs and the creation of a "binational" state, in which the two peoples would share power. Premised on the liberal notion of democratic pluralism, binationalism was at odds with the Zionist objective of founding a *Jewish* homeland. Furthermore, the Arabs showed no interest in it, contending that they needed no help from Jews to rule over *their* land. Though a few Jews were initially sympathetic, binationalism was largely discredited by the 1930s, when recurring bloodshed seemed to make very clear that the sharing of power between Arabs and Jews simply would not work.

Partition was a concept first placed on the table on the eve of World War II by the British, recognizing that their Mandate over Palestine could not last much longer. Its logic was that if Jews and Arabs could not live at peace together in Palestine, perhaps they could live there separately. Nowhere in the Middle East was there a tradition of liberalism or experience with democratic pluralism. Overwhelmingly Muslim, the region contained ancient communities of Christians, Druzes, Jews, and schismatic sects of Islam. For the most part, relations among them were peaceful. But they invariably lived apart from one another, their contacts largely limited to commerce. Most had rights of autonomy, permitting them to govern their internal affairs. Each knew where its turf ended and its neighbor's began. Partition was thus consistent with regional practice.

After the war, the British formally proposed the idea. In announcing their impending departure, they urged the United Nations to replace the Mandate with two sovereign states, Jewish in the heavily Jewish areas, Arab in the predominantly Arab areas. Months of acrimonious debate and politicking in world capitals followed. In November 1947, the United Nations—backed by the United States and the Soviet Union, its dominant members—approved the proposal in a close vote. The Arabs, denying the U.N.'s authority, rejected the decision outright. Their belief, of course, was that the Jews had no rights over Palestine at all. The Jews, disappointed that they did not have all of Palestine but relieved that they had some, gave partition their endorsement.

In the years before the partition vote, Zionists, Mainstream no less than Revisionist, had come to interpret the Balfour Declaration's promise of "the establishment *in** Palestine of a national home for the Jewish people" as a title deed to *all* of Palestine. They conveniently forgot that the Balfour Declaration also stipulated: "nothing shall be done which may prejudice the civil and religious rights of existing non-Jewish communities in Palestine." Jabotinsky, the Revisionist leader, fiercely opposed partition during his lifetime, calling it a betrayal of the Zionist ideal, and after his death Begin was no less implacable. Ben-Gurion, the Mainstream realist, was willing to live with half a loaf. He rejoiced in its premise, the establishment of a sovereign Jewish state. He also argued that the narrow frontiers of the British plan were not necessarily final.

If homeland-versus-state was the issue that divided Mainstream Zionists from Revisionists until the middle of World War II, partition became the issue that most bitterly separated them after Israel's independence. Partition, in fact, is the issue that most bitterly divides them today.

The conception that Revisionists brought to Zionism was fundamentally territorial. More on historical than religious grounds, they argued for restoration of Jewish rule within *Biblical* boundaries. In the absence of scholarly agreement on these boundaries, they asserted a sovereign right over Britain's entire Palestine Mandate, a claim that reached as far as the Iraqi border. When Britain in 1922 divided the Mandate administratively, separating the land east of the Jordan River from Palestine, the Revisionists charged a betrayal of the Balfour Declaration. In their anthems, Revisionists sing even today of an Israel on *both sides* of the Jordan. Officially, they renounced this claim only a few years ago. In fact, there are many Revisionists who have not renounced it still.

*Author's italics.

The Revisionist perspective of the 1947 partition vote was that the Jews, having lost the area *east* of the Jordan River to British machinations, were being asked by the U.N. to give up much of the land to the *west*. Mainstream Zionists were less concerned with the size than with the character of the homeland. They had no interest in the trans-Jordan area at all. They considered the Jordan River the "natural" border of historical Palestine. Their real priority was to establish a country where Jews, clearly the majority, could indisputably rule.

The region immediately west of the Jordan River—the West Bank, which the Revisionists called by the Biblical names Judea and Samaria—was heavily populated by Arabs. Ben-Gurion cared less about settling it than settling the Negev, the nearly uninhabited southern desert where in his later years he made his home. Other Zionists considered the fertile Galilee in the north, in which Arabs to this day predominate, to be more important. Though they acknowledged that partition was a territorial compromise, Mainstream leaders rejected the contention that accepting it was a sellout. In excluding several hundred thousand Arabs from the Jewish state, it in fact served their demographic objectives.

The conventional Mainstream view of partition was expressed to me by Rabin: "I believe in the historic right of the Jewish people to live all over the land of Israel. That is why—for religious, political, historical and moral reasons—the Jewish state can be only here in this place, and not in Birobidjan or Uganda or somewhere else.* But I have no interest in Israel's sovereignty over all of the land. Why? Not because the world opposes it or the Arabs oppose it but because I want a *Jewish* state—not in name alone and not by its Biblical boundaries but by its way of life. For me, the Zionist dream must be achieved by education, building, agriculture, industry, science. There is a contradiction between a Jewish state defined by boundaries and a Jewish state defined by its way of life."

*Birobidjan was established, and since abandoned, as a Jewish autonomous region of the Soviet Union in 1928; Uganda was offered to the Zionist movement by the British for Jewish settlement in 1903 and rejected.

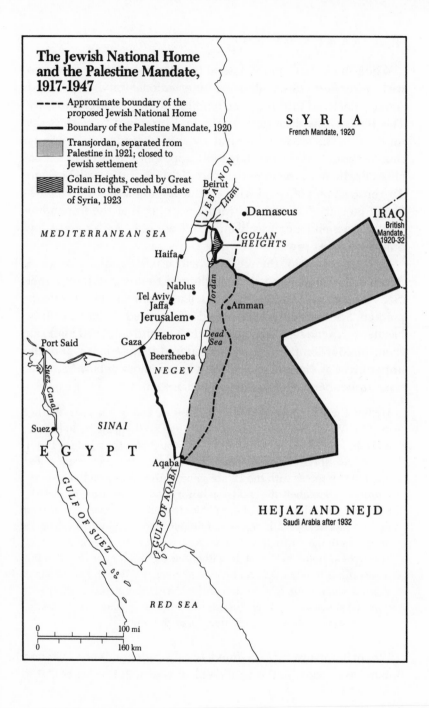

The Jewish National Home and the Palestine Mandate, 1917-1947

- - - - Approximate boundary of the proposed Jewish National Home

────── Boundary of the Palestine Mandate, 1920

▨ Transjordan, separated from Palestine in 1921; closed to Jewish settlement

▧ Golan Heights, ceded by Great Britain to the French Mandate of Syria, 1923

SYRIA
French Mandate, 1920

LEBANON

Litani

Beirut

•Damascus

MEDITERRANEAN SEA

GOLAN HEIGHTS

IRAQ
British Mandate, 1920-32

Haifa•

Nablus•
Tel Aviv
Jaffa•
Jerusalem•

Jordan

•Amman

Hebron•

Dead Sea

Port Said•

Gaza•

Beersheeba•

NEGEV

Suez Canal

Suez•

SINAI

EGYPT

Aqaba•

GULF OF SUEZ

GULF OF AQABA

HEJAZ AND NEJD
Saudi Arabia after 1932

RED SEA

0 ————— 100 mi
0 ————— 160 km

When the U.N. General Assembly voted to partition Palestine, with Jerusalem designated an international city, the Jewish Agency declared the vote to be binding on the Jewish community. The Revisionists dissented angrily and promised to redress this misdeed. "The acts of betrayal by misled leaders—all will be shunted aside," said a proclamation, apparently written by Menachem Begin, from the underground. "Historic justice will be done. The entire Land of Israel will be returned to the Jewish people— for all eternity." His words were a warning that the impending war of independence was likely to pit not only Arab against Jew but Jew against Jew.

On May 14, 1948, the day the British left Palestine for good, Ben-Gurion proclaimed the founding of the new state of Israel. (See Appendix B.) Unlike Rabin, Geula Cohen was bitterly disappointed. She considered the boundaries crafted at the U.N. to be hardly worth the sacrifices she and the underground had made for Zionism. More important, she considered them a betrayal of the imperatives of Zionism itself. This is her memory of how her emotions responded to Ben-Gurion's declaration:

> My heart was dancing, of course, because we had sovereignty, but not my feet. We didn't have Jerusalem. We had no Bethlehem, no Nablus, no Hebron, all these places I fought for. I fought for the whole of Israel.
>
> Now the enemy was dead and we were still alive and being called upon to join forces with the Establishment, the organized Jewish community.... Somehow the rudder of history had slipped from our hands. So confident had we been of our ability to control the course of events that we had deliberately refused to prepare for the inevitable struggle for power in the future Jewish state. Now we were being asked to make ourselves at home in that state without any possibility of refashioning it according to our own ideals. Victory over the British had brought about the liberation of a portion of the Jewish homeland . . . the partition of Palestine. . . . I felt the infinite grief of a slaughtered dream. . . . It was only obvious to me that I had to go on.

When Ben-Gurion proclaimed Israel's independence, Yitzhak Rabin was already on the battlefield, at war with the Arabs. After the U.N. vote in November, the British simply abandoned their peacekeeping responsibilities and stood by while Jews and the local Arabs fought out their differences among themselves. For several months, the two sides skirmished for tactical positions, in villages and city neighborhoods, at road junctions and on hilltops. Meanwhile, the Arab states—Egypt, Jordan, Syria, Lebanon, even the more distant countries—mobilized for an invasion, waiting only for Britain's departure. This was the war that Rabin and the Haganah had for nearly a decade been preparing to fight.

Ben-Gurion recognized, with some misgivings, that the new state would depend, at least for a time, on Revisionist forces. As the British packed to go, some five thousand experienced fighters emerged from the underground. Ben-Gurion had erred, Rabin told me, in having sent so many men of military age to Europe during World War II. Despite frenzied last-minute efforts, the Haganah, still operating in semisecrecy, had not yet integrated its available manpower and organized its units for the combat ahead. As the official army of the state, it was supposed to have the Irgun and Lehi units under its command, but Ben-Gurion had little confidence that the underground was prepared to accept official discipline. From the start, serious problems developed between Mainstream and Revisionist forces.

As 1948 opened, the two groups were fighting side by side to break a Palestinian siege of the Jewish sector of Jerusalem. Rabin, now deputy commander of the Palmach, had been assigned the dangerous mission of running supply convoys through the gamut of Arab villages along the city's mountainous approaches. In April, the Irgun and Lehi commands sought and received authorization from the Haganah to take Deir Yassin, a village on the Jerusalem road from which the enemy poured heavy gunfire on the convoys. In military terms, the mission succeeded. It ended, however, with more than two hundred Arabs, including many women and children, brutally slain. The Haganah promptly disclaimed responsibility for the operation.

Word of the killings spread quickly among the Arabs, triggering a panicky flight. In the weeks after Deir Yassin, hundreds of thousands of Arabs—as much as two thirds of the local population—left the sector assigned by the partition plan to the Jews. The exodus dramatically transformed Palestinian demography, providing the new state, with the substantial Jewish majority to which it aspired, far ahead of any schedule it might have foreseen.

The Revisionists certainly favored the departure of the Palestinians, but whether expulsion was part of their mission at Deir Yassin is unclear. In a message of congratulation to the Irgun troops, Begin declared: "Continue thus until victory. As in Deir Yassin, so everywhere, we will attack and smite the enemy. God, God, Thou hast chosen us for conquest." Whatever Begin's enthusiasm, however, the documentation fails to prove that he planned the massacre of the Arabs, and in his memoirs, he denies any such suggestion.

To imagine, however, that only Revisionists thought of driving out the Arab population would be far from accurate. Israeli scholars now acknowledge that Ben-Gurion himself promoted expulsion. Rabin revealed as much in a statement in his memoirs that was excised by Israeli censors. It was subsequently published, without denial, by the *New York Times*. In an account of the capture of Lod, Rabin wrote:

> We walked outside, Ben-Gurion accompanying us. [Yigal] Allon [commander of the Palmach] repeated his question. "What is to be done with the population?" B-G waved his hand in a gesture which said: "Drive them out.". . . "Driving out" is a term with a harsh ring. Psychologically, this was one of the most difficult actions we undertook. The population of Lod did not leave willingly. There was no way of avoiding the use of force and warning shots in order to make the inhabitants march the ten to fifteen miles to the point where they met up with the [Arab] Legion.

The official Zionist position has consistently been that the Arab leadership, by radio and in official proclamations, encouraged the Palestinians to flee, promising them a prompt return to a land free of Jews. Whatever the Arabs did, however, the evidence is clear that the Jewish role in the Palestinian exodus was far from passive.

The exodus created a refugee problem that in four decades has not been resolved. To this day, the Palestinians assert the right of return to their homes in Israel, which if exercised would place the Jews in a minority. It is a demand to which no Israeli government can accede. Ironically, Begin and his followers, who provoked the flight at Deir Yassin, have been the most willing since 1967 to jeopardize its consequences by absorbing into Israel the inhabitants of the captured territories. Mainstream Zionism, which still condemns Deir Yassin, is at least logically consistent in seeking to preserve the consequences of the Arabs' departure. It rejects not only repatriation of the refugees but the incorporation of land that will bring a million more Palestinians into the Jewish state.

"My conscience is completely clear when it comes to the Palestinians," Rabin told me. "In 1947, the U.N. proposed a partition plan. It was determined then that there would be two sovereign states here, a Jewish state and an Arab state. We agreed. Our leaders accepted the partition plan. Had the Arab states, and particularly the Palestinian leadership, accepted the proposal, I believe we would have been living in peace and tranquillity since then. The Arabs believed they would be able to destroy the state of Israel, but they failed. It is the Palestinian leadership that bears responsibility for the Palestinian tragedy. The Palestinians chose the wrong leaders."

What obviously made Ben-Gurion furious at the Revisionists was not the flight of the Arabs but the nasty repercussions the Deir Yassin massacre had around the world, at a time when the new state needed all the outside support it could get. Ben-Gurion proclaimed the incident a stain upon Zionist ideals, and had the Irgun officers responsible for the operation arrested. His posturing incensed the Revisionists. Though the arrested officers were subsequently released, the affair further aggravated the Zionist schism. Even as they fought Arabs, the conflict between Mainstream Zionists and Revisionists refused to go away. In fact, it leaped to a dramatically deadlier level.

Two months after Deir Yassin—a month after the declaration of independence—the confrontation within Zionism turned bloody. By then, the armies of the Arab states had crossed Israel's frontiers and combat was heavy. Fighting shoulder to shoulder with the Haganah were ex-underground units which, by mutual agreement, had begun to merge into the regular army's structure. Israel at that point was outnumbered, its supplies were short and the outcome of the war was by no means certain. Nonetheless, Jews fought Jews.

On June 11, Ben-Gurion learned from a BBC broadcast that the *Altalena,* a ship belonging to the Irgun, was heading in the Mediterranean east from Marseilles, carrying some nine hundred Revisionist volunteers and enough weapons to turn the war in Israel's favor. When confronted, Begin admitted he knew about the approaching ship—*Altalena* was Jabotinsky's nom de plume—but he maintained that the cargo was intended for the entire Israeli army. He then proceeded, however, to demand 20 percent of the weapons for underground units, which Ben-Gurion refused. Representatives of the two sides were still bargaining when the *Altalena* arrived off the Israeli coast.

With the ship lying at anchor at Kfar Vitkin, a small port north of Tel Aviv, Begin demanded that the Irgun be permitted to unload. The demand triggered a savage sequence, the responsibility for which is veiled in a mass of conflicting assertions. The most innocent interpretation holds that the bloodshed was the product of blunders in the negotiations between the two sides. A more personal interpretation has it that Ben-Gurion and Begin, sworn enemies by now, were engaged in a high-stakes contest to humiliate each other. A third interpretation contends that the *Altalena* was at the heart of a Revisionist plot to overthrow the state.

It is unlikely that there will ever be agreement on the truth.

What is clear is that the cargo was potent enough to have made the Revisionists the most powerful military force in Israel. Ben-Gurion had no intention of knuckling under to any plan to have them take possession of it.

Before agreement was reached, Irgun fighters began unloading the cargo from the *Altalena,* using small boats to take the weapons ashore. When Ben-Gurion learned what was happening, he ordered Haganah forces to surround and close in on the port. Begin, in command on the beach, rejected instructions to give up the unloaded arms and, instead, he retreated to the ship, which steamed out to sea. The *Altalena* then turned south toward Tel Aviv, shadowed by patrol boats. Meanwhile, on the shore, firing started between the two forces and continued until the Irgun contingent surrendered. Some two dozen Revisionists and eight regulars were either killed or wounded in the fighting.

While the *Altalena* was at sea, Ben-Gurion's cabinet reached a formal decision to seize the ship, making resistance an act of civil insurrection. When the ship docked at Tel Aviv, the Haganah first fired at a motor launch that was bringing in crates, then turned its guns on the ship itself. Meanwhile, within the city, Irgun fighters, many of them deserting from the regular units into which they had recently been integrated, rallied to defend their comrades at sea and on shore. The fighting was chaotic, and for a few hours, the Irgun was actually in control in the city. But late in the day, a shell struck the *Altalena* and it began to sink. Begin, one of the last to disembark, reached shore safely, then broadcast an order to his men to end the fighting. By then, nearly one hundred Israelis, most of them Revisionists, had been killed. The Haganah won the battle, but the cargo that remained aboard went down with the ship.

Israelis do not much like to remember the *Altalena* or to recognize the significance of the brief civil war it provoked. Ben-Gurion, at this crucial moment in the struggle against the Arabs, was prepared to kill Israelis to establish the state's authority. He had no doubt the *Altalena* meant insurrection. Israel's history books treat the episode slightingly. Most memoirs of the period, Begin's excepted, glance over it. Rabin, who commanded a Palmach unit that fought on the beach, does not mention it at all. Yet nothing in Israel's lifetime more vividly expressed the schism between Mainstream and Revisionist Zionism. The *Altalena* incident left a heritage of hatred, which thrives to this day.

As a Revisionist, Geula Cohen is remarkably tolerant of Ben-Gurion's conduct in the *Altalena* affair. She concedes he was a builder of institutions, determined to create a strong central government. During the Mandate, in the absence of Jewish authority, military and political bodies had grown up with allegiance only to themselves. What consoles Cohen is that Ben-Gurion was equally uncompromising with the Mainstream's bodies, though with less bloody results. The Palmach, on the left, was as ruthlessly integrated into the state military structure as, in the weeks after the *Altalena,* was the Irgun on the right. Ben-Gurion was determined to fuse them into the formal structure of the state, and for the most part he succeeded.

"He didn't want to take any risk," Cohen said of Ben-Gurion, "and I understand him. Everyone was afraid that the guns will talk more than the mouth to bring Begin to power. Ben-Gurion was not right, I think, about Begin's intentions because Begin would never make a rebellion. He thought Begin was an antidemocrat, and he was wrong. Begin was a superdemocrat, and I am against his superdemocracy. But Ben-Gurion was right, politically, to cut Begin down, even to cutting with blood. I was on the other side then. But now I see things from a different perspective. I can understand Ben-Gurion's motives."

By the end of 1948, Israel had beaten the forces that had come from the Arab nations to destroy it. It held 20 percent more land than the U.N. had allotted to it. It had closed the gaps between Jewish enclaves, making contiguous the territory under state control. It had improved its strategic position by shortening its defense perimeter. It had also taken possession of West Jerusalem,

Israel's Frontiers, 1949-1967

Jewish State, as defined by the United Nations partition of Palestine, November 1947

Territory conquered by Israel, 1948-49

Boundaries of Israel according to the armistice agreements of 1949

LEBANON

SYRIA

Damascus

Kuneitra

Acre

Safed

Haifa

Tiberias

Nazereth

Ein Gev

Afula

Beth-Shan

Jenin

Tulkarm

Nablus

MEDITERRANEAN SEA

WEST BANK

Tel Aviv

Jaffa

Lod

Annexed by Jordan, 1950

Ramla

Jericho

Amman

Ashdod

Jerusalem

Jordan

Proposed International Area

Gat

Bethlehem

GAZA STRIP

Gaza

Hebron

Dead Sea

Occupied by Egypt

Khan Yunis

Ein Gedi

JORDAN

Rafah

El Arish

Beersheeba

Revivim

El-Auja

NEGEV

EGYPT

SINAI

Elat

Aqaba

0   50 mi

0   80 km

SAUDI ARABIA

which it promptly annexed and declared to be the eternal capital of the Jewish state.

But Egypt was in control of the Gaza Strip, and Jordan held not only the West Bank but the eastern half of Jerusalem, including the Old City. Furthermore, Jordan had placed barriers along the demarcation line, sealing off its half of the city and barring the access of Jews to the Wailing Wall, Judaism's most important shrine. Israel's army, at that time, was in a position to drive the Arab forces out of all of Palestine. Instead, Ben-Gurion chose to make peace.

Begin wrathfully denounced Ben-Gurion's choice. "They have carved up not the territory but our very soul," he declared. For him, for Geula Cohen, for Revisionists generally, the decision to abide by the principle of partition meant that Israel's independence was incomplete. The end of the fighting did not diminish their dedication to the Revisionist vision of the state.

In *1949: The First Israelis,* the Israeli writer Tom Segev tells a story of a military parade planned for downtown Tel Aviv to celebrate the first anniversary of independence. Some 300,000 Israelis, one third of the country's population, flooded into the city, far more than anyone had foreseen. In the immense confusion that ensued, it became apparent that unless the route was cleared by force, the parade could not take place. So Ben-Gurion canceled the parade. Many Israelis felt embarrassed for their new nation, and Ben-Gurion himself wrote that the holiday had been ruined.

But *Ma'ariv,* the Tel Aviv daily, found consolation, even "sublime beauty," in the day's events. It noted that in Hitler's Germany the parade would not have been canceled. "It may be," said the paper, "that it was supposed to be the people and not the army that filled the road. The parade failed because, while we wanted a military parade with all our hearts, we are nevertheless Jews."

I repeat the story because it describes a more innocent Israel than we have come to know, less efficient but also less cynical. It was an Israel of humane dimensions, where hope was fresh for forging a nation in which warm Jewish values prevailed.

In this Israel, in the early glow of statehood, Revisionism went into eclipse. Begin never stopped proclaiming that Mainstream Zionism had betrayed the Jews. He lamented the loss of Judea and Samaria, and campaigned "to liberate the homeland from Jordanian rule," by which he meant extending Israel's borders to the Jordan River and beyond. But in those days, the Revisionist dream seemed irrelevant. Israelis were too preoccupied with the problems of making the nation work to think much about expanding it. They were trying to create a "normal" nation.

After the war, Begin formed the Herut (Freedom) Party, but his appeal, far removed from the national consensus, seemed to be limited to the faithful. After each election in the postwar era, Ben-Gurion used to say he was ready to form a coalition with "all parties except Herut and the Communists." Even after Ben-Gurion retired, Labor maintained the policy of excluding Herut, except for a brief period during the emergency of the Six-Day War. The policy lasted through thirty years of Labor's preeminence, during which few questioned the permanence of the electorate's commitment to Mainstream Zionism.

To the Arabs, and to other opponents of Zionism, Begin's words raised troublesome questions about Israel's *real* territorial designs. In the Middle East, Arabs and Jews alike tend to quote the most thunderous statements from the enemy's camp as evidence of his intentions. The Arabs maintained tirelessly in the years after Israel's independence that Israel would not long be satisfied with partition, citing Begin as evidence that Zionism was inherently committed to expansion. Israel's friends scoffed at the contention, and the issue remained untested during the first two decades of the new nation's history. It acquired immediacy only with Revisionism's revival in the euphoria that followed the Six-Day War.

3

Turnabout

JOHN FOSTER DULLES, President Eisenhower's secretary of state, passionately courted Egypt's Gamal Abdel Nasser throughout 1955. His design was to introduce American power into the Middle East, an area of the world that until then had remained remarkably uninvolved in the cold war, now a decade old. Dulles, who took a more rigorously anti-Soviet line than Eisenhower did, talked not just of containing but of rolling back Russian power. The Middle East, as he saw it, was part of the "soft underbelly," where the Soviet Union was extremely vulnerable.

Having been promised American arms, four countries on Russia's southern flank—Iraq, Turkey, Iran and Pakistan—had by then agreed to permit the basing of Western aircraft within range of major Soviet cities. All were Muslim countries. From that, Dulles reasoned that Muslims were, strategically, the key to keeping the Russians off balance in the south, a deterrent to their moving into the Mediterranean Sea, the Suez Canal, the Persian Gulf. Israel had no place in Dulles's design. The missing piece in his strategic mosaic, as he saw it, was Nasser's Egypt.

Israel's absence from America's plans for the Middle East seems odd from today's perspective, when a special relationship between the United States and the Jewish state is taken for granted. In our own time, Washington is committed to Israel's survival, providing it with weapons while assuring its economic viability. A shared culture and a common posture toward the Soviet Union, reinforced by the unique access provided by American Jewry to American political power, make the intimacy of the relationship seem normal and natural.

We forget that for some years after Israel's independence, neither American policymakers nor American public opinion showed much commitment to Israel's well-being. Americans generally did not seem very interested in the Jewish state. President Truman's support had been critical to the favorable vote at the U.N. on the creation of Israel, but in 1947 American policy turned to preserving the West's sources of oil in the Arab countries. It was not until late in the Eisenhower presidency, nearly a decade after Israeli statehood, that a shift in the distribution of power in the Middle East produced a sign of change in strategic thinking, though not in attitude. In all, the full transformation of American policy to what it is today took more than a quarter century to unfold. Since there now is no more critical factor than the Israeli-American relationship—loosely called an "alliance," though there is no document that makes it such—in determining the fate of the Middle East, it is worth examining the process by which it gradually came about.

For a moment, after Israel's War of Independence, it appeared there might actually be a peace settlement in the Middle East. While their armies were still in the field, Israel and Egypt met to negotiate a military armistice. It was important to the Arabs that Egypt, the most powerful of the Arab countries, set any precedent. Under United Nations supervision, Egyptian and Israeli delegations convened for talks in January 1949, on the Mediterranean island of Rhodes. Yitzhak Rabin, then a lieutenant colonel, was a junior member of Israel's delegation.

Officially, the talks were "indirect," since no Arab state would formally acknowledge Israel's existence, and the delegates addressed their statements to the American diplomat Ralph Bunche,

then serving as the U.N.'s mediator. But before long the delegations were bargaining with each other directly. Within a few days,
Rabin recalls, the members actually became comfortable with one
another, personal relationships developed among them and the
talks became almost cordial.

When Israel and Egypt on February 24 signed an armistice
agreement, it seemed clear that after a transitional period a peace
treaty would follow. The agreement said as much. The borders for
which the signatories settled at Rhodes were drawn, more or less,
along the lines that divided the armies when the fighting ended,
but borders at that time did not seem like a major issue. All the
parties treated them as subject to revision under some permanent
peace accord. The Rhodes document called itself "an indispensable step toward the liquidation of armed conflict and the restoration of peace in Palestine." It was assumed that further steps
would not be far behind.

Over the next few months, Israel signed similar armistice agreements with Lebanon, Jordan and Syria. Jordan in 1949 went even
a step further, joining Israel in preparing the text of a formal peace
treaty. The Israeli government was unmistakably prepared, at that
moment, to conclude a permanent agreement, based on borders
that followed the armistice lines. Some Arabs were clearly ready
to join them in the signing.

There were problems, of course. Jerusalem's international status
had vanished in the fighting, and Jordan was in possession of the
Old City, site of the holy Wailing Wall and other Jewish shrines.
The Israelis, however, seemed so confident of a prompt resolution
of differences with Jordan that, in the armistice talks, they had not
pressed for a formal guarantee of access to the Old City. The
oversight was to come back to haunt them. Still, at the time, the
territorial questions that were so important to the Revisionists and
have since become an insuperable barrier to peace did not appear
serious. In separate talks at the U.N., the two sides even roughed
out the framework of a settlement of the refugee question.
Nonetheless, Rabin said, he left Rhodes with a sense of foreboding.

"After we concluded the details of the agreement," Rabin re-called in his talks with me, "I sat with Mahmoud Riad—later on he became Egypt's foreign minister and secretary-general of the Arab League—and I asked him, 'Why can't we have peace right now? Why do we need this transitional period? We are ready to make peace along the cease-fire lines, to be the permanent bound-aries between us.'

"He answered, 'No, we cannot accept you. An armistice, that's one thing. But to make peace with you would mean that we have to accept that you are here to stay. We are not ready. The situation in our country and in the Arab world will not permit it. We cannot yet live in peace with you.' "

Events quickly showed that the hopes for peace were prema-ture. The defeat, having humiliated the Arab world, placed in jeopardy the governments that had been responsible for it. Disaf-fected Arabs pointed a finger at old elites, accusing them of cor-ruption and ineptitude. Nationalist indignation ran high, and ex-tremism began to flourish. In short order, the kings of Jordan and Iraq and the prime ministers of Egypt and Lebanon were assas-sinated. In 1949 the republic in Syria and in 1952 the monarchy in Egypt were overthrown by military coups. In the wake of the defeat, the Arab world was groping angrily for a new way.

The million Palestinian refugees in the region were an embar-rassing reminder to the Arabs of the defeat. More than half lived under the crown of Jordan, about equally divided between the East Bank and the West Bank. Another 200,000 were installed in the Gaza Strip, which Egypt administered. The rest had found refuge in Syria and Lebanon.

The Arab governments, already fragile, recognized the refugee problem as a powder keg inside their dwelling places. They had no desire to take on financial responsibility for the maintenance of these outsiders, much less integrate them into their own soci-eties, but they could hardly drive the Palestinians away. The course they followed was to combine a minimum of hospitality, as evidence of their nationalist virtues, with strident proclamations of the refugees' right to go back to a homeland freed of Israelis.

The refugees, save for the handful of rich among them, were thrust into wretched conditions in the wake of the war, stunned and puzzled by their misfortune. They were, for the most part, assembled in squalid camps, where their first shelter consisted of tents. Later they were lodged in cement-block or mud-brick housing. The U.N., which had voted in 1947 to establish Israel, had passed a resolution after the War of Independence proclaiming the refugees' right of repatriation. Acknowledging responsibility for the refugees' plight, the U.N. paid for their support, while keeping alive their hopes of returning home.

Once over the initial shock, some of the refugees tried wandering back across the armistice lines, often innocently, to their old villages. Others crossed over expressly to pilfer and vandalize Israeli settlements. In time, young men organized themselves into bands of *fedayeen* to conduct raids on Israel, during which they committed pillage and murder.

The Israeli public was dismayed to learn that neither sovereign independence nor victory in war had ended its vulnerability to Arab violence. To stop the practices, the government at first assigned border police, who employed means that were generally limited and passive. Their tactics produced deadly encounters at armistice lines, with heavy casualties, without diminishing infiltration. Then the army was assigned to take over, initiating a more deadly era. The army made clear it would not be bound by the tactics of passive defense, or the limitations of the armistice borders.

The army's aggressive style provoked renewal of a debate that dated back to before the War of Independence. On a lofty level, the terms of the debate were self-restraint versus retaliation, purity of arms versus intimidation of innocents. In blunter language, the issue was Israeli counterterror. The debate had once defined basic differences between Mainstream Zionism and Revisionism. It had separated the Haganah from the Irgun. Counterterror had been the issue in Ben-Gurion's dispute with Begin over Deir Yassin.

Now Israelis, edgy over the dangers of daily life, were not as ready as before to endorse military and legal niceties that once seemed intrinsic to Zionist morality. Though they had given a mandate to govern to Mainstream Zionism, they applauded the harsh retaliatory dogmas of the Revisionists. Few dissented when General Moshe Dayan, the army's chief of staff, announced a policy of massive reprisals. The Arabs, Dayan said, would henceforth have to calculate the "cost in blood" of their raids by acknowledging that Israel's reaction was likely to claim many innocent victims.

Israeli strategists were themselves divided over indiscriminate retaliation, uncertain whether it deterred or encouraged terrorism, whether terrorists cowered or accommodated when such attacks occurred. What was clear was that the public demanded that the government *do something.* Israeli forces, Dayan said, would go after targets wherever guerillas might be, among or apart from civilians, within Israel's borders or in the territory of the neighboring Arab states. Most Israelis applauded this course.

The army's first major operation took place in October of 1953, when a young officer named Ariel Sharon led a unit of commandos into the village of Qibya in the West Bank. The Israelis killed a few Jordanian soldiers and blew up most of the houses. Sharon said that Palestinians, unknown to his troops, were hiding inside the houses. Sixty-seven civilians died. The action brought Israel's first serious condemnation from the United Nations Security Council. The United States voted with the majority.

The Revisionists pronounced themselves satisfied with Qibya, and demanded more of the same. Under Begin's leadership, they maintained a drumbeat attack on the Labor government, impugning not only its policies in countering terrorism but its patriotism and courage. Begin himself led a near revolt in the streets of Jerusalem when the government, desperate for funds and after much soul-searching, agreed in the early 1950s to negotiate with Germany for financial reparations. Branding the negotiations immoral, he deliberately revived the old Revisionist saw that Mainstream Zionism had disregarded the fate of European Jews before and during World War II. Meanwhile, Begin goaded the government, calling for increasingly audacious military action, particularly against Egypt.

Israel's relations with Gamal Abdel Nasser's revolutionary regime, after it overthrew the Egyptian monarchy in 1952, had for a time been uncontentious, even quietly cordial. Ben-Gurion responded positively to evidence that Nasser, anxious to concentrate on advancing the revolution's social and economic objectives, was considering some accommodation with Israel. But the refugees remained a sensitive political issue in Egypt, as they did throughout the Arab world, and Nasser increasingly tolerated the use of the Gaza Strip for attacks by Palestinian *fedayeen* reaching deep into Israeli territory. In retrospect, it may be fair to say that Israel did not do enough to encourage Nasser's overtures. On the other hand, given the dynamism, the radicalism, the headstrong nationalism of Nasser's revolution, it seems unlikely there was ever a real prospect of reconciliation with Egypt. Inevitably or not, relations between the two governments deteriorated.

Nasser's most serious provocation was in fortifying Sharm el Sheikh, at the entrance to the Strait of Tiran, in order to blockade the shipping headed for the Israeli port of Elath. Nasser claimed the right of control over Egyptian territorial waters and, outside the region, the danger to his closing the strait was unappreciated. In those days, Elath chiefly handled oil from Iran, but Israel had invested heavily to make it generally usable to oceangoing vessels. In isolating it, Nasser cut off Israel's maritime commerce to Africa and the east, a potentially crippling blow in the struggle for economic growth to meet the needs of a rising population. In Nasser, Israelis saw a despot of increasing hostility, exercising life-or-death powers over them.

In this atmosphere of deteriorating relations, Israel chose to make a particularly daring move. On February 28, 1955, it sent a brigade of troops into the Gaza Strip to attack the Egyptian army's headquarters. In the fighting, Israel killed thirty-eight Egyptians and blew up a complex of military installations. Unquestionably, the raid was Ben-Gurion's response to demands for action by Israel's impatient public, prodded by the relentless agitation of Begin and his followers. In Israel, it was seen as just another round in the ongoing conflict of terrorism and counterterrorism. But to Nasser, it was a major escalation of the Egyptian-Israeli quarrel, a strike not at terrorists but at sovereignty, and a blow to Arab dignity, of which he had made himself custodian. In forcing Nasser's hand, the Gaza attack was a long step toward another war.

It was at this point that Eisenhower, holding Israel to blame for the rising strife, gave Dulles, his secretary of state, a free hand to join with Britain in creating an all-Islamic alliance in the Middle East. Named the Baghdad Pact, it was to mobilize the "northern tier" of countries—Turkey, Iraq, Pakistan, Iran—to threaten Soviet security with locally based American aircraft and defend against Soviet invasion with local forces using American arms. Dulles's eagerness to have Egypt join was based not so much on military as on political grounds. He reasoned that without strong Arab endorsement, the alliance faced the risk of being undermined from within. In the unstable Arab world, Nasser seemed best able to deliver that endorsement.

In such an alliance, Israel's presence would, to say the least, have been anomalous. Understandably, Israelis worried. It seemed apparent that in being left out, Israel would be more at the mercy of the Baghdad Pact than would the Soviet Union. But when Israelis proposed that Washington admit their country to the NATO alliance or, as an alternative, sign a bilateral mutual defense agreement, Dulles turned them down cold.

To win Nasser, Dulles had to show that Washington considered Egypt more important than Israel. He had to persuade Nasser that Egypt's chief threat came not from Israel but from Communism, which meant that he could hardly turn around and strengthen Israel's military capabilities, especially after the Gaza raid. An American-Israeli alliance would simply reconfirm the magnitude of the threat that Egypt already saw from Zionism. These months, when Dulles was wooing Nasser, were the grimmest in an American-Israeli relationship that had not been very good from the start.

It is interesting to note that immediately after statehood in 1948, Israel's government had shown no more enthusiasm than Washington for an intimate relationship between the two countries. The United States and the Soviet Union had both been crucial in the U.N. vote establishing Israel's sovereignty, and Soviet-bloc countries had supplied the bulk of the arms that permitted Israel to win the War of Independence. Ben-Gurion spoke of "nonidentification" with the two power blocs, if only to keep open the channels of emigration for an estimated three million Jews still living in the Soviet Union. Washington, anxious to stay in the good graces of the Arabs, who controlled most of the world's oil, made no effort to challenge Israel's even-handedness.

Nonetheless, Israel gravitated westward. Within the framework of today's American-Israeli front in the Middle East, it seems odd to recall that high officials in the State Department had warned President Truman, on the eve of the U.N. partition vote in 1947, that an independent Israel was destined to ally with the Soviet Union. With American support in the balance, Chaim Weizmann, then the leader of world Zionism, wrote a celebrated letter to Truman, firmly denying such a contention. It is true that in those days most Israeli leaders were immigrants from Eastern Europe, and among them were philosophical Marxists. But whatever fondness they may ever have had for Russia had long since vanished, and with Stalin's adoption in the early 1950s of a vicious anti-Semitism reminiscent of the czars, Moscow gave up any claims to Israel's sympathy. Mainstream Zionism, though socialist, had raised Israel as a Western political democracy. Israelis never felt they had much in common with Soviet Russia.

There were other political considerations in Israel's westward drift. Long before independence, Mainstream Zionist leaders had reasoned that to survive, a Jewish homeland would need the protection of a major outside power. In the early days, the natural candidate was Britain. In campaigning among the British for the Balfour Declaration, they had argued that in return for a security umbrella, a Jewish homeland could serve as a way station on the route to India and a Western beachhead in the Middle East. With this bargain in mind, the Zionists, in the peace negotiations after World War I, supported Britain in its quest for a European condominium over the Middle East. Jews turned a deaf ear to the Arabs, who believed Britain and France had promised them immediate independence. Few Jews are aware today that Zionism sided with colonialism, against Arab nationalism, after World War I. Few Arabs forget it. Even Jabotinsky, in those days, was willing to see a Jewish homeland nestled securely within the British empire.

The world after Israel's independence, of course, was not what the Zionist fathers, or the British, had anticipated. Britain, having turned the reasoning of the Balfour Declaration on its head by taking up the Arab cause in the struggle over Palestine, had shattered its bond with Zionism. The British showed no signs of wanting to repair the breach, but that hardly mattered. By the 1950s, it was clear Britain was no longer a world power, and Israel was in the market for another patron.

France, immediately after the War of Independence, showed an interest in taking the assignment. The French, at the time, were angry with the Arabs, whose stubbornness had forced them to give up Syria and Lebanon, their own Middle East colonies. In Egypt, it was no secret that Nasser had designs on the Suez Canal, which the French considered vital to their security. France was also fighting to suppress rising independence movements in its remaining colonies in North Africa, movements which Nasser, in his self-appointed role as champion of Arab nationalism, was openly backing. The French were convinced that Nasser's support was keeping alive the bloody rebellion in Algeria. France saw an interest, then, in furnishing Israel with modern arms, including its first jet aircraft.

The United States, during this period, was busy picking up the debris of the crumbling British empire in the Middle East. In taking over responsibility for preserving the West's sources of oil, Washington had to cultivate the Arab states. Within its own political system, pro-Israeli pressures, much weaker than they have since become, stirred up little popular support. In 1950, the Truman administration joined Britain and France in a "Tripartite Declaration," which aimed at avoiding an arms race in the region by promising to supply limited and balanced weaponry to both sides. Israel returned the gesture by endorsing American intervention in Korea in a U.N. vote in 1950, a vote regarded as a break with Israel's policy of nonidentification. The result, however, was disappointing to Israel, eliciting from Washington neither the economic aid nor the arms for which it hoped.

Limited as Truman's support of Israel was, Eisenhower's first term as President represented even further retreat. The Jewish state never felt more alone. The hostility of the Arab states was implacable. Hardly a day passed without the infiltration of terrorists to kill and pillage, plant mines, set fields afire. Though immigration had more than doubled Israel's population, economic growth was falling steadily behind. When the German government offered to help by paying reparations for the ravages of the Nazis, Begin and his followers led angry crowds in such a ferocious assault on the Knesset that the state itself seemed to totter. The American government was not alone in this period in wondering whether Israel—besieged, impoverished, divided—was actually viable.

No doubt Eisenhower shared Dulles's conviction that the Arabs were a more promising ally, as well as Dulles's uneasiness at the prospect of losing the Middle East and its oil to Communism. But Eisenhower was also deeply disturbed at Israel's growing militarization, and the tactics of indiscriminate retaliation Israel had adopted in its fight against Arab terrorism. If the demon of Dulles's moral indignation was Communism, Eisenhower believed the foundation of American foreign policy had to be more than anti-Communist. Having spent his life in the army, he had acquired a deep aversion to military aggression. Eisenhower was angry about the attack in 1955 on Gaza, which he considered part of a pattern of incendiary behavior that Israel had adopted in dealing with its neighbors.

In contrast to the Presidents who succeeded him, Eisenhower was not loath to translate his vexation with Israel into action. He talked openly of the need for reexamination of Israeli frontiers, for repatriation of the Palestinian refugees, for relocation of Israel's capital from Jerusalem to Tel Aviv. Israelis could scarcely contain their dismay when his administration endorsed a ceiling on immigration to the new state, as if unaware that there was no concept more central to Israel's sense of itself than the "right of return." (See Appendix C.) One time, he suspended Israel's small economic aid allocation until work was stopped on a hydroelectric project that would have diverted water from the Jordan River. Another time, he threatened to cancel the pledge made in the Tripartite Declaration to ensure an arms balance in the region.

Yet despite Eisenhower's stern handling of Israel, Nasser turned thumbs down on participation in the Baghdad Pact, leaving Dulles apoplectic. Nasser's decision was not arbitrary. Whatever Dulles might argue, Egypt's foe was Zionism, not Communism or Moscow. If Egypt had a big-power enemy, it was not Russia but Britain, which had occupied the country for most of a century, and from whose dominion Egypt had only recently freed itself. Worse than British partnership in the Baghdad Pact was Iraq's. The Iraqi monarchy was a British client, and Egypt's rival for leadership in the Arab world. In retrospect, it may have been a monumental blunder for Nasser to miss what was probably the Arabs' last chance to isolate Israel from the West. He surely did not appreciate how the Baghdad Pact could be useful in his fight against Israel. But Nasser saw no interest for Egypt in aligning with the Western powers, and as Israel breathed a sigh of relief, he turned his face eastward.

While Dulles maneuvered to salvage his labors, Nasser placed ambitious new schemes on Egypt's agenda. By now, Nasser's vision had gone beyond consolidating his revolution at home to exporting it to the Arab world, and perhaps further. In the spring of 1955, he traveled to Bandung in Indonesia, where he joined with other third world leaders in founding the "nonaligned" power bloc. Though ostensibly independent of both East and West, the movement emitted a reflexive hostility to the old colonial powers. If it was not pro-Communist, it was surely anti-Western. Nasser made a strong impression in Bandung and left with international stature. His performance much enhanced his market value in Moscow.

In September 1955, Nasser made the stunning announcement of the agreement that brought the Soviet Union into the Middle East. The two governments had signed a pact which provided that in exchange for Egyptian cotton, the East Bloc states would send Nasser planes, guns, tanks, warships and ammunition. A flow of arms of the magnitude foreseen in the agreement inevitably had to transform the strategic balance in the Middle East. Dulles may have introduced the cold war into the region, but the Russians had quickly seized the advantage. The Moscow pact seemed clearly destined to shift the equilibrium not only between Arabs and Israelis but between the superpowers in the Middle East arena.

Israel was, of course, dismayed by the agreement. Begin promptly initiated a campaign in behalf of a "preemptive war." Ben-Gurion was more cautious, but did not rule out military action. Both men were persuaded that unless an effort was made to thwart Nasser's designs, Egypt and the Arab world would soon have enough weapons to overwhelm the Jewish state.

Dulles was stupefied by his defeat. His labors over the Baghdad Pact had yielded precisely the opposite of what he had planned. The Russians were in Cairo, and Nasser was making ready to turn the balance of power in the Middle East in their favor. For a year Dulles persisted in trying to rescue his Baghdad scheme, continuing his courtship of Egypt, ignoring Israel. Finally, he gave up and, in a fit of mindlessness, triggered a shock whose tremors would go beyond the Middle East to shake the foundations of the NATO alliance in Europe.

For years, the United States had been working with Cairo on a project of great importance to Egypt, construction of a high dam on the Nile at Aswan. Suddenly, on Dulles's command, Washington withdrew the offer to finance the project. The Russians promptly announced they would provide Egypt with the money, so the project continued. Meanwhile, Nasser retaliated by nationalizing the Suez Canal. For all the nasty words he used, the nationalization actually did the United States little harm. Its real target was Europe. To Nasser, nationalization was the final step in Egypt's emancipation from colonialism, and the evening of a score not so much with America as with the West.

France and Britain, however, were not prepared to submit to Nasser's control over their vital sea lanes, any more than Israel was ready to tolerate Egypt's acquisition of a mighty war machine. For the French, the moment also appeared opportune to put an end to Nasser's support of the unrelenting Algerian rebellion, a devastating drain on the country. Though still uncomfortable dealing with the British, the Israelis had established excellent working relations with the French, who threw open the doors of their arms depots to the Israeli military forces. Israel was now ready to act. So were France and Britain, who laid aside their once bitter colonial rivalry with a plan to teach Nasser a lesson.

In a surprise attack on October 29, 1956, the Israeli army struck south and west at Egyptian forces, and within a few days had won a tremendous victory. Israel cleared the terrorist bases in the Gaza Strip, captured the entire Sinai peninsula and reached the Suez Canal. Among its prizes was Egypt's fortress at Sharm el Sheikh, the guns of which had enforced the blockade of the Strait of Tiran. The port of Elath was open once again. Two days after the Israelis hit, French and British air squadrons bombed Egyptian military installations, then landed paratroops along the canal. Before the paratroops completed the mission of seizing the canal, however, the operation had set off a political storm within the NATO alliance.

Yitzhak Rabin, by happenstance, played only a slight role in the Sinai war. Already among the top officers of the Israeli army, he was, at the time of the campaign, commander of the northern front, far from the battlefield. But he did not hesitate to say that the war, brilliantly though it was conducted, was in his view a serious political mistake. In our talks, this was his explanation:

"In the 1950s, I studied military affairs for a year in the Royal Staff College at Camberley, in England, where we Israelis developed many of our strategic concepts. We studied Clausewitz, who contended that the purpose of war is to destroy your enemy's armed forces, so that you can impose your political will on him. During World War II, the Allies followed this axiom and we wondered if we could do it too. It was worth a national effort, two or three years to do nothing but build armed forces to win one good war, to capture all the Arab capitals and impose peace. Clausewitz's formula would justify making such a war.

"When Ben-Gurion was convinced, or dragged, in 1956 to join with the French and the British, he believed that together they would make a new political order in the Middle East. He thought the war would bring down Nasser, and we would get the whole of the Sinai as part of Israel. After the victory, he made a statement in the Knesset about the rule of the Kingdom of Israel over the Strait of Tiran. Nonetheless, the war failed to reach any far-reaching political goal. Why?"

Rabin proceeded to explain that in contrast to World War II, the Arab-Israeli conflict did not meet the classical standards for the application of the Clausewitz theory. He did not mention that a small country like Israel, tough as its army might be, could destroy all the Arab forces and still lack the means to impose its political will. Arabs outnumber Israelis in the Middle East about thirty to one. Cairo, four or five times more populous than all Israel, could by itself swallow up a huge occupation force. With enormous reserves in population and territory, the Arabs can fight on indefinitely, after their armies are destroyed. Rabin contended that the several years of respite from future war that Israel won in the Sinai campaign may not have been worth the losses. The blame for Israel's failure to win the political victory that Clausewitz described Rabin assigned to the superpowers, whose intrusion in the Middle East turned Clausewitz upside down.

"Comparing the basic difference between the Allied forces in the Second World War and Israel in the Arab-Israeli conflict, the conclusion I came to is that between the Allied forces and God, no one existed. But between Israel and the Arab countries, there are the superpowers, and they can stop us from even thinking of doing what they themselves did to the Axis countries. Israel must fight wars for its defense, but there is no purpose for Israel to initiate a war because, since we cannot impose our political will or totally eliminate the enemy's motivation to go to war, there would be no justified political goals."

With the Israeli army sitting on the east bank of the Suez Canal, Eisenhower provided Rabin with the evidence to validate his contention. Outraged by the attack, Eisenhower stated flatly that France and Britain, as well as Israel, had engaged in violations of international legality that were more terrible than any of Nasser's misdeeds. Unusual as such indignation toward allies may be in diplomacy, there was scarcely any doubt about Eisenhower's sincerity. He imposed stringent pressures not only on Israel, a country to which he felt no great attachment, but on the French and British, his World War II comrades in arms. He insisted on the immediate and total evacuation of Egyptian territory. With the capture of the canal half completed, London meekly concurred. Left no option, France followed suit.

Ben-Gurion, however, proved tougher to crack. He was under heavy pressure from Eisenhower to move in one direction, but from Israelis to move in another. Begin, who had demanded that the government launch the war, kept public opinion at a high pitch, proclaiming that Israel must return none of its spoils. In Israel's possession was not only the entire Sinai, including the Gaza Strip, but a mass of captured Soviet war materiel. Begin argued particularly for retention of the Gaza Strip, which he called "a liberated part of the homeland." To the Revisionists, the war was vindication of Jabotinsky's contention that Zionism could attain its territorial objectives through military power. Politically, it was not easy for Ben-Gurion to walk away from the fruits of Israel's victory.

But Eisenhower would not soften his stand. He warned he would break relations with Israel, and when the Russians threatened to take matters in their own hands, he announced that Israel would have to stand alone if attacked. Many Americans found him unduly rigid. On Capitol Hill, Senator Lyndon B. Johnson led a campaign to provide Israel with security guarantees in return for withdrawal. His position no doubt influenced Eisenhower, and prefigured American policy after the Six-Day War, during Johnson's own term as President. But faced with Eisenhower's intransigence, Ben-Gurion knew he was licked. As Rabin put it, "When Ben-Gurion realized he had failed, he decided to cut losses and confine himself to very limited goals."

Israel gave in slowly, withdrawing its forces in two steps from the Sinai but holding on to the Gaza Strip and Sharm el Sheikh. Finally, the United States and Israel hammered out a compromise on the remaining issues, which was far different, in at least one crucial area, from what Eisenhower had originally conceived. The agreement, for the first time, focused major American attention on Israeli security concerns.

The agreement provided for basing a United Nations Emergency Force (UNEF) on Egyptian territory. The force was to have a dual mission. It was, first, to keep units on the border of the Gaza Strip to guard against infiltration into Israel of Palestinian *fedayeen*. Second, it was to stand watch at Sharm el Sheikh, to keep the Strait of Tiran open to ships headed for the Israeli port of Elath.

Historically, the provision concerning the Strait of Tiran became the more important, for it carried with it a peacekeeping commitment from the United States. Eisenhower, dedicated internationalist though he was, had strongly opposed American involvement in the Arab-Israeli conflict. But whatever his misgivings, he endorsed formally and publicly an aide-mémoire from Dulles to the Israelis that pledged the United States, in the event of a new blockade of the strait, "to exercise the right of free and innocent passage and to join with others to secure general recognition of this right." (See Appendix D.) Thus, standing behind the United Nations peacekeeping force at Sharm el Sheikh was America's word.

The pledge was by no means nominal. Addressing a problem left unsettled in the armistice agreement at Rhodes, it placed the United States at Israel's side, in legal terms, in affirming that the Strait of Tiran was an international waterway. It went farther in promising that the United States would use its power to enforce those terms. Israelis who argued against the withdrawal from the Sinai, and particularly against the return to Egypt of Sharm el Sheikh, expressed skepticism about whether the United States could be relied upon to keep the promise. But Ben-Gurion stood on the agreement. A decade later, on the eve of the Six-Day War, the test of America's word would come.

Meanwhile, Eisenhower's decision, understood in the West as bailing Nasser out of disaster, was in the Arab world perceived quite differently. By conventional diplomatic standards, Eisenhower had taken an unprecedented action, less reflective of America's national interest than of his own personal morality. He had punished America's friends and rewarded its enemies.

Nasser did not respond with gratitude. On the contrary, he adopted a stance—perhaps more common to politics in the Middle East than elsewhere—based on passion, if not pure fantasy. Nasser laid claim to being the conqueror of giants, and when the armies of Britain, France and Israel retreated from the Sinai, crowds in the capitals of the Arab world cheered hysterically. Eisenhower had transformed Nasser into a hero of mythological dimensions. His new stature encouraged him to demand increasing recognition as leader of all the Arabs, and to give an aggressive redefinition to Arab nationalism. It was to make Nasser much more dangerous than before, to both Israel and America.

As for Ben-Gurion, the record is blurred on whether he had contrived deliberately to draw the United States into Israel's struggle in the Middle East. Dulles's misjudgment had set the stage. The secretary of state, unable to lure Egypt into the Western camp, had touched off a chain reaction that brought the Arabs into the Russian camp. Whatever Ben-Gurion's designs, Washington was left with the cold war imperative of having to acquire an agent of its own in the region. It had no real choice. Dulles's debacle required Washington to turn to Israel.

But by now Israel was no longer looked upon as second best in the Middle East. It was America's good fortune to have learned in the Sinai campaign, while its own interests were not directly at stake, of the Arabs' limitations in combat. In contrast, Israel's performance on the battlefield was splendid, suddenly transforming it into a much more desirable asset than Egypt in a military alliance. Dulles's blunder over the Baghdad Pact had changed the basis of American strategic calculations in the Middle East, but it was Ben-Gurion's skill and endurance that persuaded Eisenhower to consent to a new relationship. Israel, in persuading an American President to guarantee maritime passage through the Strait of Tiran to Elath, made it unlikely the United States could remain aloof from any future Middle East war.

4

Six Portentous Days

Relatively calm in the decade after the Suez campaign, the Middle East, seen in retrospect, was in transition toward a confrontation of grander dimensions. The United States had introduced the cold war into the region in 1955, and shortly afterward, the Soviet Union stole the initiative. In the years that followed, Arabs and Israelis slid steadily deeper into opposing cold war camps. The involvement of the superpowers guaranteed that the next explosion—which was to take place in 1967—would be of greater magnitude and have wider repercussions than either of the Arab-Israeli wars that preceded it.

The Russians encouraged Nasser, convinced by their Marxist dogmas that, as a revolutionary, he shared their commitment to victory over the West. They provided him with bombers and fighters, tanks, helicopters, submarines and other naval craft, artillery and antiaircraft missiles. They also poured powerful weapons into Syria and Iraq, anti-Western regimes that lined up behind Nasser and his fiery, anti-Israeli nationalism.

Still, none of Israel's Arab neighbors was eager for another round of war. Though Palestinian terrorism fueled a cycle of violence in the region, Syria and Jordan were preoccupied with internal disarray, and Nasser himself was bogged down in a nasty conflict in Yemen. None was ready for combat against Israel. As for the Soviets, they were apprehensive that a Middle East war, which risked unleashing Arab rages they had never learned to control, could ultimately involve themselves. Persuaded by Marxist doctrine of the inexorable gravitation of colonialized peoples into their orbit, the Russians were confident of achieving their objectives without war.

Compared to the Arabs, Israel was still very much on its own. The United States remained reticent about narrowing the gap in its relations with the Jewish state, not only while Eisenhower was President but even under his successor, John F. Kennedy. After de Gaulle came to power in 1958, settled France's war in Algeria and resumed old friendships with the Arabs, Israel's special relationship with Paris also withered. The Israeli air force still used French aircraft, equal to any the Russians furnished the Arabs, but France was stingy with replacement parts, and to keep up in the arms race, the Israelis now had to scrounge. Through German channels, thanks to the ties established during the reparations talks, Israel acquired American helicopters, tanks and artillery. It also bought tanks from the British. In the early 1960s, the United States consented to make a few exceptions to its embargo, and sold Israel some antiaircraft missiles directly. By 1967, Israel was far from the superpower client that the Arabs had become but, dependent solely on the West for its arms, it had unmistakably taken a side.

Trouble approached almost unnoticed, stoked more by political rivalries among the Arabs than by any immediate aggravation in Arab-Israeli relations. A coup in Syria in February 1966 brought to power a radical military regime, resentful of Nasser's influence, anxious to prove itself. In January 1967, the Syrian army engaged the Israelis in an extended artillery duel across the Golan Heights. A few months later, Syria challenged Israel in the air over the Galilee, and six of its MiGs were shot down. The Russians took the loss as a defeat not just for their weapons but for their stature in the region. To even the score with Israel, they persuaded Nasser to demonstrate Egypt's support of Syria by redeploying his troops at the Israeli border. Though apparently meant as a gesture, the move conveyed a threat of war, and precipitated a chain of events that no one knew how to stop.

Egypt's forces, exhausted by their fighting in Yemen, were in no way prepared to attack Israel in the Sinai. But in his self-appointed role as spearhead of Arab nationalism, Nasser could not back away. For more than a decade, the United Nations contingent that was created under the terms of settlement of the 1956 war had been on Egyptian soil. In the Arab world, foreign troops were still a symbol of colonial submission, and in the taunting give-and-take among rivals, Nasser had long been ridiculed for allowing the U.N. force to remain. There is evidence he preferred to sidestep the Russian request but found himself trapped. On May 18, 1967, Nasser demanded evacuation of the U.N. troops based in the seaside fortress of Sharm el Sheikh.

Sharm el Sheikh, which controlled passage through the Strait of Tiran, had been a cause of the war of 1956, when it was captured by the Israelis. Only after the United States promised to resist any blockade of Elath had Israel agreed to evacuate it. U.N. Secretary-General U Thant apparently failed to grasp its importance. He consented promptly to Egypt's demand, squandering whatever opportunity delay might have provided to help Nasser get off the hook. The momentum of events was now out of control. When the U.N. force departed, Nasser dispatched his army to the cannon of Sharm el Sheikh and, repeating his provocation of 1956, declared the strait to be closed. Throughout the Arab world, street crowds cheered wildly when Nasser defiantly announced, "We are ready for war."

Nasser's decision to expel the United Nations forces, violating the guarantees provided by the United States to Israel after the war of 1956, clearly required an American response. President Johnson, who as a senator had been a strong supporter of Israel, did not deny that the United States was bound by Eisenhower's pledge of innocent passage to Elath. He recalls in his memoirs that he even contacted Eisenhower, living in retirement in Pennsylvania, who confirmed that the United States had made a firm commitment. A week after Nasser closed the strait, Johnson stated publicly that Washington considered Egypt's blockade illegal and a serious threat to peace.

But Johnson faced a dilemma. He had already involved the country in one unpopular war, which consumed most of its energy and military resources, and he was not prepared to get it involved in another. Vietnam was the Johnson administration's albatross. When Israel presented him with a notice of American indebtedness, he acknowledged its validity but lamely replied that without endorsement from Congress and public opinion, he was powerless to pay.

Johnson's response was to hedge, his tactic to promise to organize an international flotilla—composed of the ships of the Western nations—to steam through the Strait of Tiran. Thus would the right of free passage be affirmed. But the pledge that had been made to Israel in 1957 was America's, and the response from other governments was tepid. The Israelis gave the United States several weeks to execute its plans, without discernible results. In his memoirs, Johnson claimed he was making headway when the Israelis concluded that further delay would only jeopardize the opportunity for tactical surprise. Out of conviction that the pledge was meaningless, Israel decided to act alone.

To act against the enemies of the Jews, and if necessary to act alone—that was why the state of Israel had been created in the first place. In the Jewish mind, the situation in the spring of 1967 seemed classic. The Jews, menaced by their enemies, were now abandoned by their friends. Was this not the story of the Holocaust? It was the scenario for which the Jews demanded a state of their own. The crisis reaffirmed the Jewish disposition, cultivated during centuries of anti-Semitism, to believe that in crisis the Jews could count only upon themselves.

Indeed, Johnson's default elicited a full range of atavistic insecurities among Israelis. Was Israel a second-class member of the family of nations? Would Johnson have done the same if Israel were not the *Jewish* state? Did Christians care if Israel and the

Jews were destroyed? The deep uneasiness of the times played to the "muscular" Zionism of the Revisionists, who proclaimed that Jews must rely on their arms alone. Undermining the value of America's word, Johnson's failure exalted Israel's trust in the gun. This prelude to the Six-Day War was to have a lasting impact in militarizing Israel's outlook toward the outside world.

What finally cast the die, however, was not Nasser's army, which was known by Israeli intelligence to be no great threat, but King Hussein's. Few Americans have understood the importance of the Jordanian decision. In the account in his memoirs of the events leading to the war, Johnson does not even mention it. But on May 30, the Jordanian king, roused by a sense of Arab solidarity, laid aside his long rivalry with Nasser and, with much fanfare, flew to Cairo to place his forces under Egyptian command. His decision fundamentally changed the strategic balance.

It was not the fighting capacity of Jordan's soldiers that worried Israel's generals so much as the proximity of Jordan's guns to Israel's highly populated industrial centers. Egypt, to wage war against Israel, had to cross the Sinai, straining fragile lines of communications and supply. The Syrians, though nearer, had to descend from the Golan Heights, which presented its own logistical problems. Though the Egyptians had larger forces, and the Syrians were tougher fighters, both were regarded as a lesser threat than the Jordanians. Jordan's army, based on the West Bank, was within rifle range of Israel's heartland.

Jordanian units had the capacity in a quick thrust to cover the nine miles from the frontier to the sea, cutting Israel in two or three, severing the factories of Tel Aviv from the major port at Haifa. They could also isolate West Jerusalem, the nation's capital. The only road that connected Jerusalem with the rest of the country lay adjacent in many places to Jordan's border. From their existing emplacements, Jordanian guns covered all of Israel's large cities, and fully two thirds of Israel's population. The same guns could also drop shells on the airport at Lod, which in a crisis was Israel's only link to outside help.

It is difficult, in the light of the victory that ensued, to recall the anguish that enveloped Israel in the first week of June 1967. With every able-bodied man from eighteen to fifty in uniform, along with a large proportion of the women, Israel had to move quickly, or risk being smothered economically. The margin that separated life from death appeared paper thin. The Arab world was united. Washington vacillated and the remainder of the community of nations had made clear it planned to do nothing. Jewish reflexes, not just in Israel but throughout the world, summoned up the specter of a second Holocaust.

Ben-Gurion was now in retirement and Levi Eshkol, who had succeeded him as prime minister, was perceived as a man of less strength, decent but vacillating. Eshkol, to rally the disparate fragments of the nation, decided to form a government of national unity. Yielding reluctantly to what had hitherto been unthinkable for a Labor prime minister, he invited Menachem Begin into the government. With Begin came Moshe Dayan, esteemed as Israel's preeminent strategist, as minister of defense. The cabinet was now organized for conflict. In an atmosphere of cool desperation, these men shaped Israel's decision to respond to the inevitability of war with a preemptive strike.

At dawn on June 5, the Israeli air force swooped down in a surprise attack on Egyptian air bases. Israel's plan was to go first after Egypt, its most formidable enemy, while urging King Hussein to keep Jordan out of the fight. Within hours, Israel had knocked out Nasser's entire air force, effectively settling the contest. Over the next few days, Egypt's army, operating without cover, was decimated by Israel's air and ground forces.

Notwithstanding Israel's appeal, Hussein joined the war, unaware that the outcome had been determined before his forces fired a shot. When Jordanian artillery shelled Jerusalem and Tel Aviv, Israel struck. In a three-day offensive, it captured the Old City of Jerusalem, destroyed Jordan's army and occupied the entire West Bank. Before the last battle against Jordan had been fought, the Israelis turned on the Syrians, who appeared impregnable in their bastion on the Golan Heights. In the most brilliant military exploit of all, the Israelis stormed the Heights, and by the end of the week, Syria, too, was defeated.

In fighting both on land and in the air, Israel had demonstrated its superiority over the combined power of its Arab neighbors. It ended the war in occupation of territory more than three times its own size. It was in possession of what its generals called "strategic depth," with a defensive perimeter that included Egypt's Sinai peninsula and Gaza Strip, Syria's Golan Heights and Jordan's West Bank. Israel, which had appeared outmatched in 1948 and again on the eve of the Six-Day War, had suddenly become invulnerable to the full power of the Arab world.

It is Moscow's line that the Israeli government, certain of victory, somehow cajoled the Arabs in 1967 into providing a pretext for war. Some Arabs assert it too. The argument has become grounds for a claim that Israel's occupation of Arab territory was the fruit of calculated aggression.

Yitzhak Rabin, who in 1967 was chief of staff of the Israeli armed forces, laid out in a conversation with me what was basically Mainstream Zionism's doctrine of war.

"When I was on the general staff—and for eight years I was either number two or number one—no government ever gave instructions to initiate a war," Rabin said. "The purpose of the military strength of Israel was, first, to make sure that we stayed alive and, second, to shift the struggle from the battlefield. Our orders were to defend the country from attack, to destroy the attacking force, and then to acquire as much land as possible, to create conditions to shift the Arab-Israeli conflict to the negotiation table."

Nothing in the record of the events that preceded the Six-Day War belies Rabin's statement. To suggest that Israel had a responsibility to show further restraint than it did in the spring of 1967 is to forget that the Arabs, led by Nasser, had never ceased in bloodcurdling threats to proclaim the goal of its extinction. Nasser's stated purpose in mobilizing was to drive the Jews out of

Israel's Conquests in the Six-Day War, 1967

Israeli territory, 1949-1967

Israeli conquests, June 5-11, 1967

Beirut

LEBANON

Damascus

SYRIA

Kuneitra

GOLAN HEIGHTS

Haifa

MEDITERRANEAN SEA

Nablus

WEST BANK

Damia Bridge

Tel Aviv

Jordan

Amman

Jericho

Allenby Bridge

Jerusalem *EAST JERUSALEM*

Gaza

Hebron

Dead Sea

GAZA STRIP

Beersheeba

JORDAN

Port Said

El Arish

Ismailia

Suez Canal

Suez

S I N A I

E G Y P T

Elat

Aqaba

GULF OF SUEZ

GULF OF AQABA

SAUDI ARABIA

Strait of Tiran

Sharm el Sheikh

RED SEA

0   60 mi

0   100 km

the Middle East. His own assertion that Egypt was "ready for war" was invitation enough to Israel to strike first. That Israel, to attain a tactical advantage, attacked before all possibilities of resolving the crisis were exhausted is clear. That Israel's generals were more confident of defeating the Arabs than they conceded to the public is apparent. Certainly, the Arab leaders blundered in provoking an attack on their unprepared armies, but the claim that Israel tricked them into it is farfetched. No credible case can be made for it.

Egypt's defeat in the Sinai in June of 1967 had been, in large measure, foreshadowed on the same battlefield a decade earlier. But no one, not Rabin or anyone else, foresaw the magnitude of the Israeli victory, or the political explosion that would be detonated by it.

The Six-Day War radically changed the Middle East conflict, both militarily and politically. It resulted in gains for the winner too huge to be digested, costs to the losers too embarrassing to confront. It left Israeli forces on the doorsteps of Cairo, Damascus and Amman, with no armies to defend them. From the shattered fragments of the conflict emerged a structure of relations among the nations of the Middle East dominated by Israel's military power, hardly healthier for the victor than for the vanquished.

The war transformed the perception of Arabs and Israelis, both of themselves and of each other. The change in political geography created a new reality, psychological as well as physical, affecting the daily existence of millions of people. The environment in which Arabs and Israelis lived would never be the same. For better or worse, regional powers and superpowers henceforth would be guided by the consequences of the Six-Day War in all their deliberations on the future of the Middle East.

Let us now take another look at the Middle East conflict in terms of the three tiers we examined earlier—East versus West, Israel versus the Arab states, Zionists versus Palestinians. The Six-Day War was a conflict of states. Its outcome transformed relations between Israel and the Arab nations. The change at the other two levels was much less decisive.

In East-West terms, the Six-Day War was clearly a Western victory, but neither camp modified strategy significantly as a result of the outcome. Except that the United States moved to fill the gap left by France, East and West remained willing providers for their respective clients. Both were careful to avoid war themselves, but when the fighting was over, Washington and Moscow—the former to preserve the results, the latter to reshape them—remained equally ready to serve up their surrogates to another round of battle.

As for the popular conflict between Palestinians and Zionists, Israel's victory made matters only worse. The strategy of the Palestinians had been to entice the Arab world into combat for their cause, and they succeeded, but the victory that was supposed to follow eluded them. The geography of defeat, however, improved their means of waging warfare on their own. In substituting occupation for partition, Israel acquired within its sphere of control more than a million new enemies. The constant grinding of Palestinians against Israelis in the West Bank and the Gaza Strip sharpened nationalist emotions. At the same time, proximity offered a range of accessible targets. The war brought the struggle between Zionists and Palestinians no closer to an end. On the contrary, it created a situation that invited more terrorism, and more instability.

In terms of the encounter between the sovereign states of the Middle East, however, Israel's victory could hardly have been more decisive. That is not to say that Arab governments rushed to sue for peace. On the contrary, they decided for a time to live with their losses, in the hope of somehow reversing them. But the hope was never serious. Persistent though they were in refusing peace, they were no longer a menace to Israel's survival. The formalities of peace were irrelevant. The clear lesson of the war was that if diplomacy was to catch up with reality, the Arab states would have to accept terms providing not only for Israel's recognition but for its security. At no time since the Six-Day War have Israel's neighbors presumed to threaten its national existence.

In the last hours of the Six-Day War, Prime Minister Eshkol put the world on notice in stating to the Knesset: "Let this be said—there should be no illusion that Israel is prepared to return to the conditions that existed a week ago. . . . We have fought alone for our existence and our security, and we are therefore justified in deciding for ourselves what are the genuine and indispensable interests of our state."

Eshkol's statement quietly asserted Israel's pride in its victory, while barely concealing a reproach to those who had failed to keep a promise. The words summed up the pervasive sentiment among Israelis that relations between the Jewish state and its Arab neighbors must never again be what they were before. It gave notice that as far as Israel was concerned, the United States had defaulted on the right asserted by Eisenhower in 1956 to reorder the outcome of the war. Whatever President Johnson's intentions, Israel would not consent to having the fruit of its victory snatched away from it again.

In looking back at the period immediately after the war, it is fair to say that the Israeli government had not made up its mind what to do about the captured territories. That was not true, of course, of the Revisionist minority. But most Israelis seemed to assume that the booty of war would be returned as part of a bargain in a peace settlement. As Yitzhak Rabin said, Mainstream Zionism considered the goal of making war to be making peace. Arab diplomacy, of course, did not take warmly to the idea of trading its territory for a political settlement. The Arabs' hope was that a higher authority—meaning the superpowers, deliberating at the United Nations—would reverse the war's consequences, as Eisenhower had once done. But Israel could not forget that in 1956 all it had received for the territory it had captured was a pledge on which the United States had reneged, and a decade later it faced another war which placed its survival in question. Israelis thought they were justified, this time, in retaining their conquests until they could obtain more.

From the start, however, Israelis could reach no consensus on their demands. The minimum was security, since there was no dispute that the state should no more be in jeopardy. But there were conflicting strategies of security, and even deeper conflicts on what was to be attained beyond security. The victory, in fact, appeared to provide such a range of options that the debate over peace in the Middle East would thenceforth be conducted more over the clashing views of Jews than over the long-standing differences between Jews and Arabs. The bitterness of the debate soon established that it was easier for Israelis to resist any movement toward a settlement with the Arabs than to reach an agreement on terms among themselves.

Abba Eban, in a conversation with me, said, "There has been nothing more breathtaking and, I think, inspiring in Israel's history than the proposals we made after the Six-Day War." Eban, foreign minister during the war, said the Arabs were notified that "everything is negotiable" in return for peace. The assertion, which in one form or another he has often repeated, was disingenuous. Like most Mainstream Zionists, Eban was committed to the reestablishment of partition, to a vision, as he put it, that "takes Israel's smallness for granted." So were most Israelis, at least in the first days. Common sense should have impelled the Arabs to move quickly, before Israel became infatuated with grandeur. Since the Arabs did not move at all, however, Eban's claim was never submitted to a test.

Indeed, in saying "everything is negotiable," Eban himself made clear he did not mean *everything*. Israel, as he knew, was not ready to give up all the captured territory for peace. For deeply emotional reasons, an undivided Jerusalem, free of the barriers that since 1948 had separated Jews from the Old City, was a *sine qua non*. Israel's government, having abolished these barriers the day the city was taken, two weeks later formally annexed Arab Jerusalem. There were few Israelis, then or since, prepared to advocate a return of any part of the city to Arab rule.

In his memoirs, Eban further qualified the "everything" by acknowledging that any boundary agreement negotiated with
Egypt and Syria would have had to include "changes for Israel's
security." Neither the Israeli government nor Eban made more
than a vague allusion to what the changes would be. Most Israelis
seemed determined to hold on to Sharm el Sheikh, which Israel
had twice captured in order to keep open the port of Elath. They
seemed also to agree on the Golan Heights, from which Syrian
artillery had long made a nightmare of life in the eastern Galilee.
These two, along with East Jerusalem, looked like rock bottom.
Insistence on holding them conveyed the vision of a settlement
consisting not of territory *for* peace but territory *and* peace.

Eban, in fact, went further still, for in dwelling on the generous
terms Israelis were willing to extend to Egypt and Syria, he left the
clear implication that the terms offered to Jordan for the West
Bank would be harsher. On the matter of the West Bank, Eban
said, "no similar consensus" on the return of the territories existed
among Israelis. Jordan's lands, he said, "raised problems that transcended strategic interest." His veiled words were a reminder of
the ideology of Begin's Revisionists, who intended to seize the
opportunity lost in 1948 to make the West Bank an integral part
of the country.

The Revisionists, after the Six-Day War, were no longer the rank
outsiders they had been only a few weeks before. Begin, now a
minister without portfolio in the government, had a voice in all of
the cabinet's deliberations. Furthermore, the ideological distance
between the Israeli majority and the Revisionists had narrowed
discernibly. It was not that the Revisionists had changed, but that
large numbers of Mainstream Israelis had been moved much
closer by the Six-Day War to Revisionism's commitment to absorb
the West Bank.

Jordan's participation in the war had done much to change
Israeli perceptions. Acquiring territory, a cause once identified
with the ideological ardor of Revisionism, suddenly merged with
the cold calculations of military thinkers. Jordan, though quickly
defeated, had given Israel a serious scare. The shelling of Tel Aviv

and Jerusalem was a reminder of how close the Arab armies stationed on the West Bank had been. Among the conclusions Israeli strategists drew from the Six-Day War was that control of the West Bank was indispensable to Israel's security.

The issue, moreover, was not Jordan alone. In moving its frontier eastward, Israel also acquired strategic depth against Iraq and the Gulf states, containing reserves of Arab manpower. The new border offered defenses behind two natural barriers, the Jordan River and, running parallel to the west of the river, a rugged chain of mountains tenable by small forces against attack. The strategic price such barriers exacted lay in blunting the attributes that had made the Israeli army so formidable against more populous neighbors. Natural barriers converted Israeli forces, who had won a great victory through superior speed and mobility, to the concept of static defense in depth. Nonetheless, Israeli strategists were unable to resist the temptation of creating a buffer zone in the region where the country was most vulnerable. Almost overnight, strategic and Revisionist thought came together, making the West Bank the hinge of a common political front.

For Mainstream Zionists, the West Bank presented a dilemma from which Revisionists were spared. Yitzhak Rabin understood the risk to the Jewishness of the society that incorporation of the Arabs of the West Bank presented to Israel.

"Since 1967, I have opposed Israeli sovereignty over the entire West Bank," Rabin said in his talks with me. "With sovereignty, we would have to give Israeli citizenship to the 800,000 Arabs who reside there. If we did not, it would be apartheid, and no Jewish state can have such a racist policy. There is no purpose in having a Jewish state if it is not free and democratic.

"But if we give the Arabs the vote, we'll shift Israel from being a Zionist country to a non-Zionist country. Israel has an obligation to Jews all over the world, to the Jews of the Soviet Union, to any Jew who is oppressed, to any Jew who wants to come here to resist assimilation. Israel cannot give up this duty, or ask the Arabs to share it."

Rabin, however, was not just a Mainstream Zionist. He was also the soldier who as chief of staff led the victorious armies in the Six-Day War. His deepest professional commitment was to Israel's security. The loss of Israel's Jewish character would mean defeat of Mainstream Zionism's dream, but an Israel in permanent jeopardy could never attain the dream. How could Israel reconcile being Jewish with being secure? The answer favored by Rabin, and supported by Labor Party leaders in the wake of the Six-Day War, was a program of "territorial compromise" known as the Allon Plan.

"Under the Allon Plan, we will make changes in the boundaries of the West Bank to meet Israel's basic security needs," Rabin told me in one of our talks. "That is to say, we will retain the Jordan valley and the eastern slopes of the Judean-Samarian hills, which have very little population. I also include Jerusalem, which is not a security problem, but it is the heart of the state. I am talking about 35 percent of the land of the West Bank. The other 65 percent I am ready to give back within the context of peace. This territory includes 85 percent of the population. To me, that is a solution. I don't believe there is anything holy about boundaries."

Rabin's words conveyed the sharp distinction between his Mainstream position and Revisionism's mystical nationalism, aimed at recreating Biblical-era Israel. Indeed, Rabin likes to refer to himself as a "dove," in his willingness to accept the commitment to exchange territory for peace. And yet, despite the contrast in outlook, he made common cause with the Revisionists, and in time became known as a relentless hard-liner.

Inevitably Rabin, even while faithful to the philosophy of Mainstream Zionism, was shaped by his training as a soldier. When the superpowers, after the fighting, began to discuss a possible peace settlement based on exchanging the captured territory for Arab political concessions and international security guarantees, Rabin scoffed. The experience of the war had convinced him that no treaty with the Arabs, much less a pledge from the international community, would ensure Israel's security.

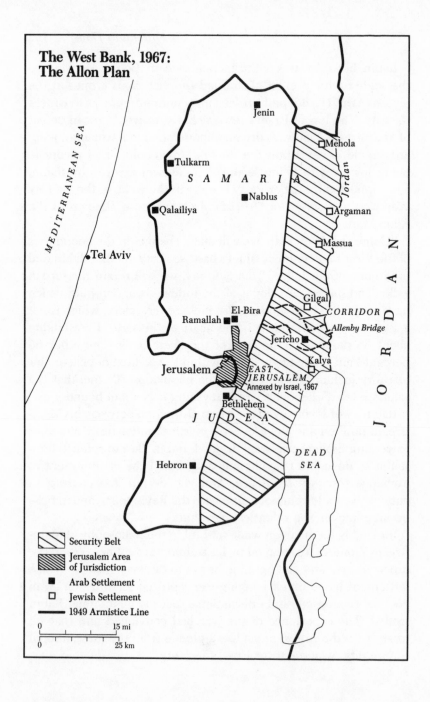

The West Bank, 1967: The Allon Plan

MEDITERRANEAN SEA

Jenin

Mehola

Tulkarm

SAMARIA

Jordan

Nablus

Qalailiya

Argaman

Tel Aviv

Massua

Gilgal

CORRIDOR

El-Bira

Allenby Bridge

Ramallah

Jericho

Jerusalem

EAST
JERUSALEM
Annexed by Israel, 1967

Kalya

Bethlehem

JUDEA

JORDAN

DEAD
SEA

Hebron

Security Belt

Jerusalem Area
of Jurisdiction

■ Arab Settlement

□ Jewish Settlement

1949 Armistice Line

0   15 mi
0   25 km

Rabin, like Jabotinsky's Revisionists, put his trust in Jewish arms. Though his demands were less stringent than the Revisionists', his minimum boundaries, nonetheless, required significant Arab concessions of territory. Rabin's objective was to make a state that the Jews could defend, whatever the hostility of the Arabs, without help from anybody else.

Israel was hopeful, at first, that the magnitude of its victory would somehow persuade the Arabs of the wisdom of a settlement. The Six-Day War, however, had claimed not just Arab armies but Arab self-esteem. In buoyantly announcing that he was "waiting for a phone call," Defense Minister Moshe Dayan only showed how he failed to understand the peculiar dynamic of the defeat. The boast confirmed to the Arabs that the peace Israel had in mind was one in which the vanquished came to the victor for terms. Arab leaders, satisfied Israel had already seized more land and population than it could effectively rule, reasoned they had little more to lose by digging in their heels. They would not suffer further humiliation by marching to the negotiating table to surrender. So the phone call never came.

Had Nasser been a greater man, or perhaps a lesser one, he would have acknowledged the barrenness of an Arab agenda so long concentrated on Israel's destruction. Instead, in August of 1967, he called together in Khartoum the Arab heads of state, from whom there emerged a landmark resolution. It vowed "nonrecognition of Israel, no conciliation nor negotiation with her and the upholding of the rights of the Palestinian people to their land." (See Appendix E.) These were the celebrated "three noes" of Khartoum, which crushed the prospect that out of the debris of battle might rise some sensible progress toward peace. At Khartoum, Nasser sought to convey an illusion that the war had in no way modified the Arabs' grand design.

Yet a fundamental change had taken place at Khartoum, so subtle it is not clear that the Arabs themselves at first discerned it. There, the shift away from bombast began. On the eve of the

Six-Day War, Nasser had proclaimed that his "object will be the destruction of Israel." In contrast, at Khartoum the Arab leadership promised—even in pronouncing the "three noes" and rejecting a peace conference—to recover the occupied territory, not in battle but "in joint political and diplomatic action." Thenceforth, Arab governments would often enough speak of war, but with the object of improving their leverage to compel Israel to return lost territories. The talk of destroying Israel itself virtually disappeared.

The Khartoum conference, notwithstanding the "three noes," demonstrated that the Six-Day War had broken a psychological barrier. It was not that Arabs became more tolerant of Zionism. Rather, they learned they had no choice but to tolerate Israel's existence. The recovery of the lost land became the new objective, transforming the rhetoric and, with it, the real goals of Arab leadership.

It is a reasonable premise that the Arabs' shift began as no more than a tactic. Yet for many Arabs, hearing the new, more limited objective proclaimed over and over again, while talk of Israel's destruction vanished, inevitably created a fresh truth. It is a truth on which a whole generation of Arabs has now been raised. If it did not convert the Arab mind to approval of Israel, it surely narrowed the distance between rejection and acceptance. If asked directly in 1967, most Arabs would, like Nasser, have answered that nothing had changed. Some would offer the same answer today. But the shift in goals that took place in Khartoum contained an implicit admission by the Arab world that Israel had become part of Middle East reality, likely to be around for a long time. It was a signal that the Arabs had found room in their worldview for Israel's legitimacy.

From the very start of the Six-Day War, President Johnson adopted a diplomatic position sharply different from that of Eisenhower in 1956. The Soviet Union, the moment the magnitude of the Arab defeat became apparent, began calling desperately at the United Nations for a cease-fire. The United States responded by deliberately temporizing, so that the Israeli army could sweep the battlefield clean. When the Soviets threatened to intrude with their own forces to rescue their clients, Johnson warned that American forces were ready to go to Israel's defense. Washington's policy at the U.N. very quickly disabused both Russians and Arabs of the notion that Eisenhower's course would be repeated, enabling the losers once again to avoid paying the price of their defeat.

After the cease-fire, Johnson explicitly endorsed Israel's refusal to evacuate the captured territories without compensating Arab concessions. "An immediate return to the situation as it was on June 4 . . ." Johnson declared, "is not a prescription for peace but for renewed hostilities." His stand was an acknowledgment that Eisenhower's policy, whatever its moral justification, had simply led nowhere. Johnson accepted the Israeli view that the Six-Day War should not be wasted, as the Sinai war had been, but must somehow be utilized to promote a lasting peace.

Well before the fighting was over, the Soviet Union understood that its foothold in the Middle East had been shattered. Having armed and trained the military forces of Egypt and Syria, Moscow watched as the Israelis disgraced them with French aircraft and a hodgepodge of Western ground equipment. The Kremlin's decision from the first day, when it was already clear the Arabs could not reverse the rout, was to airlift no equipment to the battlefield. The decision left Syrian gunners whose artillery was destroyed with no guns to shoot, and Egyptian pilots who survived the surprise attack with no planes to fly. To save their ten-year investment in the Arab world, the Russians decided they would have to put all their effort into the postwar battle, with both diplomacy and arms.

The Soviet Union's war diplomatic strategy in the weeks that followed the fighting was to play aggressively the role of the Arab patron, using Eisenhower's high moral arguments of 1956 to block Israel's acquisition of territory. The Six-Day War, however, was not the Sinai campaign. The Arabs had forfeited the reservoir of sympathy available to them a decade earlier. Nor did anyone mistake the Kremlin's expediency for Eisenhower's morality. Within the U.N., there was, in fact, a reaction that the Arabs were getting what was coming to them. More important, unlike the paradox of 1956 when the Kremlin had Washington as its U.N. ally, it now had Washington as its adversary, thwarting its every maneuver to undo the damage of the battlefield.

Yet it is worth noting that the Soviet Union, though it severed diplomatic relations, did not attack Israel's legitimacy. A midwife at Israel's creation in 1948, it had long since shifted its favors to the Arabs, but it never adopted the Arab line that Israel had no right to exist. Once the war began, Soviet delegates viciously condemned Israel as an aggressor, calling for the passage of resolutions demanding unconditional withdrawal to the pre-1967 borders. Unable to win the backing of the third world countries, their efforts failed dismally. Still, the Soviet Union did not retreat on the issue of Israel's right to nationhood.

It was the American position that represented the more dramatic change. President Johnson's decision to back Israel to the hilt has several explanations. Israel, after its spectacular victory, became popular with Americans, and thus worth Johnson's attention to cultivate at a time when his own policies in Vietnam were growing more unpopular. Johnson reasoned that the American-Jewish community, largely alienated over Vietnam, would respond favorably to an openly pro-Israel policy. But it is surely true that he was also moved by a bad conscience at having shirked his pledge to Israel, to which he had long been sympathetic, on the eve of the war. In contrast, few Americans had sympathy for Nasser, especially after the fit of petulance in which he blamed Washington for starting the war and broke diplomatic relations. Nasser was a figure Americans were quite willing to hate.

But whatever the domestic political implications, it was also true that events had not been kind to the vision Eisenhower had imposed on the Middle East. Had Nasser fulfilled his dream of crushing the Jewish state, the Russians would have reigned supreme in the region. Had Russia exacted as its fee from Nasser its own control of the Suez Canal, the United States would have been forced to choose between launching a major war or looking on as bystander while the Soviet Union squeezed Western Europe. Israel's victory in the Six-Day War enabled the United States to keep its hand in the Middle East. At a time when American resources were severely strained in Vietnam, Israel appeared as an ally ready to cover American interests in the region. Once Johnson decided to go with Israel, the United States never turned back.

Still, American policy in the Middle East had more than a single prong, and Johnson never abandoned the Arabs, either. In the 1950s, the Russians made the mistake of cutting themselves off from Israel, and in 1967 they joined the Arabs to break diplomatic relations. The move profoundly reduced their influence in the region. In contrast, Washington has maintained its presence in the Arab camp. The United States can hardly forget that the Arabs provide the West with most of its oil. They occupy a strategically crucial landmass. They are the core of Islam, a force that reaches from Morocco to Indonesia and into the Soviet Union itself. The Kremlin, for whatever reasons, might choose to abdicate its role among Israelis. But Washington, even in cultivating an alliance with Israel, has chosen never to let its influence among the Arabs go by default.

This policy has created contradictions often difficult to reconcile. Dulles tipped America's preference decisively to the Arab side. Johnson tipped it back. The Nixon administration, which followed Johnson, talked of being "even-handed," then decided it would not be. As practiced by a series of Presidents, the American approach has been at one moment to serve as advocate of Israel, at another to try a hand as mediator, at still another to promote a program in the Arab world.

In making their policies, Presidents have had to calculate not only American interests abroad but their own interests at home, taking special account of the political influence of the American-

Jewish community. The shifting has inevitably confounded friends and puzzled adversaries. It has invited a permanent tug-of-war, sanctioned in a democratic society, involving the White House, Congress and the diplomatic bureaucracy, all pulled by competing forces at home and abroad. It has conveyed an impression, often quite accurate, of indecision, even confusion. The uncertainty of American policies has been an enigma for Israel as well as the Arab states, inevitably straining relations in both.

After the Six-Day War, the United States came down unequivocally in favor of the principle promoted by Israel of exchanging territory for peace. Further, it accepted the Israeli contention that borders would need some modification in the interests of security. Nonetheless, it established a conceptual barrier against a temptation already being articulated in Israel to keep the territories permanently in the place of peace. Officially, Washington has never departed from the position that the territorial changes brought about by the Six-Day War were temporary.

In a candid explanation of policy, Johnson said soon after the war, "We are not the ones to say where other nations should draw the lines between them. . . . It is clear, however, that there must be secure and there must be recognized boundaries. . . . At the same time, it should be equally clear that boundaries cannot and should not reflect the weight of conquest." Johnson called for "honest negotiations," leading to agreement based upon "just compromise" on international borders.

As the months passed, the arguments within the Israeli cabinet over borders did not abate. Views ranged from Eban's willingness to return nearly all the land to Begin's unwillingness to return any. The lowest common denominator was an insistence on "defensible borders," but as long as the Arabs remained committed to the Khartoum Declaration, Israelis had no need to decide what these borders would be. Washington refused to recognize Israel's annexation of the Arab sector of Jerusalem. And though, in practice, it has acquiesced in the occupation that began in 1967, it has never departed formally from its commitment to the principle it championed immediately after the war, the exchange of land for peace.

The United Nations debated the adoption of a principle of its own throughout the summer of 1967, while battling raged unofficially between Israeli and Egyptian forces on the canal. Then, in October, after weeks of sporadic firing and skirmishing, Egyptian missiles sank the Israeli destroyer *Eilat*. Israel retaliated with a heavy shelling of the Egyptian port of Suez. Superpowers and belligerents alike recognized then that the warfare, even if unofficial, was getting out of hand, and none of them was ready for a major resumption of combat. Washington and Moscow then applied pressure, each on its own client, to come to an agreement on a text.

Resolution 242, finally approved by the Security Council in November 1967, would henceforth serve as the chief reference point for all discussion of an Arab-Israeli settlement. (See Appendix F.) It was negotiated with the recognition that unless some sort of agreement was reached, tension was likely to mount rapidly, not only between Arabs and Israelis but between East and West. This recognition gave Washington and Moscow their own interests in getting an agreement, apart from that of their clients. Resolution 242 was necessarily a multifaceted compromise, in which two sets of allies had to agree on terms among themselves before the two sets of adversaries could strike their bargain.

Not surprisingly, the document left Arabs and Israelis still very far apart. Yet it was an achievement, in committing all four parties for the first time to settling their differences through negotiations. And whatever its inadequacies, it also committed them to the principle of exchanging territory for peace.

Resolution 242, in its preamble, stated as dogma "the inadmissibility of the acquisition of territory by war." As both the United States and the Soviet Union saw it, this was to be the guiding principle for a Middle East that would be stable enough, at the very least, to assure no conflict between themselves.

The substance of Resolution 242 came in its statement of the right of "sovereignty, territorial integrity and political independence of every State in the area and their right to live in peace within secure and recognized boundaries." This assertion, to which the Arab delegates agreed, effectively dismissed any contention that Israel did not legally exist. The trade-off exacted by the Arabs was contained in the provision requiring "Withdrawal of Israeli armed forces from territories occupied in the recent conflict." It was an affirmation of the territory-for-peace concept, though the terms were wrapped in ambiguity.

The ambiguity lay in the expression "from territories," which was deliberately written to be imprecise. The Arabs insisted it meant *all* territories. Eban argued on Israel's behalf that in the absence of "the" before "territories," the expression conveyed the acceptance by the United Nations of the doctrine of territorial revision. In fact, the superpowers deliberately left the wording unclear so that both Arabs and Israelis would be free to uphold their positions before their own constituencies. No more specific provision could possibly have received the approval of all the parties.

The two sides were brought to a clever compromise in the implementing provision, after a fight over the symbolism of recognition. The Arabs wanted the resolution to be "self-executing," which would have absolved them of a need to meet with Israelis across a table. Israel insisted on direct negotiations between the parties. The resolution as adopted required the U.N. Secretary-General to name a special representative to maintain contact with all the states of the region to implement its terms. In requiring agreement between the parties themselves, it satisfied the Israeli condition aimed at forcing the Arabs to concede a semblance of recognition. In waiving a requirement for *direct* talks, however, it followed precedents set by the Arabs to avoid their having to face the recognition issue head-on.

The Johnson administration was happier with Resolution 242 than the Israelis were. The Labor Party majority was ready to endorse it but Begin, speaking for the Revisionists, argued that he could not now consent to a resolution that called for return of the West Bank, since he had argued during the nineteen years of partition that it was Israel's. Not being a member of the Security Council left Israel free to equivocate. The Israeli cabinet authorized the United States to vote for the resolution, while withholding formal approval of its own. Israel's course was to take no stand at all rather than risk a bitter internal fight over the terms of peace. It was a course followed often in the ensuing years and Johnson, though annoyed, concurred in it.

Shortly afterward, Johnson provided the hard proof of support that many Israelis considered crucial to their new relationship with Washington. Yitzhak Rabin grumbles that Johnson, before agreeing to provide Israel with weapons, attempted to make a deal with the Russians to limit the arms race in the Middle East. Rabin was not interested in any policy of mutual restraint, and he vowed he would not be satisfied until Israel had supply channels that were immune to the whims of Presidents.

It did not take Johnson long, however, to recognize what Soviet policy was. Responding to a rapid buildup of Russian arms in the Arab world, he approved the sale to Israel of American tanks, helicopters, missiles and, most important, Phantom fighter-bombers, which were to prove the most lethal weapon in the Middle East. The United States was at last Israel's chief arms supplier. The decision gave birth to a bond that both nations have since called an alliance, casting the United States as Israel's permanent diplomatic, economic and military protector.

The superpowers had now completed a structure in which to conduct their own struggle in the Middle East. Under the arrangement, they were involved in the region on an almost day-to-day basis. Soviet and American interests had become as much a factor in the policy decisions of the region as those of Arabs and Israelis. The two had signed on as cold war surrogates.

5

Ratcheting Up

Two new administrations took office at the start of 1969. Richard Nixon, who had been Dwight Eisenhower's Vice-President for eight years, succeeded Lyndon Johnson as America's President in January. Golda Meir, who was Ben-Gurion's foreign minister when Israel stood up to Eisenhower at the close of the Sinai campaign, was named prime minister on Levi Eshkol's death a month later. Their dealings were often contentious, but, together, these two would fire a tougher and harder texture in the complex American-Israeli relationship.

Yitzhak Rabin was by then Israel's ambassador to the United States. He had been appointed by Eshkol the year before, in recognition of his services as chief of staff during the Six-Day War. In Washington, as in Israel, Rabin was admired for his analytical mind, his gift for grand strategy and his sober political calculations, but he was too blunt and too distant to be liked. As ambassador, Rabin was never at ease with the gentle, easygoing Eshkol. Nor did he get along with his foreign minister, Abba Eban, who was more eloquent and sophisticated, a conciliator by temperament, a man who gauged Israel's security more in political than military terms. Rabin had a different view from Eban's of his mission in the United States.

"I arrived in Washington," Rabin said in our interview, "with

the knowledge that for the first time, there was a strategic understanding between the United States and Israel. In simple words,
it was 'no withdrawal without a political solution.' I had in mind
to make sure it would not be easy to change the realities that came
into being from the Six-Day War.

"I also had a goal in weapons procurement. What I tried to
achieve was not just an increase in the quantity and quality of arms
but a change of attitude, a change of policy. Every war the Arabs
lost had given them an impetus for accelerating the arms race.
They became dependent on the Soviet Union for more and better
military hardware. In Israel, we had to keep our relative strength.
We had to maintain our control. I wanted a clear-cut commitment
from the United States government to Israel to supply whatever
was needed to maintain the balance of power."

With the accession of Mrs. Meir, Rabin came into his own as
ambassador. The only woman among Israel's "founding fathers,"
Golda Meir had made a reputation during her years in Labor Party
politics as a relentless partisan with a razor-sharp tongue. She was
named foreign minister after the Egyptian-Soviet arms treaty in
1955 because Ben-Gurion considered her alone, among his associ-
ates, tough enough to confront the crisis. When she was chosen
prime minister, it was out of respect not for a quick mind but for
a fierce tenacity. In her total absence of artifice, Mrs. Meir compelled affection, which Rabin never managed to do. Nonetheless,
the two, much alike in their bluntness of personality and simplicity
of values, formed a strong bond of trust.

Like Rabin, Golda Meir was uncomfortable with Eban, the foreign minister, whose conciliatory disposition she saw as softness,
whose intellectuality she took as reproach. As a result, she established a direct link with Rabin in Washington, enabling him to
bypass ministry channels. Rabin thus became an independent
force, with the embassy as his power base. What is more, his
military background and his access to Mrs. Meir made him the
equivalent at home of a national security adviser, and thereby a
major influence in Israeli cabinet deliberations.

Rabin had met the new President for the first time some years before, during a visit by Nixon to Israel. Rabin was head of the army, and Nixon was then in the political wilderness. He has said Nixon never forgot that while most Israeli politicians turned their backs, the Israeli army offered him the "red carpet treatment." Rabin recalls the two met again in mid-1968, shortly after he arrived in the United States. It was during the presidential campaign, and he was making calls on the candidates, he said, to solicit their views on supplying Israel with arms. He came away uneasy from his meeting with Hubert Humphrey, the Democratic candidate. Nixon's views, in contrast, were "almost uncanny" in paralleling official Israeli positions.

In his memoirs, Rabin quotes Nixon as saying, "I believe it necessary to reach an understanding with the Soviets, and I am convinced that the only language they respect is the language of force. You can't reach an agreement with them unless you do so from a position of strength. . . . The correct view of American-Soviet relations also holds true for Israeli-Arab relations. You will find considerable understanding from me in everything connected with guaranteeing Israel's strength."

Rabin says he answered, "We too believe that it is vital to reach agreement with our adversaries in the Middle East. But negotiations can only begin when Israel speaks from a position of strength and has concrete backing."

Nixon's national security adviser was Henry Kissinger, a former Harvard professor, who, like Rabin, was preoccupied with questions of grand strategy. Kissinger's jurisdiction in the White House ranged across the East-West conflict, with particular emphasis on ending American involvement in Vietnam. Kissinger did not have a Middle East policy, as such. And, though Jewish, he showed no particular sympathy for Israel. Israel's position in the Middle East was of concern to Kissinger only as a factor in America's global relations. He saw the advantages the United States had acquired through Israel's victory of 1967 as a weapon to be used against the Communists in bargaining over Vietnam. Kissinger was obsessed by the superpower game, and saw Vietnam, arms control, Cuba, East-West trade, the third world, and European security as cards to be played in it. That is also the way he saw the Arab-Israeli conflict.

Yet Mrs. Meir and Rabin on the one hand and Nixon and Kissinger on the other had much in common. In contrast to the Israelis, the two Americans were complex and devious, and in everyday dealings the two sides often grated on one other. But the four shared a *weltanschauung.* All exalted power over conciliation as a means of resolving international differences, and none was averse to using armed force whenever it promised to be useful. Nixon and Kissinger in the framework of the cold war, Mrs. Meir and Rabin in the Arab-Israeli struggle, were hard-liners together.

But just as Mrs. Meir had Eban, an intellectual outsider, in her camp, Nixon had William Rogers, a Wall Street lawyer who was his secretary of state. If there was an Eisenhower disciple in the Nixon administration, evoking memories of 1956, it was Rogers. While Nixon was Vice-President, Rogers was attorney general, and the two of them, working under Eisenhower, became close friends. A man of courtesy and decency, Rogers rejected Kissinger's inflexible linkage of diplomacy to the promotion of marginal advantages in the cold war. He considered a Middle East settlement a self-evident good, not just for the Arabs and for Israel but for the United States too. A settlement, he believed, was worth a major American effort. Rogers failed to understand Kissinger's antagonism to this position any more than he understood why Israel would prefer territorial possession to peace.

At the start of the Nixon administration, it looked as if Rogers's view on the Middle East would prevail as policy. Before inauguration, Nixon sent William Scranton, former governor of Pennsylvania, as his personal envoy on a fact-finding tour of the Middle East. Scranton returned with a recommendation that American policy in the region become more "even-handed." Israel interpreted these innocent-sounding words as a warning that Nixon was preparing to abandon Johnson's policy of defending its interests, perhaps to adopt an approach more like Eisenhower's. While taking care to avoid tensions with the new President, Mrs. Meir protested. Nixon quickly backed away, and saw to it that Scranton's phrase was stricken from his administration's lexicon. But Israel had by no means heard the last of Rogers's approach.

"In the spring of 1969, a confrontation between the United States and Israel was always over the horizon," Rogers said in a talk with me. "I thought we ought not sit still and risk a conflict with the Russians. Resolution 242 was a good enough framework for settling the problems of the region, and Israel knew damned well that was our position. But Israel had no interest in changing the status quo. We weren't going to force them to do anything, and we never thought of withdrawing our support. But it was obvious to any practical person that it would be a major setback to the United States if the Arabs should turn against us."

Rogers told me he was bewildered at Israeli claims of betrayal in Scranton's proposal of an "even-handed" American posture. "I interpreted the phrase, and I think this is accurate," he said, "as meaning fair and equitable. Certainly in legal terms, even-handedness is required. The scales of justice themselves show an even-handedness." He said he did not grasp why the American supporters of Israel would be so aroused to indignation. Rogers said he was determined from the moment he took office to work for a settlement to the Middle East conflict that would be fair to both Arabs and Israelis.

Meanwhile, reports from the Suez Canal left no doubt that the Soviet Union had come a long way since the Six-Day War in rebuilding Egypt's armed forces. Though Moscow had denied Nasser's desperate plea to send Russians to fly Egyptian planes and command Egyptian troops, it had nonetheless integrated Russian technicians into virtually every level of the Egyptian military structure. These technicians had brought not only Soviet combat aircraft, tanks and guns with them but Soviet battlefield doctrine. This doctrine prescribed that Egypt keep Israel's forward lines off balance and on the defensive. It committed the Russians more directly than before to the outcome of the fighting.

As early as the summer of 1967, the lobbing of artillery shells at Israeli emplacements across the canal had become commonplace, and by October, when Egypt killed forty-seven Israelis in the sinking of the destroyer *Eilat,* casualties on the two sides were already in the hundreds. Egyptian commandos regularly crossed the canal in boats to attack Israeli installations and ambush patrols. Egyptian patrol craft fired at Israeli shipping off the Sinai coast. Even Egyptian aircraft were used, to bomb and strafe Israeli troops. Egypt's campaign, contrived with Russian help, made clear to Israelis, and to Washington, that the occupation, if it was to be long, was not going to be easy.

Having taken some months making up its mind about the response, Israel, by the fall of 1968, had selected a program designed for a protracted stand on the canal. The savage warfare had required the Israeli cabinet to choose between two alternatives: a static defense in fortified positions at the water's edge or a mobile defense with the bulk of forces based on the high ground in the rear, out of artillery range. It was no secret that at the waterline Israeli forces would be vulnerable not only to artillery bombardment but to surprise amphibious attack. Such a defense assured constant casualties, and wasted the army's strong attribute of mobility. But a defense from the rear would present the Egyptians with a standing invitation to seize beachhead positions. To drive them back into the water would take time and heavy losses in equipment and personnel.

With its military circles more or less equally divided, Israel's political leadership tipped the decision to a hugely expensive network of tunnels and forts to be known as the Bar-Lev line. The cabinet reasoned that if Israeli forces moved to the rear, the Egyptians would seize the opportunity to vault across the canal to grab a piece of the Sinai, then call for an immediate cease-fire. If they succeeded, Israel's rigorously held strategy of giving up territory only in return for peace would be in ruins.

Whatever the merits of this reasoning, the decision committed the Israeli army on the Suez front, as on the Jordanian front, to a static defense, the military posture at which it was weakest. It was a signal that Israel was willing to make whatever sacrifices were necessary to avoid withdrawal from the Sinai. But it made Israelis into sitting ducks for Egyptian guns. The Bar-Lev line led inevitably to the War of Attrition, the fourth major encounter in the Arab-Israeli struggle. It also set the stage for the catastrophe of the Yom Kippur War, the fifth.

Egypt immediately recognized that the Bar-Lev line, by placing the Israeli army in a trap, played to its strength. Egypt's army had plenty of firepower and was at its best in stationary warfare. It had far greater reserves of manpower than Israel and was prepared to take substantially more casualties. In April of 1969, Nasser proclaimed the abrogation of the cease-fire of 1967, and the War of Attrition officially began. Besides the relentless artillery bombardments, each side searched boldly but vainly for tactics to break the deadlock. When Egypt stepped up its amphibious crossings, jeopardizing Israeli lives along the length of the canal, Israel escalated by striking from the air at targets well behind Egyptian lines. But neither side much intimidated the other, and the war became bloodier.

In Washington, Nixon was bothered by the ramifications that the bloodshed might have for the superpowers. That was when Rogers saw an opening to promote his own Middle East position. In 1969, at the time Nixon took office, the United States was still painfully embroiled in Vietnam. Kissinger's assignment was to find a way out, but until he did, the scraping of East against West at the canal presented the risk of a second war. Nixon liked the prospect no more than had Johnson in 1967. When Rogers proposed to explore with Moscow the possibility of defusing the danger by bringing Arabs and Israelis together, Nixon, over Kissinger's objections, granted him the opportunity.

Kissinger was an admittedly ambitious man, and Rogers's overture represented a setback in his personal campaign to control Nixon's foreign policy. But beyond that, Kissinger was not willing to have the United States and the Soviet Union divide the world, or even the Middle East, in half. He wanted more. Committed to combat with the Russians, he was determined to make America the dominant power in the Middle East, and he was not interested in a peace settlement that provided otherwise. As Kissinger saw it, any meeting between Israel and Egypt as equals would be taken as evidence that the Russians since 1967 had shifted the scales of power in the Middle East in their client's favor. Since by this reasoning any agreement would have been a Russian victory, he preferred no agreement at all.

Furthermore, in terms of military strategy, he concluded that the United States would not necessarily gain from an agreement. Since the Six-Day War, the wreckage of ships sunk in battle had barred all passage through the Suez Canal. On its eastern bank, Israel's army stood guard, obstructing clearance operations. It was true that interruption of the Suez trade route was costly to Western Europe, which had to stretch new maritime lanes around Africa to get oil from the Persian Gulf. Still, in the judgment of military analysts, it was the Russians who stood to gain the most by the canal's reopening.

For some years, Russian warships had been cruising in the warm waters of the eastern Mediterranean, calling at Arab ports, making their presence felt by the American Sixth Fleet. Meanwhile, at home, Russian naval yards were turning out new ships at a rapid pace. The Russians' apparent purpose was to challenge Western dominance not only in the Mediterranean but in the oceans of the world. Strategists spoke routinely of the growing Russian naval capacity to encircle Western Europe from the south.

A reopened Suez Canal seemed to offer the Russians still further naval options. It would give them the means to outflank the West's oil fields in the Gulf. It would also increase the vulnerability of China, recently transformed from Moscow's ally to its enemy, and even of the American forces in Vietnam. Pursuing such strategic options would, of course, entail huge risks, and the Soviet Union had never shown a disposition to take major risks. Still, the canal offered a range of new possibilities, from which Moscow would be free to pick and choose. In Kissinger's eyes, an opening of the waterway, accompanied by Israel's retreat from Suez, would present the Soviet Union with the temptation to advance its global aims.

Thus, within the Nixon administration, the lines were drawn over Middle East policy. In Kissinger's view, Washington had to keep Israel standing firm against Egypt at the Bar-Lev line, while tolerating no further Soviet incursion into the region; to Rogers, the battles being fought at the Bar-Lev line were a threat to ignite World War III. To Kissinger, the United States, for at least as long as it was entangled in Vietnam, had no choice but to depend on Israel as its cold war surrogate; to Rogers, Washington had to deal even-handedly with Israel and the Arabs, to reduce the danger of superpower conflict. According to Kissinger, Israel was the guardian of the American national interest; according to Rogers, Israel placed obstacles in the way of a peace settlement of which it would itself be a beneficiary. He saw the United States as beneficiary, as well.

Once he received Nixon's authorization, Rogers contacted Moscow, proposing a joint brokerage of Arab-Israeli negotiations based on Resolution 242. The agenda the two agreed upon included talks on the Syrian and Jordanian borders, but in view of Nasser's preeminence and the fighting on the canal, the emphasis was on the Egyptian-Israeli frontier.

In the ensuing months, Soviet and American representatives met repeatedly, exchanging position papers, occasionally making progress on joint positions. But Moscow perceived Nixon's interest in the talks to be, first, their linkage to agreements to get American forces out of Vietnam and, second, their impact on the Soviet Union's own painstakingly cultivated influence in Egypt. On neither count did Russia intend to accommodate. On the other hand, it soon became apparent to the Americans that the Soviet objective was to obtain Israeli territorial withdrawal from the Sinai in return for few if any Arab concessions. So an agreement became more elusive, while the War of Attrition worsened.

Meanwhile, Kissinger, skillful at bureaucratic warfare, did his best to sabotage Rogers's negotiations, and Rabin quietly conspired with him. Israel, kept informed but not consulted on Rogers's talks, warned that it would not be bound by the results, and repeatedly expressed displeasure that the talks were taking place at all. With Kissinger's encouragement, Rabin sneered openly at Rogers's agenda, proclaiming it an "erosion" of American resolve in the Middle East. In public statements, the American government deplored the War of Attrition, with its growing death toll. But privately, Kissinger urged the Israelis to fight on, convinced that bloodying the Russians' chief client in the Middle East somehow advanced the American position in Vietnam.

To Israeli "hawks," the War of Attrition, if tragic for the lives lost every day, was also an opportunity for Israel to prove itself indispensable to America's global objectives. They cited the war as evidence of Israel's contribution to the United States in the superpower struggle. Their real goal, of course, was to discourage Washington from imposing any pressure for territorial compromises. They wanted Israeli steadfastness at the canal to deliver the message that occupation of the territories was vital not just to Israel but to America's cold war interests.

Rabin, clearly among the "hawks," used the war as an argument in Washington for acquiring weapons. Arms procurement, he told me, was the "bread and butter" of his work as ambassador. He said Kissinger was consistently sympathetic to his efforts to obtain America's finest weapons on the best possible terms, while the State Department was much less so. Occasionally, he noted self-mockingly, State Department officials had to remind him that arming Israel was not the only goal of American foreign policy.

Rabin does not contend, at least from the perspective of nearly two decades later, that the positions Israel took in the debates on peacemaking were always reasonable or even wise. Nor does he deny that Israel occasionally shared with the Arabs the fault for the long failure of the parties to the Middle East conflict to negotiate a settlement.

"I believe we tried, though maybe not hard enough, to find a settlement," he said. "I would add that though our demands might have been too much, I believe the Arab world was not ripe for peace. I believe both sides lacked the minimum confidence to reach a solution. Still, I will not deny that in Israel there were people in the government who did not care about peace. The mood in the cabinet was based on a conviction that we had become the third great power in the region, if not in the world."

Rabin was correct in saying the Arabs in 1969 were no readier than Israel for peace. The two superpowers learned to their disappointment during their months of talks that they would be unable to guarantee delivery of their respective clients to meet and accept terms, even if they were able to resolve on terms between themselves. The Arabs still refused to sign a contractual peace agreement, and the Israelis had not been persuaded to evacuate territory. Though the superpowers themselves narrowed their differences during the bargaining, they clearly failed to commit their clients to even the roughest premises of a settlement. And so no formal American-Soviet mediation came out of the talks.

But Rogers, unwilling to concede failure, decided on an audacious stroke and, on December 9, 1969, unveiled in a public speech the program that was officially designated the Rogers Plan. Rogers's intention in the speech had been to put the United States decisively on record in favor of a negotiated settlement based on Resolution 242. But Kissinger's baneful hand was visible from the start. The very name conveyed the message that the "Rogers Plan" was not the Nixon administration's program but the secretary of state's. The conclusion for all to draw was that its objectives were not a central concern of the United States government. Objectively, the prospect of success of the Rogers Plan was no greater than that of the joint Soviet-American proposal, which had already failed. But with the President openly positioned at a distance, it never had a chance.

"Our policy is and will continue to be a *balanced* one," Rogers declared in his announcement of December 9. "We have friendly

ties with both Arabs and Israelis. To call for Israeli withdrawal as
envisaged in the U.N. resolution without achieving agreement on
peace would be partisan toward the Arabs. To call on the Arabs
to accept peace without Israeli withdrawal would be partisan toward Israel. Therefore, our policy is to encourage the Arabs to
accept a permanent peace based on a binding agreement and to
urge the Israelis to withdraw from occupied territory when their
territorial integrity is assured."

If Rogers was the Eisenhower disciple in the Nixon cabinet, his
statement was nonetheless a far cry from United States policy of
1956, when Eisenhower insisted that Israel surrender the territorial gains of the Sinai campaign without a complementing Arab
move. The Rogers Plan was consistent with President Johnson's
characterization of a unilateral return to the prewar borders as
"not a prescription for peace but of renewed hostilities." It was
well within the framework of what Yitzhak Rabin described to me
as the "strategic understanding between the United States and
Israel" that existed at the time, based on the principle of "no
withdrawal without a political solution."

In sketching his vision of a Middle East at peace, Rogers went
beyond the vague formulation of Resolution 242 to propose specific guarantees of access by Israel not only to the Strait of Tiran
but to the Suez Canal. Addressing Israeli objections to an "imposed" settlement, he made clear he favored negotiations between the parties themselves over international guarantees. On
the issue of Israeli security, he went even a step further. He persuaded Nixon to sweeten the Rogers Plan with an offer of "hardware for software," which in the jargon of the day meant the
United States would furnish extra arms to Israel to compensate for
whatever risk was created by the evacuation of territory.

Yet the Israeli government went into a frenzy over the Rogers
Plan. What stirred up Israeli tempers was Rogers's assertion that
"any changes in the pre-existing lines should not reflect the weight
of conquest and should be confined to *insubstantial* alterations
required for mutual security." The words were almost identical to
those Lyndon Johnson spoke shortly after the Six-Day War, but

Israel denounced the formulation as itself constituting an "imposed" settlement, in depriving them of a free hand in determining their own borders. Rogers's statement represented no change in American policy, which Israel had long since formally accepted. But Israel's temper was ignited at Rogers's pointed notice that "We do not support expansionism."

With Mrs. Meir leading the charge, Israel took only a day to reject the Rogers Plan, declaring that the concept of "insubstantial alterations" was inadequate for realigning frontiers. At the same time, she contemptuously dismissed Rogers's suggestion that Israel might be engaged in "expansionism." The Israeli cabinet characterized the Rogers Plan as a retreat from America's support of Israel's claim of the right to "defensible" borders. In a formal statement, the cabinet said, "The proposal by the U.S.A. cannot but be interpreted by the Arab parties as an attempt to appease them at the expense of Israel." Nasser, however, failed to see the appeasement, and so joined with the Israelis in turning the Rogers Plan down cold.

"The Rogers Plan was the political result of the War of Attrition," Rabin said. "The Soviet Union and Egypt believed their position on the Suez Canal was so good that they backed out of any form of negotiations. Israelis had not found the answer militarily. American resolve was eroding. We were at a loss. I said to my government, the problem is the political implication of Nasser's capacity to continue the strategy of war. I said the only response was to force Egypt to stop, not just by attacking their forces but by threatening their regime.

"Threatening their regime meant bombing, the deep penetration of their country. You couldn't bomb the sources of their armaments. That was in the Soviet Union. I advocated bombing big factories and military targets deep in Egypt, and the sources of their electric power. We had to do something to change the strategic situation, or we would lose more and more in the United States."

In January 1970, a month after announcement of the Rogers Plan, Israeli Phantoms began bombing in the Nile delta, in the suburbs of Cairo and far south in the Nile valley. Israel's new strategy was given the name "deep penetration," and Rabin took credit for originating it. Rabin acknowledged that the strategy divided the Israeli cabinet bitterly. A group led by Foreign Minister Eban did not want to risk alienating Washington. This group queried him relentlessly, he said, on whether an understanding with the American government had been reached. Rogers's State Department clearly regarded the Israelis as reckless and, officially, the American reaction was cool. But in both his memoirs and his talks with me, Rabin maintained that Washington's inner circle— by which he meant Nixon and Kissinger—was secretly delighted with Israel's behavior.

"In relations between a superpower and a small country," Rabin said, "you don't get permission for something like this, for in giving permission the superpower takes over the responsibility. We could not ignore the United States or do anything contradictory to American interests. But we could not ask for a green light, either. It would be stupid to believe we could.

"Therefore, after the first deep penetration raid, I waited. I didn't expect applause. But if the United States doesn't like something, they know how to say it. They know how to say to Israel, 'We don't like it.' But no voice came.

"Then came the second raid, when we bombed a big factory. We were using bombs produced in the United States, and one of them did not explode. Dayan panicked, and transmitted classified information about the fuse to the Egyptians. I received a call from Kissinger and I was told, 'Be more careful with your bombing and with American secrets. We don't want the Soviets to get them.' The cabinet was scared by that. So I decided on another move. I went to Kissinger at the White House and I said, 'We are in the process of heavy bombing and we need an acceleration in the shipment of bombs.' "

Rabin said, snapping his fingers sharply, "I got it like *that*. . . ."

"Now, if somebody wanted to get American permission to bomb, that would be stupid. He would not understand the role Israel has to play and how to play it. But not hearing anything after the first raid, being told after the second, 'Be more careful with your bombing,' and getting a large accelerated shipment of bombs after the third, what else did I need?"

Whatever his satisfaction with the American response, Rabin was dismayed by the unwillingness of the Egyptians to give in when confronted by Israel's "deep penetration" strategy. Nasser responded by running to Moscow, proposing the War of Attrition be ratcheted upward another notch. The Russians abandoned their early caution and, whatever understandings they had reached with Rogers during the months of two-power discussions, they decided to go along with Nasser's proposals.

By February 1970, Russia's new surface-to-air missiles—SAM III's, in military terminology—had started arriving in Egypt. With them, for the first time, were Soviet combat personnel, chiefly fighter pilots and missile crews. By March, ten thousand Russians were in Egypt, and Soviet involvement in the Arab-Israeli wars had reached a new level. In strategic terms, Moscow had marked up a cold war advance. Russian soldiers had finally reached the banks of the Suez Canal.

The Israeli air force quickly learned to respect the deadly power of the Soviet-operated SAM-III's. After suffering heavy losses around Egypt's major cities, Israel had no choice but to turn to Washington to make up its deficiencies, both in aircraft and in electronic gear. Meanwhile, the Egyptians were moving the ground emplacements for the missiles farther eastward, to buttress the already substantial margin in manpower and artillery they enjoyed on the canal. The Egyptian-Soviet response had not only defeated Israel's deep penetration strategy but, by the spring of 1970, had placed Israel's capacity to defend the Sinai itself in serious jeopardy.

Russia at that point offered to pocket its profits. It proposed a deal to Washington in which it would freeze the movement of the SAMs in return for an end to the deep penetration raids. The hitch in the terms was that the War of Attrition would have continued, leaving Egypt free to exploit the advantage in firepower that it enjoyed before the deep penetration began. Rogers was willing to take the deal, though it represented a significant Israeli defeat. Kissinger, sneering at Rogers's faintheartedness, refused. Rabin recalled Kissinger's summoning him to a secret meeting with Nixon at the White House, at which he expected to discuss the latest Israeli request for airplanes.

"Nixon turned to me," Rabin said in our talk, "and asked, 'Have you considered attacking the ground-to-air missiles [SAMs] of the Soviet Union?' I was shocked to hear a direct question about military operations against the Soviet Union, especially while he kept in abeyance a decision about the additional Phantoms we had asked for. When I said 'No,' he added, 'Sometimes a decision like that is hard for a superpower to take.' I came out of the meeting with the distinct impression that he wouldn't mind at all if our Phantoms attacked Soviet installations."

Rabin had some precedent for his impression. A year before, Nixon had secretly ordered a series of heavy bombing raids on Cambodia. Rabin never knew whether or not Nixon meant the remark as a dare to Israel, but, he said, he chose not to follow up the hint. Nixon understood, nonetheless, that the warfare at the canal was growing more perilous every day. In April 1970, the first Soviet-piloted MiGs showed up, and Israelis shot several down in dogfights. Now, with more Russian air units arriving, the prospect of conflict increased between the superpowers themselves.

Meanwhile, after a year of trying, Nixon's hopes for easing pressures in Southeast Asia had gone unfulfilled. Kissinger had made little headway in Vietnam negotiations, and Nixon's own decision to extend the fighting into Cambodia had been both unsuccessful and unpopular. Rogers's response to the reversals in Southeast Asia was to step up his advocacy of the need to reduce tensions between the superpowers. To Kissinger's dismay, Nixon reacted by authorizing the secretary of state to undertake yet another Middle East peace effort.

On June 19, 1970, Rogers proposed a ninety-day cease-fire on the canal, in conjunction with negotiations, based on Resolution 242, directed by Gunnar Jarring, the U.N.'s special representative. The proposal, called the Rogers Initiative to distinguish it from the Rogers Plan, seemed simple enough. It committed the parties, in Rogers's terms, only "to stop shooting and start talking."

Mrs. Meir's instinct was to reject the Rogers Initiative as she had earlier proposals. But Rabin was more realistic. Though personally responsible for the deep penetration plan, he understood the dangerous changes on the canal that the raids had provoked. Far from ending the War of Attrition, Israel's strategy had intensified it. Israeli casualties were staggering and the economy was faltering. The reserve forces were in a state of permanent mobilization, paralyzing the country. In the face of all this, Israel's government appeared, even to its own supporters, to have become unjustifiably rigid. Rabin flew home for an emergency meeting to appeal to Mrs. Meir for prudence.

"Golda didn't understand the military meaning of what was happening," Rabin said. "Neither did Dayan. The Russians had the upper hand in terms of moving the missile system where they wanted. We were not equipped with a weapons system, and neither was the United States, that could bring about a victory of the Phantoms over their missile system.

"What held the Russians in check was not Israel's military capability but the warning of war with the United States. That is what many Israelis tried to ignore. They looked at it in such a narrow way. But we had attacked, and we failed. We didn't have the capacity to tell the Russians, 'Don't move the missiles.' We had to come up with a political solution. That's where the Rogers Initiative came in."

Despite the admission of strategic failure, Rabin insisted the deep penetration strategy had yielded a major reward for Israel, the product of his success in bringing the superpowers to the brink. "Basically," he said, "without deep penetration, we would have lost the War of Attrition worse than we did. By escalating from local to superpower involvement, we at least brought the fighting to a halt." Clearly, the superpowers, seeing the prospect of a military confrontation between themselves, had decided the War of Attrition could not go on.

But the benefits, as Rabin saw them, did not stop there. A near conflict between the superpowers was not enough to deter Nixon —or, at least, Kissinger—from warming up the cold war in the Middle East. While negotiations over the Rogers Initiative were at their most sensitive point, Kissinger made the assertion that the objective of American policy was "to expel" Soviet combat forces from the Middle East. It was an ironic boast, since Kissinger himself, in endorsing the deep penetration strategy, had contributed mightily to bringing Soviet combat forces to Egypt. His conduct recalled Dulles's blunder years before, in bringing the Russians to Egypt in the wake of the collapse of the Baghdad Pact. Kissinger was so combative, in fact, that when Moscow offered to join as a cosponsor of Rogers's cease-fire proposal, he persuaded Nixon to refuse the offer.

Kissinger was also behind Nixon's decision, announced during the "deep penetration" crisis, to loosen American control over the machinery of Israeli military procurement. To Rabin, this was Israel's real reward. During more than a year in office, the Nixon administration, though it approved most of Israel's arms requests, nonetheless reserved the right to link them to Israel's attention to American interests. The system irritated Rabin, who liked neither the requirement that Israel forever justify its policies nor the squabbles with the United States that inevitably ensued. Then Nixon changed the system, endorsing the principle of long-term arms authorizations, which would insulate Israel from regular review. This was the chief objective Rabin had set for himself in his role as ambassador.

Nixon first indicated that he was considering a new arrangement in a television interview on July 1. "Once the balance of power shifts where Israel is weaker than its neighbors, there will be war," Nixon said. "Therefore, it is in U.S. interests to maintain the balance. . . . We will do what is necessary to maintain Israel's strength vis-à-vis its neighbors, not because we want Israel to be in a position to wage war—that is not it—but because that is what will deter its neighbors from attacking it."

The statement actually said more about Nixon's view of the cold war than of the Arab-Israeli struggle. It meant that Nixon would continue to play close to the edge of superpower confrontation. It represented a clear departure from Rogers's view that America's interest lay in imposing tight controls over the Middle East arms race, reflecting instead Kissinger's contention that a heavily armed Israel was America's strongest asset in the superpower conflict. Nixon's vision substituted a policy of armed confrontation for the philosophy of Resolution 242.

"President Johnson had never declared this policy officially," Rabin said, interpreting Nixon's words to me. "President Nixon made it clear that the United States takes it on itself to maintain the military balance between the Arab countries and Israel." Rabin said Nixon repeated this pledge in a secret letter to Mrs. Meir, confirming that the American interpretation of the meaning of the July 1 statement matched Israel's. Though the squabbling between the United States and Israel was far from over, a new step had been taken in the relationship. "We took it as a commitment," he said, "a commitment that no future President would be able to avoid or to ignore."

Despite the new arms policy, the indomitable Golda did not submit easily to the Rogers Initiative. Rogers had conditioned his cease-fire effort on the Israeli cabinet's ending its three years of equivocation, to formally endorse Resolution 242. Without such an endorsement, he said, the talks that were to follow had no prospect of success. Begin's Revisionists repeated their warning that they would quit the government if she submitted to Rogers, and her instinct, as usual, was to give political unity precedence over

a peace overture. She also knew that in Washington she had Kissinger on her side. But then Nixon weighed in, announcing that,
strongly as he supported Israel, he also had American interests to
protect. He was fully behind the Rogers Initiative, he said, and
would not look favorably on its rejection.

Mrs. Meir tried one more ploy. Gauging the Israeli public's
weariness of the war, she audaciously told Rogers she would take
half his package: the cease-fire without the negotiations. Rogers
politely refused.

The Israelis, meanwhile, counted on the likelihood that, while
they procrastinated, Nasser would kill the Rogers Initiative. He
had taken much of the heat off them six months before by rejecting the Rogers Plan. In fact, when the Initiative was first presented
to him, Nasser spurned the proposal. But then he flew to Moscow,
where the Russians apparently told him they were as concerned
as the Americans about a superpower war over the Suez Canal.
Indeed, in talks in Washington, the Russians had hinted at a willingness to yield to prudence by bringing pressure to bear on
Nasser. On his return to Cairo, Nasser reversed his earlier statement and announced his acceptance of Rogers's terms.

Mrs. Meir now had no choice but to give in, though before she
did she succeeded in exacting one crucial concession. In return for
Israeli acceptance, she told Rogers, she wanted an American
pledge that the Egyptians would not take advantage of the cease-
fire to move their SAM installations forward, where they could
control the air directly over the canal. Rogers found the request
reasonable and promised Mrs. Meir a "standstill" on the missiles,
not foreseeing that it would turn his diplomatic designs to scrap.

His acceptance of Mrs. Meir's condition, however, cleared the
way for the Israeli cabinet, at long last, to endorse Resolution 242.
Begin, faithful to his long-standing promise, announced he could
not be a party and submitted his resignation. On August 6, the
cabinet followed the lead taken by Nasser in voting to approve
Rogers's cease-fire terms. The shooting at the canal then came to
a stop.

But Nasser's new sense of military power, acquired in his victory in the "deep penetration" crisis, promptly crushed the agreement's political promise. Despite his pledge of a "standstill," Nasser began immediately to move Egypt's SAM emplacements forward, where for the first time they were in a position to dominate Suez's skies. When Washington protested to Moscow, the Russians replied that they had no obligations to enforce an agreement to which, thanks to Kissinger, they were not a party. In fact, the Russians were assisting the Egyptians in the missile redeployment, confirming Israel's worst anxieties. In fooling Israel, Nasser destroyed any hope that the Rogers Initiative would prove to be a move toward peace.

Israel actually proposed to take ground action to undo the missile move. But the Nixon administration, with Kissinger's acquiescence, decided it was wiser to accept Egypt's *fait accompli* than to retaliate, which no doubt would have led to resumption of full-scale fighting. Kissinger persuaded Nixon to make amends to Israel by sending more weapons, and under the circumstances Rogers had no choice but to concur. Thus the cease-fire held, but it led to a surge in the regional arms race, a very different result from what Rogers had envisaged.

Mrs. Meir, citing Egypt's violation, then refused to participate with Nasser in the peace talks, which were to have been the second step of the process, and Rogers was in no position to dispute her decision. As a result, Israel, whose withdrawal from the canal seemed a reasonable prospect when the Rogers mission began, now appeared likely to be at the water's edge indefinitely, looking across at both Egyptian cannon and SAM missiles. Within a few weeks of the agreement, the confrontation at the canal, though unaccompanied by gunfire, was more threatening than before.

The Rogers Initiative, which began as a triumph for American diplomacy, ended as an embarrassment for the Nixon administration, and a personal defeat for the secretary of state. But Kissinger and Rabin were not displeased. Kissinger saw the aggravated tensions between the superpowers at the canal as leverage he could somehow put to use in his Vietnamese negotiations. Rabin took satisfaction in receiving the weapons that kept the tensions in force. The two gloated over tying the hands of the enemy—the Soviet Union for Kissinger, Egypt for Rabin—and claimed perpetuation of the status quo as an achievement. Neither had any remorse about Rogers's setback, unaware that three years later the canal would explode again with the roar of Egyptian cannon and the flames of SAM missiles. Though it is conjecture whether the Rogers Initiative held out real promise for peace, its failure certainly accelerated the movement toward another war.

Yet in the short run, Kissinger and Rabin were vindicated in their belief that Israel's proper role was to serve as America's military outpost in the Middle East. In September 1970, just after the cease-fire, a series of events occurred that transformed political relationships in the Arab world, and reinforced America's impression that Israel was unique in the region in its reliability and solidity.

The disruptions of September began with protests by the Palestinians, who denounced Nasser's endorsement of the cease-fire as abandonment of their cause. But Egypt was inaccessible and too strong to be a target of retaliation by the Palestine Liberation Organization, "umbrella" of the Palestinian resistance movement. Jordan, where a million Palestinian refugees lived, was more vulnerable. Furthermore, a victory in Jordan, in making the PLO a major force among the Arabs, would be more important.

Jordan, the least bellicose of Israel's neighbors, was on good terms with the West, and wanted to stay that way. King Hussein, its leader, understood that within its borders the PLO had for some years been building a power base among the refugees, with the barely concealed goal of overthrowing him. The PLO's reasoning was that without the monarchy, it would have an unassailable power base of its own, from which it could turn Jordan into an aggressive, "rejectionist" state. When its agents hijacked three

Western airliners, and landed two of them at a desert airstrip near Amman, the king faced the choice of becoming an accomplice of PLO terrorism or provoking a showdown.

The odds in a showdown did not appear to be in the king's favor. When he went looking for help in the Arab world, Nasser was nowhere to be found. Syria, another of the Soviet Union's Middle East clients, lined up openly with the PLO. Iraq, a third, had forces based in Jordan, and he was uncertain how they would respond. The king had a well-trained army, but many of its members were Palestinians, of whose loyalty he was unsure. Practically speaking, he could count with assurance only on the faithful bedouin of his own realm.

But Israel also had a large stake in preserving the Jordanian monarchy from the PLO's designs. So did Nixon and Kissinger, who chose to see the impending inter-Arab war as a new chapter unfolding in the ongoing superpower struggle. Hussein's decision was to take on the Palestinians to preserve his throne as it was. When he ordered his army to attack the PLO's units in Jordan, the West was on his side.

The Arab world has named the period "Black September." The PLO called for the refugees in Jordan to rise up, while the king staunchly rallied his followers. Questions about the Palestinians' loyalty were answered during the ensuing bloodshed. Most ignored the PLO's call. The Palestinian soldiers fought, and the civilians either supported the monarchy or fled from the battles. Thousands on both sides died in the fighting, and the PLO was put to rout.

But while the outcome was in doubt, the United States and Israel stood guard, backing up Hussein. The American Sixth Fleet steamed menacingly off the Syrian coast, and the Israeli army covered Jordan's flank against a possible Syrian invasion. In fact, a Syrian tank column did cross the border, but the Syrian air force apparently had second thoughts about taking on the Israeli air force, and, without air cover, it retreated back into Syria when it met Jordan's armor. Throughout the crisis, Kissinger and Rabin worked closely in Washington at coordinating joint American-Israeli efforts. The outcome was more than a triumph for Hussein. By cold war standards, it was also a victory for the West.

Once again, Israel had played a crucial role in protecting Western interests, which Kissinger cited to Nixon as proof of the Israeli army's value to American interests. The conclusion drawn from the episode by Israel was that whatever its recent losses in the War of Attrition, the Arabs, in total disarray, were in far worse condition. Kissinger emerged from "Black September" with the upper hand in his contest with Rogers. As for Nixon, he drew from the experience the conclusion that Rogers's objective no longer made sense, and he abandoned altogether the goal of bringing Israel and the Arabs to the peace table.

In the same month, Nasser died. I happened to be in Israel at that moment, and I recall how somberly Israelis responded. I saw no jubilation. The country, in fact, seemed a trifle anesthetized by the news. Nasser, paradoxically, had provided a certain security. For all his bluster, Israelis felt they had taken his measure. Having grown accustomed to him, they were uneasy at his departure.

On the basis of my talks with Israelis, I wrote a report in the *Washington Star*, from which I take a few paragraphs.

JERUSALEM—For the world outside Egypt, the key question today is not so much who will succeed Gamal Abdel Nasser, but what influence the Russians will have on the direction of the Arab states after the succession.

That is how the issue is shaping up for Israelis as they emerge from the shock that followed the news of Nasser's fatal heart attack. Israelis are not rejoicing at the death of Nasser, though he was their most formidable foe. Rather they are trying to assess the effect they know this event must have on war and peace in the Middle East.

I was struck by how little talk I heard about whether Nasser's death would present new prospects for a peace settlement. Experts on Egypt in the Israeli foreign ministry introduced me to the name of Anwar Sadat, the vice-president, but they dismissed him as insignificant. They characterized him as a transitional figure, with neither a following nor a philosophy, and they said he would not last. Later I learned that their thinking coincided with the opinions of experts in most Western governments. In the same column, I wrote:

> Disliking strong men around him, [Nasser] prepared no successor. In contrast to him, all of those given a chance to become Egypt's new leader look like second-raters, or worse. . . . Vice President Anwar Sadat starts with the advantage of having moved constitutionally into Nasser's office. But he is considered an incredible incompetent whom Nasser kept around out of regard for loyalty.

I found it personally discouraging to note, at that moment, that Israelis seemed to have stopped talking about peace, seemed even to have stopped hoping for peace. Jaded by victory, Israel seemed to have become too cynical for peace. Peace was made out to be the relic of an earlier era. Israelis treated it as something not to be enjoyed but to be suffered. In the debates that had taken place in Israel since the Six-Day War, the concept of peace had become distorted, not just by the Revisionist opponents of the government but by the Mainstream Zionists themselves. Golda Meir had made peace seem like a national punishment.

By now, all Israelis understood that peace would entail painful political disruptions and require wrenching territorial sacrifices. Living in their Golden Age, they saw no justification for either. Thanks to the United States, they found it easy to be strong enough to intimidate the neighbors, and hard to chart a course among themselves to reach any diplomatic accommodation. The path of least resistance was preservation of the status quo. Israelis asked not for peace but only for a respite from war, which Nasser's death and the accession of Sadat seemed to assure.

In Nixon's Washington, Rogers, the bearer of peace, was finished. Kissinger, bearing arms, was riding high. Few Israelis were willing to contemplate the possibility that this was not the best of available worlds.

6

War of Atonement

On JULY 18, 1972, Anwar Sadat astounded the world by notifying Moscow that Egypt no longer wanted on its soil the fifteen thousand Soviet citizens, uniformed and civilian, who served as the backbone of the Egyptian military establishment. No less astounding, the Soviet Union rather meekly concurred.

Sadat's action reversed the direction in which the Arab world had been moving since Nasser negotiated the first arms agreement with the Russians in 1955. In strategic terms, he removed Soviet forces from the banks of the Suez Canal, where they had been positioned since the War of Attrition in 1970. At the same time, he broke the hold the Soviet Union had established and had continued to expand throughout the Arab world. Sadat thus presented the United States with a victory of major proportions, one that Israel could not possibly have achieved in its behalf, and that Washington had no means of achieving on its own.

Sadat's decision was all the more electrifying in that it was in no sense the settlement of a debt to the United States. At that very moment, the Nixon administration, preparing for presidential elections, was publicly accelerating arms shipments to Israel, while distancing itself from peace negotiations. If Sadat's decision was a long-term investment in American policy, it was surely not the product of any encouragement received from either Nixon or

Kissinger at the White House. What Sadat handed the United States was a gift, for which he exacted no payment, demanded no change of objectives, required no promises in return.

In his memoirs, Kissinger characteristically takes credit for Sadat's move. He argues that since he had repeatedly outmaneuvered Moscow in the course of negotiations over détente, Sadat came inevitably to the conclusion that Washington could offer Egypt more than the Soviet Union did. But such a conclusion on Sadat's part was not inevitable at all. The Soviet Union's program of military assistance to Egypt was continuing, notwithstanding détente. Had the more cynical Nasser still been head of state, and Kissinger followed the same course, the Russians would surely have remained lodged where they were. If anything, Sadat acted not because he drew the right conclusion from Kissinger's maneuverings with Moscow but because, as he later learned, he drew the wrong one.

Sadat's decision was based on his own reading of the best means for regaining the Sinai, as well as the other territories the Arabs lost in 1967. In mid-1972, when détente appeared to have become the hub of Soviet policy toward the West, he became convinced the Russians were no longer willing to apply the necessary coercion, diplomatic or military, to get the territory back. He disliked the Soviet Union, and resented its efforts to determine Egyptian policy. By taste, he preferred the United States, and he had an appreciation for America's leverage with the Israelis. Sadat shifted his allegiance out of a conviction that the United States, unlike the Soviet Union, had not only an interest in but the power to attain a settlement in the Middle East.

Sadat's action, however, made sense only if the United States used that power. Expelling the Russians would have only transient meaning if Washington failed to see it as not just a victory but an opportunity. Sadat presented the United States with the means. In providing American diplomacy with credible access to the Arab capitals, he placed Washington in a powerful position to broker an exchange of land for peace, a Pax Americana. The benefits to the United States seemed to him self-evident. He opened to Washington the prospect of achieving the preeminence it sought in the region through friendly relations with both Israel and the Arab world. The resulting stability would put an end to the risk of superpower conflict, which had accompanied every Arab-Israeli war. Sadat assumed it was an opportunity that Washington would seize. But, in both the immediate and the long term, he was mistaken.

He was mistaken because the United States for which he opted was not the one that he got. Sadat had calculated that once he made his shift, Washington would be governed by the perspective of even-handed peacemaking associated with William Rogers, a perspective that carried the promise of satisfying the reasonable demands of the two sides in the Arab-Israeli conflict. What he got, instead, was Kissinger's cold war outlook, which was not satisfied with a quiet American preeminence in a stable Middle East. Kissinger's objective was nothing less than to forge an instrument for humbling the Soviet Union. It was Kissinger's rather than Rogers's perspective that was in the ascendency then and, for the most part, has dominated American foreign policy considerations ever since. Except for a brief period when Jimmy Carter joined him, Sadat alone among leaders has gone out on a limb for peace, starting in 1972 and throughout the years that have followed.

The United States never seized the opportunity that Sadat held out to it. Whatever the exertions of peacemaking in the ensuing years, Washington's vision of superpower rivalry made certain that the two sides in the Arab-Israeli conflict would wind up more polarized than before. There never was a Pax Americana. In fact, there was never a *pax* at all. Israel is less secure for it, and in the conditions of instability that have persisted, American preeminence in the Middle East is notably less at the end of the 1980s than it was when Sadat sent the Russians packing at the beginning of the 1970s.

Sadat gave his notice to Moscow nearly two years after the truce in the War of Attrition and the death of Nasser. During those two years, he had steadily shaped a new Egyptian approach—and planted the seeds of a new Arab approach—to the issue of a Middle East settlement. In a series of public declarations, he made clear that in return for restoration of the Sinai, he would go far to meet Israel's security concerns. Unfortunately, the world did not take notice of his words until after he launched a savage war in 1973. His overtures evoked no response from the United States in these years, and only disdain from Israel.

One prominent Israeli, it should be noted, dissented. Defense Minister Moshe Dayan, the most astute and influential member of Golda Meir's cabinet, argued that Israel should make an offer to Sadat, as a test of his intentions. Dayan even presented the cabinet with a plan to draw the Israeli army back from the Suez Canal, beyond the range of Egyptian artillery, in order to persuade Egypt to invest in peace by rebuilding the cities along its banks. The idea would have meant abandonment of the defensive system based on the Bar-Lev line, which many members of Dayan's general staff had long considered extremely dangerous, anyway. But in cabinet discussions, Prime Minister Meir found the proposal much too audacious, and despite Dayan's considerable influence, she kept it from ever being presented to Sadat as a formal offer.

So the cease-fire of 1970 dragged on, interrupted now and then by an exploratory peace mission led by the U.N. special representative, Gunnar Jarring, or by some other intermediary, equally well-meaning and equally ineffectual. What mattered to the Israelis was that they continued to receive American arms, while Sadat, having severed his connection with Moscow, appeared to them to have waived his military option. Only innovative leadership in Israel could have shaped a positive response to the new Egyptian approach and, Dayan apart, it was sorely lacking in Mrs. Meir and the men around her. The Israelis, deeply divided on the issue of territorial withdrawal, calculated the political costs of meeting Sadat partway, and remained faithful to the policy of doing nothing.

As for the Middle East policy of the Nixon administration, the best one could say was that during Sadat's first years, the President's mind was elsewhere. Nixon was preoccupied with Vietnam peace talks, then with the opening to China, then with the pursuit of détente with Moscow. Kissinger, insisting that the elements were not in place for a Middle East settlement, dismissed all proposals to involve Washington in Arab-Israeli peacemaking. He maintained that a favorable atmosphere for negotiations would emerge only through "linkage" to East-West issues that carried higher priorities. Nixon and Kissinger dismissed Sadat's peace overtures as a diversion from their own worldwide agenda, already ambitious enough.

Only Secretary of State Rogers, by now an outsider within the administration, kept trying. He prodded the Israelis to receive Jarring, shortly after Sadat took office. He also introduced several sensible innovations in procedure, which he hoped might break down the resistance of the two sides.

Building on Dayan's proposal to the Meir cabinet, he brought to discussions of a Middle East settlement the concept of the "interim agreement," which provided for Israel to cede a strip of territory on the east bank of the canal deep enough to permit Egypt, with some degree of security, to rebuild several cities along the western edge. Meant as the start of a step-by-step process toward peace, it was to replace the futile efforts to implement Resolution 242 in a single stroke. Kissinger, of course, did his best to scuttle the "interim agreement" proposal when Rogers placed it on the agenda. Two years later, however, the proposal became his own model in the negotiations that followed the Yom Kippur War. He even dared rebuke Israel for having turned Rogers down.

Rogers also sponsored the notion of "proximity talks," a plan to close the gap between the Israeli and Egyptian positions on direct negotiations. Israel insisted on direct negotiations in order to establish, in the symbolism of diplomacy, a measure of Arab recognition of its legitimacy. That, of course, was precisely the reason that Egypt rejected such a procedure. Rogers suggested that Israel and Egypt lodge representatives in adjacent rooms of some hotel, while the United States would act as a catalyst, carrying messages between them. Though no more than a stratagem, it had a face-saving component for both sides. After a flurry of consideration, however, "proximity talks" died like so many earlier efforts to initiate settlement negotiations.

In 1971, Rogers himself traveled to the Middle East to meet with Sadat and Mrs. Meir. No American secretary of state had visited either Egypt or Israel since John Foster Dulles, two decades before. Rogers, first of a long parade of American diplomats who in the next ten years would be captivated by Sadat, left Cairo hopeful of the prospects for peace. After meeting with Mrs. Meir a few days later, he left Jerusalem with a quite different feeling. Conciliatory by nature, a lawyer trained to mediate differences, exquisitely polite and a trifle formal, Rogers found little in common with the caustic Israeli prime minister, whose opinions of people and issues tended to divide sharply between the good and the evil. Their meeting was a near disaster.

"She had very strong views," said Rogers, ever punctilious, in a conversation with me. "She was an older person, and I think she felt the best thing for Israel was to have the status quo continue. I think she felt deep down inside that things were going pretty well, so why not leave them the way they were. She also felt the United States wasn't going to force her to do something she did not want to do.

"But we were guaranteeing Israel's sovereignty and its continuation as a state, and when we urged the Israelis to take a few chances in an effort to achieve peace, I think they had a corresponding obligation to the United States. If the Israelis tell themselves we are locked into the position of supporting them no matter what, then American interests become irrelevant."

Rogers's recollection of Sadat's thinking was more positive.

"At that time, Sadat and I talked about his going to get the Soviet troops out. I think I helped him reach a conclusion to do it. On his side, Sadat said, 'We don't want you to change your policy toward Israel. I understand your policy. I don't agree with it, but I understand it. We think it is important for the United States not to have a confrontation with Israel. We don't think you should force the Israelis to do anything, but squeeze them a little bit.'

"That's the expression he used, 'squeeze them a little bit,' so they will be a little more reasonable. Now, to me, that sounded like a man who was prepared to make compromises for peace."

But Nixon, prompted by Kissinger, refused to squeeze the Israelis at all. In White House deliberations, Kissinger consistently objected to Rogers's proposals that American arms deliveries be used as bait to persuade Israel to soften its positions on peace negotiations. Thanks largely to Kissinger, in the three years that followed the cease-fire at the Suez Canal in 1970, American military credits to Israel increased tenfold. Whatever Rogers's claim of American attachment to Resolution 242, the flow of arms told the Israelis that Washington had no real objection to their stringent diplomatic posture on the territories. That was all Israel had to know.

Meanwhile, in the years of abortive peacemaking that followed the Six-Day War, enormous changes were taking place inside Israel, which were to make the prospect of a settlement in the Middle East even more remote. Beneath the tranquil surface of the "Golden Age," a strong undercurrent of discord had begun to manifest itself. Israelis could not ignore the fact that despite the magnitude of their victory, their security problems had not been resolved. Recurring terrorist incidents reminded them that the Palestinian problem loomed as starkly as before. Moreover, the aftermath of the Six-Day War had loosened the hinges of Israeli society. The good life of the Golden Age had intensified factionalism, making the nation more petulant, quirkier, less tolerant, without political direction and much more intransigent in its dealings with the outside world.

The changes, which few Israelis had foreseen, were remaking the foundation on which the country conducted its daily discourse. Despite an unprecedented military victory, Israelis felt increasingly threatened in their national existence. The simple homeland of Zionist dreams had overnight become an empire containing

two million Arabs, most of them without political rights. The Jewish people, long embarrassed by their impotence, suddenly over-
flowed with hubris at their military prowess. Though no one fully
understood why, a new atmosphere had come into being, in which
old truths were under attack, and old political positions were
breaking apart. The change added a new layer to the complexities
that already existed in the quest for peace.

Politically, there burst on Israel a new Revisionist wave, which
still focused on the goals of Jabotinsky but was now more religious,
and much more populist. Its leadership remained in the hands of
right-wing Ashkenazim of the Begin model, an elite of basically
secular Jews from the old terrorist underground. But it was fortified by the accession of the bulk of the Sephardi population who,
for the first time, gave these leaders a mass following. More star-
tlingly, many of Israel's Orthodox Jews joined the wave, buttress-
ing old-line Revisionist objectives with religious zealotry, even
sanctification. The coalition that came into being positioned the
Revisionists to make their first serious bid for political power.

The rise of the new Revisionist coalition, while shifting the balance of votes to the right, also changed the rules of combat for the
conduct of politics. Israelis had always practiced their democracy
vigorously, with heavy doses of hyperbole, even of demagogy. But
the new wave of Revisionism introduced into the political arena
an element of physical aggressiveness, often passionate, sometimes violent, occasionally lawless. Begin and his disciples, underground veterans disdainful of campaign niceties, found an appre-
ciative audience after 1967 for their confrontational political style.
Sephardi youth, personally rebellious and accustomed to the mob
politics of the Arab world, had turned to them for leadership, and
responded muscularly to their fiery platform invocations. Meanwhile, Orthodox Jews, having suddenly found truth in Revisionist
doctrine, supported it with fanaticism, acclaiming the virtue of
violence committed in the exercise of God's commandments.
With the advance of Revisionism, a rage unknown to an earlier
Zionism intruded into the daily competition for position between
Jews and Arabs, and no less among Jews themselves.

The power of the Sephardim had been a latent force in Israeli politics since shortly after independence. Thanks largely to the maturing of demographic trends, it surged after the Six-Day War. The significance of these trends first caught the attention of Israelis when they acknowledged that Zionist thinkers had made a mistake in predicting a massive migration of Jews to a Jewish homeland. Some three million Jews remained locked up in Russia, forbidden to leave. Most Western Jews showed no interest in moving to Israel. These developments were contrary to conventional Zionist thinking. What Zionist thinkers had also failed to foresee was the almost total migration to the Jewish state of Jews from Muslim lands.

In its first months of independence, Israel welcomed more than 300,000 European Jews, survivors of Nazism, but after that the Western influx abated and immigration from the Arab world soared. By 1956, Israel's population had been increased threefold by the arrival of Eastern Jews. Worldwide, though Sephardim were about 15 percent of the Jewish people, inside Israel their ratio grew from barely a fifth at independence to nearly half. With a substantially higher birth rate, they had increased their ratio by the Six-Day War to more than a majority.

In Israel's early years, when resources were particularly scarce, the state housed newcomers, Ashkenazim and Sephardim alike, in makeshift camps, supporting them on a meager dole. Incapable of catering to the special values the immigrants brought with them, the leadership operated on a presumption that all would somehow hew to the ideals of Mainstream Zionism. But the immigrants were not Zionist pioneers. Whether from Europe or the Arab lands, they were for the most part refugees from oppression, not settlers inspired by a Zionist vision. For reasons of security, the state placed priority on settling them in frontier areas and on lands vacated by the Arabs. These were mostly townspeople, however, who were not drawn to the idyll of the early pioneers. They did not take well either to country life or to tilling the soil.

There were also differences between the two bodies of immigrants. The Ashkenazi refugees, adapting more easily to Israel's

Western ways, made their way to the cities, where they entered trade or industry. There they were quickly absorbed into the middle class. The Sephardim who followed them to the cities tended, in contrast, to gravitate into an urban proletariat, living in slums. As for those who stayed behind, they clustered in state-constructed "development towns," economically and socially impoverished, a far cry both from the vibrant Arab cities from which they had fled and from the Jewish homeland of their millennial dreams.

While the Ashkenazi immigrants assimilated, the Sephardim seemed doomed to be a permanent underclass. In jobs, schools, the army, they saw themselves as victimized by discrimination, but their grievances went beyond the material. As Arab Jews, they were made to feel like foreigners in a Jewish land. Mainstream Zionist leaders, insensitive to their alienation, publicly lamented the prospect of Israel's being "Levantinized" or "Orientalized." They spoke openly of the dangers presented by Sephardi ignorance of democracy and the rule of law. Rather loftily, the Ashkenazi ruling elite called upon Sephardim to transform themselves into good Israelis, like themselves.

Insofar as the Sephardim might have been called Zionists at all, theirs was a religious, even "Messianic," belief, far from the political and social ideology of the Mainstream. Socialism was remote from their experience. Democracy was little known to them and the "new" Jew was a goal to which they did not aspire. Family oriented, they bristled at the challenge to patriarchy, at the pervasiveness of women in the labor market, at the freedom given to children, Western ways which they saw as threatening to their traditions. Strongly committed to the practice of Judaism as it had evolved in Moslem lands, they were ill at ease with both Israel's Ashkenazi-dominated religious establishment and Mainstream Zionism's secular vision of society.

The Sephardim also brought to their political calculations their own view of the Arabs. Arabs today often claim to be bewildered by the hatred many Jews feel for them, since for centuries, they

say, the two peoples lived in harmony. And it is true that Jews in
the Arab world experienced no Inquisition, no pogroms, no Holocaust. But the Jews of the Arab world knew the relentless humiliation of second-class citizenship, and they did not forget it when
they reached Israel.

Though less angry than Ashkenazim at Christianity, they were
readier to blame Islam for Israel's woes. They dismissed Ashkenazi
concern for the rights of Arabs in a Jewish state as effete European
humanism. Israeli opinion polls have shown that nearly half of
Sephardim currently sympathize with anti-Arab extremist movements, more than twice the ratio of Ashkenazim. Sephardim seem
largely to have adopted the proposition that Jews should treat the
stranger in their midst as they were treated when they were
strangers. For most Sephardim, now was the time to settle old
scores.

Geula Cohen, born in Palestine during the Mandate, says she
does not remember, as a child, suffering discrimination from Ashkenazim for her Yemenite origins, though there was a consciousness of differences. In those days, Sephardim were a small fraction
of the Jews in Palestine, however. Since then, Israel has become
much more aware of being multiethnic. "I remember there was
such a problem when I was growing up," she said, "but I think
more now about being Sephardi than I did then, and I am more
proud of it."

Sephardi resentment of the Ashkenazi "ruling class" grew
steadily after independence. Ashkenazim, convinced their superior culture would by some law of nature prevail, had predicted
the fading of ethnic sensitivity as Easterners became familiar with
Western ways. But in fact, Sephardim resisted Western customs,
and ethnic consciousness increased. Furthermore, barriers between the groups were higher in the second generation than in
the first, hastening a political showdown.

The Sephardim of the immigrant generation, grateful to be in
Israel, had tended through many elections to be faithful to the
Labor Party. It was Labor, after all, that had snatched them away

from the Arab multitudes. It was also Labor that controlled the job market, the housing allocations, the social services in Israel. Their sons and daughters had a different attitude. Native born and assertively Israeli, they were less in awe and more resentful of Ashkenazi power than their fathers and mothers had been. They blamed the Labor Party for the burdens that being Sephardi imposed on them.

The Six-Day War provided Sephardim with a new grievance toward Mainstream Zionism. When Israel seized the West Bank and Gaza, overnight thousands of Arabs arrived to join the domestic labor force, and in the years of prosperity that followed, the Arabs took over most of Israel's menial work. Mainstream Zionists were troubled. A tenet of their egalitarian philosophy held that all work was honorable, that there would be no class of serfs, that Jews and not Arabs would perform the drudgery of the Jewish society. During Israel's early years, the Mainstream took pride in the fact that Jews served as policemen, garbagemen and mechanics, jobs that Jews had almost never held in the Diaspora. Then suddenly, when the labor force swept in from the West Bank and Gaza, it was Arabs who took over these jobs.

David Shipler, who for many years was the *New York Times* correspondent in Jerusalem, notes in his sensitive book *Arab and Jew: Wounded Spirits in the Promised Land* that Israelis almost never tell jokes that poke fun at their relations with Arabs. The only one he recalled, he said, concerned an old Ashkenazi pioneer who took his grandson from the city on a tour of the kibbutz where he had spent his life. As Shipler recounts it, the story went as follows:

> "See that road?" the old man says proudly to the boy. "I built it. See that house? I built it. See that field? I plowed it."
> "Oh, Grandpa," the boy says, "did you used to be an Arab?"

If kibbutzniks continued to do their own manual labor, the situation in the cities and towns where most Israelis lived changed in the era after independence. Before the Six-Day War, it was not the "Jews" but the Sephardim who did most of the dirty work, and

Mainstream Zionists, whatever their egalitarian commitments, seemed not to notice. As Arabs took over the drudgery after 1967, these Ashkenazim mourned their lost ideals. The Sephardim, in contrast, took better jobs and cheered.

Thanks to Arab day labor, Sephardim acquired a vested interest in having Israel keep the occupied territories. They have little representation in the movements to colonize them. Even with the "suburbanization" of the West Bank, relatively few have left the cities and towns of Israel proper. They have not given their allegiance to the Revisionist ideology of a Greater Israel. Their reasons are practical, which is why they have trouble understanding the laments of Mainstream egalitarians. The Arab work force offers an opportunity to Sephardim for upward mobility, and they have little patience with those who proposed to snatch it away by returning the land.

In a brilliant work of journalism called *In the Land of Israel,* the novelist Amos Oz, an Ashkenazi and a kibbutznik, interviewed many Sephardim in an effort to capture the current spirit of Israel. Oz records the words of a second-generation Moroccan Jew, to whom he spoke in a café in Bet Shemesh, a shabby development town near Jerusalem. The words tell much about the political position that many Sephardim have adopted since the Six-Day War.

> They [Ashkenazim] gave us houses, they gave us the dirty work; they gave us education, and they took away our self-respect. What did they bring my parents to Israel for? . . . Wasn't it to do your dirty work? You didn't have Arabs then, so you needed our parents to do your cleaning and be your servants and your laborers. . . .
>
> But now I'm a supervisor. And my buddy is a contractor, self-employed. And that guy there has a transport business. Also self-employed. . . . If they give back the territories, the Arabs will stop coming to work, and then and there you'll put us back into the dead-end jobs, like before. . . .
>
> Look at my daughter: she works in a bank now, and every evening an Arab comes to clean the building. All you want is to dump her from the bank into some textile factory, or have her wash the floor instead

of the Arab. The way my mother used to clean for you. . . . If for no other reason, we won't let you give back those territories.

The conflicting perceptions of the Arabs have created an interesting paradox, with important political implications. Mainstream Zionism, claiming no animosity toward Arabs, considers their presence incompatible with a Jewish state, and so has urged the reintroduction of partition. The Sephardim, acknowledging anti-Arab attitudes, reconcile themselves to the perpetuation of a large Arab minority within Israel's borders. Sephardim see no injustice in having Arabs as a permanent underclass, having themselves lived as an underclass in the Arab world for centuries. And so, responding to the pledge that the territories would not leave Israeli hands, they became Revisionists.

After the Six-Day War, Menachem Begin began to taste the fruit of his long cultivation of Sephardi soil. With his ceremonial manners and formal dress, Begin was a quintessential European, with no interest in Oriental culture. He seemed an unlikely candidate for the Sephardim's allegiance. But he was a man of simple personal style who articulated powerful political certitudes and professed traditional religious values. He also proclaimed a vigorous right-wing populism, strongly hostile to Arabs, which appealed to Sephardim.

Young Sephardim were particularly excited by Begin. They liked his theatrics on the public platform, his contempt for socialism, the harsh language he applied to the kibbutzim and to the Ashkenazi ruling elite. They were thrilled by his truculence, by his "muscular" Zionism. They loved to cheer when he spoke, and to chant aggressively and repetitiously, "Begin, Begin, King of Israel." Sometimes bands of young Sephardim broke up Labor Party campaign meetings. Led by their younger generation, the Sephardim marched into Begin's Revisionist camp.

From a different direction, Orthodox Jews also entered the camp, having been transformed even more than the Sephardim by the Six-Day War. For religious Jews, Israel's victory reversed a century of hostility to the ideology of Zionism. In a single leap, Judaic theology covered the distance from rejection of a Jewish statehood to embrace of a rabid Israeli nationalism. After the war, only a small, ultra-Orthodox segment continued to hold out against allegiance to the state. The majority of Orthodox Jewry translated God's word into Begin's politics. These Jews provided theological authority to the history-based claims of the Revisionists upon the occupied territories.

Not only Orthodox Jews, of course, entertained the notion that the triumph of the Six-Day War was a miracle, wrought by God. Almost all Jews did. How else explain that in a week, Israel was transported from the brink of destruction to the kingdom of heaven, with all of Jerusalem, including the holy Wailing Wall, in Jewish hands? The Wailing Wall was the place where Jews had traditionally stood to mourn the loss of their Temple. (Jews today, with less to lament, conventionally call it the Western Wall.) On its capture, Yitzhak Rabin, a secular man, recalled that, to him, "It seemed as though all the tears of centuries were striving to break out . . . , while all the hopes of generations proclaimed: 'This is no time for weeping! It is a moment of redemption.' " What Jew, in Israel or the Diaspora, did not rejoice? Religious skeptics, no less than religious believers, concluded that God had spoken.

But the rededication to Judaism excited by the war was soon to give Israeli society a shriller, more self-righteous tone. Israel's dominant Ashkenazi ethic was not antireligious but it had kept religion at arm's length, treating religious practice as the relic of a bygone age of Jewish subservience. Though Palestine had always contained pockets of devout Jews, few of the Zionist pioneers attended the synagogue, and even fewer of the young men and women who fought for a Jewish state in the era of independence saw their cause as religious. The first Israelis were patriots, not pietists, and though the founding fathers recognized religion in organizing the state, they allowed it to play only a minor role.

Then, after the Six-Day War, to wear a *kipa,* the knitted cap signifying religious belief, became common, even fashionable, among Israeli men. Pressures intensified for religious conformity, and for imposition of *halacha,* Jewish religious law, over widening areas of life. Uncommitted to the principle of church-state separation, Orthodox factions in the Knesset, taking advantage of unprecedented popular endorsement, applied new powers of coercion to a range of nonreligious issues. One of them was the occupied territories. With little dissent inside its ranks, religious orthodoxy proclaimed the victory in the Six-Day War to be God's command to the Jews to rule over all Palestine.

To be sure, the germ of patriotic theology first appeared long before, after the turn of the century, when a few prominent Hebrew scholars challenged the Orthodox view that Zionism was a barrier to Messianic redemption. Most notable among them was Abraham Isaac Kook, who became the first chief rabbi of Palestine's Ashkenazi community. In the yeshiva that he established in Jerusalem, he taught that every Jew who returned to the Land of Israel would help prepare the stage for the Messiah's coming. Though he did not advocate creation of a Jewish state, he argued the radical notion that every Jew had a duty to return. In effect, he endorsed Zionism as a service to messianic redemption.

Kook's son, Rabbi Zvi Yehuda Kook, succeeded as head of the yeshiva in 1935, and shaped it into a more bluntly nationalistic instrument. Well before Israel attained its independence, the younger Kook was claiming that the founding of a Jewish state would fulfill a holy commandment. Revisionist in his politics even then, he asserted that the occupation by Jews of all Palestine would hasten the Messiah's return. After independence, while other rabbis were disparaging the state, Kook urged Jews to take on the mission of enlarging the territory.

In the thrill of the victory in the Six-Day War, Kook declared from the pulpit, "We have to see the greatness of this hour in its Biblical dimension, and it can be seen only through the Messianic perspective . . . only in the light of the Messiah." Within his yeshiva, he formulated the doctrine that the war was God's signal to rebuild the Temple—destroyed by the Babylonians in 586 B.C. and by the Romans in A.D. 70—on the Temple Mount, where the Dome of the Rock and the Al Aqsa mosque, holy Islamic shrines, have stood for more than a millennium. Kook, furthermore, was not satisfied to *urge* the government to retain the occupied territories. He argued that Judaism left the state of Israel *without the right* to hand them back.

Kook's ideas became a new rallying cry in Israel's internal debate. It added a major variation to the two Zionist ideologies, Mainstream and Revisionist, which for some forty years had been in conflict. On the subjects both of the territories and of the Arabs within them, Kook's doctrine turned out to be the most radical that lived of the three.

In terms of the choices presented to Israelis in the years that followed the Six-Day War, the doctrines looked like this:

• Mainstream Zionists, for whom prolonging the occupation was a practical issue, argued that their concerns about security did not change their commitment to putting distance between Jews and Arabs. In principle, the Mainstream remained pledged to partition in order to preserve Israel's Jewish character.

• For the Revisionists, the occupation, fulfilling a historical mission, permitted the Jews to live on their own land as a nation. But while insisting that Israel retain the land, they pledged fair treatment for the Arabs living on it. The problem was an inability to fashion clear proposals that reconciled the fair treatment of the Arabs with the Jewish nature of the state.

• Religious Zionists readily solved the dilemma of the Arab minority. They reasoned, since God commanded the Jewish presence in the land, that God would endorse whatever act contributed to its fulfillment. From this dogma, they have drawn the conclusion that the Arabs had no rights at all. Radical religious groups have drawn justification from it for intimidation, violence, even fraud committed against Arabs. Rabbi Meir Kahane has taken this doctrine to its logical end by asserting a right to expel all Arabs forcibly from the Jewish state.

Claiming religious sanction, Jewish settlers in the occupied territories have in the last decade committed repeated acts of terror. They have assassinated and maimed Arab officials, bombed Arab buses and machine-gunned Arab schoolrooms. Kahane has urged an end to Israeli democracy, if necessary, to force the Arabs to leave the country. After a violent election campaign in 1984, Kahane won a Knesset seat, and his standing in public opinion polls has risen dramatically since then. Behind the violence lie the ideas of Rabbi Kook, who has assured Israelis of God's blessing not just upon a land that is *Arabenrein* but upon a Jewish *jihad*, as well.

Rabbi Moshe Levinger was the man most responsible for transforming the theology of Rabbi Kook into right-wing political activism. In the spring of 1968, a year after the Six-Day War, Levinger registered a group of ten families in a small Arab hotel in Hebron for the ostensible purpose of celebrating the Passover holiday there. Hebron is a West Bank city with shrines holy to both Jews and Moslems. Orthodox Jews consider it one of Judaism's sacred towns. It had contained a Jewish community throughout most of history, but in 1929 sixty Jews were killed in sectarian violence there and the remainder fled. Spending the holiday in Hebron was lawful, but in 1968 Israel did not yet permit Jews to move at will into the West Bank. Levinger's strategy was to defy Israeli law, and when Passover was over he proclaimed his group's refusal to leave.

The cabinet was not prepared for Levinger's stand. It was stunned, furthermore, when Israelis from every sector of the society, aroused by deep-seated religious memories, rose in his support. Levinger did not pretend that his visit to Hebron was symbolic. He declared he would settle permanently in Hebron, because God had decreed Jewish sovereignty over the West Bank, as part of the Land of Israel.

Uncertain what course to take, the cabinet equivocated. Israel had already annexed Arab Jerusalem and had announced plans to resettle the Etzion Bloc, a series of Jewish farm communities not far from Hebron, where defenders had taken heavy casualties in a battle against Jordanian forces in 1948. The cabinet had also begun carrying out the Allon Plan, a program for establishing a belt of settlements in the Jordan River valley to serve as a trip wire against invaders. True to the Mainstream beliefs of most Israelis, the state claimed its interest in West Bank settlements was security, not theology. Still, it was clear that Israel was on the move. Having resurrected the old Zionist strategy of "creating facts," the government faced Levinger, unsure itself where to stop.

Begin, the Revisionist, was Levinger's most outspoken supporter in the cabinet coalition. But Labor sensed a shift in the country's mood, and momentum was also flowing in Levinger's direction within the Mainstream. After a few weeks of debate, Eshkol's cabinet gave in, allowing Levinger not only to remain in Hebron but to found a religious school there. Later that year, after a bomb wounded worshipers at the tomb of the Jewish patriarchs in Hebron, the cabinet voted to build a Jewish town, called Kiryat Arba, on the heights above the city.

"We had to stay there," Rabbi Levinger said to me in an interview in Hebron many years later. Levinger is a spindly and ill-kempt figure, with bad teeth, thin and disordered hair and a scraggly beard, but his eyes give off a fiery charisma. We talked in his home in the ruins of an old synagogue in the Arab marketplace. His wife sat nearby and his children played around us. "We have to live everyplace in Eretz Yisrael, in our country. There is no difference between Tel Aviv and Hebron. We did not have permission to stay, but why did we need permission? In the Torah it is written that Eretz Yisrael belongs only to the Jews. Why do the Jews need permission to live in their own country? This was the beginning."

Whatever his eccentricities, Levinger proved to be a shrewd political tactician, capable of making a strong appeal to a receptive public. Many Israelis, sensing a decline in national purpose since the fight for independence, perceived Levinger and his followers as a vanguard of present-day Zionism, heirs of the pioneer tradition. In an age of growing materialism, were not Levinger's settlers, even in flouting the law, the agents of Zionist idealism? Levinger sparked latent feelings of dedication among Israelis. Even among those who were concerned about where his audacity was taking the country, there were few who did not feel at least a grudging admiration.

After the triumphant sit-down in Hebron, Levinger founded Gush Emunim (Bloc of the Faithful), a settlement movement which became increasingly demanding and increasingly powerful. As its leader, he astutely exploited the divisions that the territories had produced among both politicians and the public. His natural allies were Begin and the Revisionists. But even the Mainstream Zionists of the Labor Party—concerned with security, frustrated by the intransigence of the Arabs, tantalized by hegemony and imbued with a strategy of "creating facts" on the land—succeeded in putting up only sporadic resistance to the movement's designs.

"Levinger is a revolutionary," said Geula Cohen. Levinger's style of leadership was that of an austere Ashkenazi rabbi, a dry Talmudic intellectual. It was quite unlike the boisterous passion of Cohen, which was more characteristic of the Sephardim. Nonetheless, Cohen spoke of Levinger with awe. "At Hebron, he said, 'After me,' and they followed him. He is the most brilliant politician of this age. Sometimes he's moderate, sometimes he's very radical. He understands exactly what to do. You can't belittle him. He outmaneuvered Eshkol and Golda and Rabin and Begin too.

"Levinger symbolizes the return of Zionism to its natural course. Until 1967 it was frozen. It wasn't the settlements that were important. It was Zionism itself that was frozen. He will get his way with any Israeli government because he is right; in my eyes his is the right way. He is standing like a candle in Judea and Samaria. He is the leader of the Zionist revolution."

I asked Geula Cohen why she considered Israel's expansion into the West Bank the natural course of Zionism. She answered:

"It's not expansion, it's liberation. I know you can't agree, but to me liberating Hebron means much more than liberating Tel

Aviv or Jaffa. Okay, I understand that the Jews may have to compromise because they don't have the choice. I can understand
when they say, 'You left Judea and Samaria for many years and you
come back and another people is there.' But don't ask me why I
think they are ours. It's just that I believe they are. From a personal point of view, a Jew can be wherever he wants. But as a
nation, we have got to be here, with our roots.

"So if the Arabs want Hebron, let them fight. And if I have to
fight for it, I'll fight. It's not only that I don't have any choice. It
is also my justice, and I want to realize it. You know the statement
'Make love, not war.' It's a stupid statement, because if you love
something you fight for it. All of our lives we are fighting, because
we love this land very much."

As the presidential election of 1972 approached in the United
States, Richard Nixon, sensitive to his Jewish constituency, took
the ultimate step of ordering the State Department to abandon its
peace initiatives in the Middle East. The decision wiped out Rogers's last shred of influence, and without him there was no force
in the government prepared to seek a narrowing of Arab-Israeli
differences. Rabin, suspicious at best of George McGovern, the
Democratic candidate, willingly reciprocated Nixon's gesture. Reflecting the Israeli cabinet's satisfaction with White House policy,
Rabin tiptoed to the very edge of diplomatic indiscretion by making known to the American-Jewish community his endorsement of
Nixon's reelection. In the months before the balloting, whatever
prospects may have existed for a peace settlement were crushed
by campaign priorities.

Sadat did not miss the message. He had gambled on persuading
Washington to redress the imbalance of power in the Middle East,
which he believed stood as the chief obstacle to negotiations. He
knew by now he had lost. Far from rewarding Sadat for handing
the United States a strategic victory, Kissinger chose to profit from
the greater freedom of maneuver provided by Russia's departure
from the Middle East. The conclusion Kissinger drew from Sadat's

move was that Washington could indulge Israel with impunity. By the fall of 1972, it was apparent to Sadat that the United States, while pouring arms into Israel, had turned away from diplomacy. He reasoned he would have to go back to playing the superpower game to force America's hand.

"I think after Sadat kicked the Russians out," Rogers said, "we probably missed an opportunity. What he did was a courageous act, and if the President had taken a more active role in trying to bring about a peaceful solution, it might have accomplished something. But Nixon was so preoccupied with the Vietnam War that nothing else could get his attention. He did not want to upset the status quo in the Middle East while the Vietnam talks were still pending. Besides, there was an election on the horizon, with a feeling of 'Let's not tip over the applecart.' And after the election, of course, came Watergate."

Abba Eban, Mrs. Meir's foreign minister, also speaks of missed opportunities after the War of Attrition. In his talk with me, he called Jarring, the U.N. mediator, "almost chronically limited intellectually" and Rogers, the secretary of state, "clumsy and always hurried." "In diplomatic history," he complained, "these are the weakest characters I have ever met." While conceding that the overtures from Egypt were promising, he also blamed Sadat for not addressing, at least until much later, "the problem Israelis have with Arab credibility."

But, Eban added, "the great obstacle was Golda, who wanted the cohesion of the government much more than she wanted any international gain. She was very suspicious, very defiant, and she simply didn't believe there was a prospect of peace."

Sadat understood that Israel, believing it faced no threat from the Arab world, had every incentive to preserve the status quo. He was also a careful enough observer of Israeli politics to know that the growing force of Revisionism was pressing the prospects of a settlement ever further into the distance. When I made my first trip to Egypt a year later, I was astonished at how much Egyptian officials, even at middle levels of the bureaucracy, knew about what was happening in Israel, much more than Israelis knew about Egypt. One part of the explanation was that information about Israel, thanks to a free press, was widely available. Another part was that Israelis felt rather little need to know what was happening in Egypt. But whatever the explanation, Sadat was aware that Israel was not preparing for peace, while Israel had no idea that Sadat was preparing for war.

Scarcely noticed by Israelis, in the year after Sadat's massive expulsion Soviet forces actually returned to Egypt. They returned smaller in number and without the fanfare that accompanied their departure, but they were back. Sadat insisted that if the Russians wanted to regain a position in Egypt, it would be to serve, not to dominate, Egyptian policy. Moscow apparently accepted the condition. The Russians brought with them an abundance of new weapons, which they taught the Egyptians how to use, while this time leaving the planning and command functions for Egypt's forces in Egyptian hands. Not even the Russians were clear then about Sadat's intentions. Israelis and Americans knew even less. Their intelligence services were picking up signals of intensifying military activity, but neither one considered Sadat's intentions to be menacing.

The leadership in both the United States and Israel misjudged Sadat, failing to take seriously his determination to put an end to the situation of "no war, no peace." Certain of Israel's impregnability, the two governments basked in a sense of euphoria. Some years later, Israel was to begin the peace process with Egypt, and Kissinger was to realize his dream of being remembered as a peacemaker. But it was only after Sadat had left them no choice, by launching an attack that again brought the superpowers to the edge of conflict, and that inflicted huge losses of life on both Egypt and Israel. Only war broke the diplomatic logjam, with which Kissinger and the Israeli cabinet had so often pronounced themselves satisfied.

Israelis, almost unanimous in dismissing Sadat's conciliatory overtures, had paid even less attention to the bellicose statements with which, after 1971, he interspersed them. Whatever their worries, Israelis were comforted by strategists who assured them that Egypt, having learned its lesson in the Six-Day War, would not dare an attack. I remember during visits to Israel in the "Golden Age" that, over dinner in homes or in restaurants, Israelis routinely talked not about national security, much less about peace prospects, but about the economic boom, new cars, vacations abroad, bigger salaries. They liked being prosperous, and few of them—whether cabinet ministers or generals, scholars, journalists or diplomats—entertained the notion that their Arab neighbors had the stomach to fight. Equating distant borders with security, Israelis were sure their defense was taken care of at the Bar-Lev line. No one expected war.

During a trip to Israel a few months before the Yom Kippur crossing, I was invited by the Israeli army on an inspection tour of the Bar-Lev line. Accompanied by a uniformed escort, I was ferried from Jerusalem over the Sinai dunes at low altitude in a single-engine prop plane. After landing at a desert airstrip, my military escorts took me to see the ruins of Qantara, an Egyptian city midway between the Red Sea and the Mediterranean. Then I was driven by jeep to an underground fortress on the bank of the Suez Canal.

I had no idea, of course, what the Egyptians were planning, and in making my observations, I claim no staff officer's eye. But what I saw left me with an uneasy feeling that the situation was not quite as well in hand as Israel's official statements claimed. This is what I wrote in the *Star:*

QANTARA, Israeli Occupied Egypt—From our perch above the sandbags at the edge of the Suez Canal, we watched the Egyptian soldier in a gray fatigue uniform climb a tree to snatch an apple.

Nearby, another soldier pitched stones into the water but, at a distance of 175 yards, we could not hear the splash. The only sound that reached our ears, apart from the quietly lapping water, was the chirping of birds.

Subconsciously the members of our party—a handful of soldiers, a military escort officer and two journalists—waited tensely as the tree-borne Egyptian extended himself further into the branches. At that moment, his fate seemed very important to us. When he finally descended, apple in hand, we collectively breathed a sigh of relief.

Thus, two hostile armies confront each other across an aquatic no-man's land—and soldiers, who would surely prefer to be elsewhere, pass the time of day.

In an observation post, sandbagged on three sides and roofed as a shield from the intense sun, an Israeli corporal sits with field glasses, paper and pencil and a chart covered with diagrams of Egyptian military equipment. His assignment is to record every movement on the opposite side.

But, save for the occasional frolicking, off-duty soldier, he has little to report. The only consistent military activity he detects is the relief of the Egyptian who also sits in an observation post, undoubtedly performing exactly the same duty as he.

To the nonmilitary observer, the only substantial difference between the two banks is the heavy barbed wire the Israelis have strung along their side. The Egyptians, instead, have cut into the bank every few hundred yards.

Presumably, these contrasting configurations reflect the different strategies of the contending armies. The Egyptians are on the offensive, and the ramps are designed to enable amphibious tanks to scramble into the water and quickly establish a bridgehead on the other side. The Israelis are on the defensive, and the barbed wire is meant to deter such an attack.

For the tough little Israeli army, defense is an unaccustomed posture. In the past, its doctrine has been based on the attack, and its columns have ranged far and wide over the desert.

But now it is dug in. Its men move through trenches which wind below the levees. Its supplies are buried beneath tons of stone and sand.

To be sure, Israeli military strategists believe they could make it handily to Cairo—barely an hour's drive from the canal—by choosing either to go through the heavy defenses in front of the city or to outflank them.

Those strategists are convinced that the basic fighting quality of the Egyptian army has not improved, despite intensive Soviet training and the most up-to-date Soviet weapons. . . .

So the two armies sit in quiet confrontation. Right now, the atmosphere is relaxed.

But in their underground quarters, the Israeli soldiers lie with grenades and bandoliers next to their bunks, and they ask each other whether the canal will still be silent on the morrow.

On the morning of Yom Kippur 1973, the holiest day of the Jewish year, Sadat sent Egyptian tanks rolling down the ramps on the western edge of the Suez Canal. It had occurred to few Israelis that granting the soldiers leave to go home for the holiday would present a risk. The fortifications of the Bar-Lev line were largely empty. Against only token opposition, with guns roaring, the Egyptians crossed the water and crashed through the barbed wire on the other shore. Meanwhile, the Syrians surprised the Israeli army defending in the north by attacking in force across the Golan Heights.

The Arabs had planned their assault with an attention to detail that far exceeded the capacities which Israeli strategic doctrine had attributed to them. The Egyptians skillfully handled the new weapons the Russians had supplied. They got their infantry across the water quickly, in boats at first, then over complicated Russian bridging equipment, suffering only light casualties. The SAM missiles that had been installed after the cease-fire of 1970 deprived the Israeli air force of its customary superiority over the battlefield. Without air cover, the Israelis fought as equals, and the Egyptians matched up well. While the Egyptians were destroying the Bar-Lev line, the Syrians in the north attacked with masses of tanks. On both fronts the Israeli army retreated, suffering heavy losses.

Nixon, his powers by now seriously impaired by the Watergate scandal, had abdicated control over foreign policy to Kissinger, who in the first days responded hesitantly to the Arab assault. Only a few weeks before, Nixon had named Kissinger to replace Rogers as secretary of state, while keeping him in the post of national security adviser. No one else ever held both offices, which more than confirmed Kissinger's preeminence in shaping foreign policy. Kissinger, however, had not anticipated the war. According to the evidence, neither superpower wanted it, and both were without a plan. But rather than try to stop the fighting, and reduce the prospect of war between them, both Kissinger and the Russians decided to take their chances, gambling that an opportunity would come along from which to extract some strategic advantage.

During the first week of battle, the United States watched Israel take a battering, and only barely kept even with the Russians, who were resupplying the Arabs with ammunition and light equipment. Kissinger conducted desultory talks with Moscow on a cease-fire but neither the Soviet Union nor the Arabs, as long as their side was winning, seemed interested in a truce. In fact, neither did Kissinger. He held to the conventional view that Israel, despite its early reverses, would soon put an end to the presumptuous enemy, salvaging victory for the West. He also held back help for the Israelis, he wrote in his memoirs, "to avoid becoming the focal point of all the Arab resentments." Kissinger's account of the war conveyed his satisfaction with the prospect that a few blows to Israel would enhance American influence in the negotiating that would follow.

Kissinger's cold war juices began to flow only in the second week of battle, after the Soviet Union started to ferry in heavy arms by sea and air. Faced with a major commitment, he made up his mind to match the Russians weapon for weapon.

Though the fighting against Syria in the north had turned in Israel's favor within three days, the war was into its second week when Israel, strengthened with new American equipment, reversed the tide in the Sinai. On October 14, after the Egyptians had advanced beyond the range of the SAMs, Israel won a huge tank battle in the desert. The victory was followed by a crossing of the canal by the redoubtable General Ariel Sharon, a maneuver that threatened to encircle Egypt's Third Army, which was exposed in its bridgehead in the Sinai. During the ensuing days of fighting and dying, the momentum shifted increasingly to Israel. It was only then that the two combatants, pressed by their patrons, showed a readiness to stop.

The cease-fire in the Yom Kippur War was negotiated not by the warring parties, however, but by the superpowers. Kissinger flew to Moscow to arrange the terms. What emerged was Security Council Resolution 338, which took its place alongside Resolution 242 among the fundamental documents of the Middle East conflict. (See Appendix G.) The resolution called on the belligerents to stop firing at once, then begin "negotiations . . . aimed at establishing a just and durable peace" based on "the implementation of Security Council Resolution 242 . . . in all of its parts." A peace conference was to be convoked promptly at Geneva, "under appropriate auspices," which meant with the guidance of the superpowers.

The Arabs were by now more than willing to accept the cease-fire terms. Israel, still cool to Resolution 242 but sensitive to the wishes of the United States, swallowed Resolution 338 reluctantly. Dated October 22, it was to go into effect at once—sixteen bloody days after the first Egyptian soldiers crossed the canal.

But having grudgingly accepted the agreement, the Israelis immediately found excuses to violate it. Determined to punish Egypt for the effrontery of starting the war, they continued to move forward, tightening the ring at the rear of the Third Army, enlarging their military options to include the capture of Cairo or, at least, the surrender of Egypt's forces. Both superpowers were seriously upset at Israel's continued advance. The Russians, with their long investment in Egypt, had the most to lose. But even Kissinger now acknowledged that, given the change in conditions created by the war, the United States had a stake in Sadat. Neither was prepared for a reprise of 1967, with the Egyptians so humiliated that negotiations became impossible.

The Russians first proposed a joint Soviet-American force to stop the Israelis and separate the armies. Kissinger, perceiving a trick to get Soviet combat troops into the field, promptly vetoed the idea. The Kremlin then ordered its military machine mobilized, the opening step to unilateral intervention. Kissinger, at that point, had to choose between forcing the Israelis to retreat, which he feared the world would consider an American defeat, and matching the Russian threat, which would bring a war of the superpowers ominously close. Kissinger chose the latter.

Throwing its painstakingly negotiated "détente" with Moscow to the winds, Washington ordered a worldwide alert of American forces. It was alleged at the time that Nixon issued the order in a desperate bid to distract attention from Watergate, which was closing in around him. Kissinger has angrily denied the charge, and, in fact, the evidence to support it is slim. Kissinger had no need of Watergate to advance to the brink of war. He liked high-stakes diplomacy, and he had all the freedom he needed to move nuclear forces across the board as a challenge to the Russians. That was the way he played the cold war game.

But at the same time, Kissinger hedged, by leaning hard on the Israelis, who had by now completed the Third Army's encirclement. Over strenuous objections, he convinced them to allow a convoy to pass through their lines, carrying provisions to the beleaguered Egyptian soldiers. Two more weeks of hard bargaining followed, much of it conducted by Kissinger himself in Jerusalem and Cairo, to establish the principle of ongoing reprovisioning. Finally, an agreement was signed, leaving it to the Israeli and Egyptian military commands to work out procedures for ongoing reprovisioning themselves. As the superpower confrontation blew over, Israeli and Egyptian officers organized a meeting at Kilometer 101 on the Cairo-Suez road. It was to be the first face-to-face encounter between representatives of the two warring countries since Rhodes in 1949.

Having escaped a clash with the Soviet Union, Kissinger turned to another major concern, the international oil crisis that the Yom Kippur War had produced. Months before, Sadat had elicited promises from the Arab oil producers that in case of war, they would bring their "oil weapon" into the conflict. When Washington began the airlift to Israel in the second week of the war, they kept their word.

The Arabs imposed a total embargo on shipments of oil to the United States, while simultaneously imposing severe restrictions on deliveries to Western Europe and Japan. Though relatively independent of Arab sources, the United States responded by setting limitations on domestic oil distribution, inflicting some hardship on consumers. Its reaction was restrained, however, compared to that of the Europeans, whose dependence on Arab supplies brought them close to panic. They introduced tight rationing, which placed their economies under severe stress. They also reacted by refusing the Americans any further use of their refueling facilities for the airlift of military provisions. It took considerable ingenuity and determination for Washington to keep supplies going to Israeli forces still fighting in the Middle East.

Nor did the Arabs put the "oil weapon" away when the fighting stopped. For some years, the West's oil consumption had been rising precipitously, while oil production, particularly in the United States, dropped. The industrial countries and their agents, the international oil companies, thus ceded advantage in the marketplace to the oil producers, the most powerful of which were in the Persian Gulf. By 1973, a producers' cartel called the Organization of Petroleum Exporting Countries, dominated by Saudi Arabia, had acquired almost total control over worldwide pricing. OPEC gave the Arabs, in their role as principal producers, great leverage for influencing the course of the struggle with Israel. Not all of OPEC's members shared Arab political designs, of course, but none objected to the Arabs' exploitation of the Yom Kippur War to send international oil prices skyward.

After the fighting was over, Kissinger found himself bargaining not only with Israel and Egypt about territory and peace but with the Saudis about the price and supply of oil. In December 1973, with the embargo still in effect, OPEC announced a rise in oil prices to nearly twelve dollars a barrel, a figure that has since come to appear modest but that quadrupled the prewar price. To the Western industrial nations, the Arabs seemed to have acquired a stranglehold on the world's economy.

Indeed, as long as the Arabs were willing to endure limitations on their own income, they had the power to manipulate production to determine both price and supply. In an oil-dependent world, they seemed suddenly to have acquired the power of life-and-death control over the future of the West.

In retrospect, it is apparent the embargo of 1973 was the peak of the oil producers' intimidating power. On the one hand, their governments proved unwilling to forgo income. On the other, huge investments by the industrial nations produced a worldwide surge in energy supplies, which were supplemented by conservation measures and heavy stockpiling of supplies. The result was that by the end of the 1970s, the influence of the oil-producing countries was substantially weakened, both economically and politically. In the days after the Yom Kippur War, however, this decline was not yet apparent, and getting the oil to flow again was a top priority for American diplomacy. It seemed then that a major new factor had entered the Middle East conflict, which could conceivably deliver Israel a crippling blow.

Still, at the top of the American diplomatic agenda was the mission of turning the tenuous cease-fire in the Middle East into a more stable arrangement. The armies of Israel, Syria and Egypt remained entangled across the battlefields, their units standing as they were when the cease-fire went into effect. Though Israeli forces were poised within striking distance of Damascus and Cairo, the Egyptian and Syrian armies were still intact and in battle formation. They had been defeated but not routed, and they seemed willing to do battle again. If nothing else, the Yom Kippur War had proved to them that Israel was not invincible. Unless steps were taken to disengage the antagonists, the fighting might easily resume.

The victory Israel won in the Yom Kippur War was of far less magnitude than its triumphs in earlier wars. In the opening days, the Arab offensive had rolled forward, and Israel was unsure that the state would survive. Defense Minister Dayan, the cool commander of earlier victories, urged the cabinet to accept the possibility of catastrophe. It was the first time that Arab armies in battle had succeeded in administering a real scare to Israelis. Even after the tide had turned, the Arabs fought harder and more courageously than in any previous war. The fighting lasted three times as long as the Six-Day War, and 2,500 Israelis died, nearly three times more.

When the cease-fire took effect, furthermore, Egypt as well as Israel was in possession of territory its forces had captured in battle. What Egypt held was not Israeli but Egyptian land, and only a small fraction of what Nasser had lost in 1967. But it represented a major beachhead in the Sinai, a situation that was precisely what the strategy of the Bar-Lev line had been designed to prevent. Israel could have driven the Egyptians out of the Sinai salient only with heavy losses of its own. With the land it seized, Egypt had earned the right to bargain. Egypt had won a major strategic victory, even though in the end it was Israel that got the better of the war on the battlefield.

"The Yom Kippur War," said Yitzhak Rabin, "was not fought by Egypt and Syria to threaten the existence of Israel. It was an all-out use of their military force to achieve a limited political goal. What Sadat wanted by crossing the canal was to change the political reality and, thereby, to start a political process from a point more favorable to him than the one that existed.

"In this respect, he succeeded."

According to Kissinger's memoirs, even Golda Meir, when she was not vowing revenge, paid grudging tribute to Sadat. "He is the hero," she said. "He dared."

Thanks to the Yom Kippur War, Kissinger was finally forced to place the Arab-Israeli conflict on America's diplomatic calendar. Throughout Nixon's first term, he not only had desisted from involving himself in the complexities of the region but had connived to keep the United States from being involved at all. While Rogers was secretary of state, Kissinger had deliberately undermined every effort at making peace, hardening the Arab-Israeli deadlock.

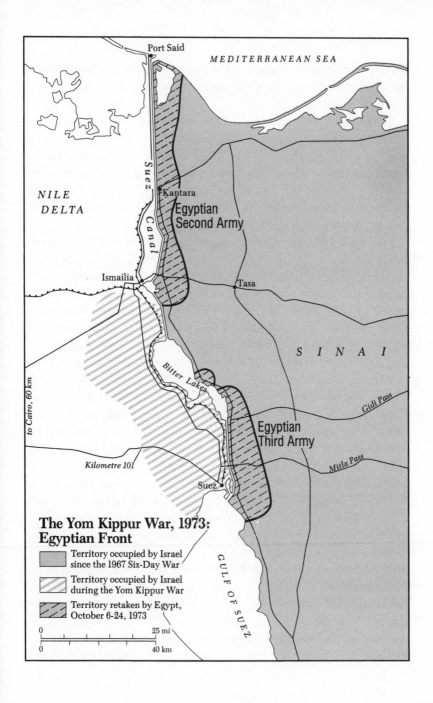

Port Said

MEDITERRANEAN SEA

Suez Canal

NILE
DELTA

Kantara

Egyptian
Second Army

Ismailia

Tasa

to Cairo, 60 km

SINAI

Bitter Lakes

Gidi Pass

Egyptian
Third Army

Kilometre 101

Mitla Pass

Suez

GULF OF SUEZ

The Yom Kippur War, 1973:
Egyptian Front

Territory occupied by Israel
since the 1967 Six-Day War

Territory occupied by Israel
during the Yom Kippur War

Territory retaken by Egypt,
October 6-24, 1973

0   25 mi

0   40 km

Nearly two years and thousands of casualties later, he had a chance
to make up for the opportunity he had lost after Sadat expelled the
Russians in 1972.

In the interval, it is true, the circumstances had improved. In
disrupting the status quo, Sadat had replaced a deadlock with a
fluid situation, ready-made for the exercise of creative diplomacy.
Israel had been traumatized, and was no longer locked into the
rigid positions it had taken before the war. Kissinger saw the
moment as a challenge to his diplomatic virtuosity. Equally com-
pelling, he was now personally in charge.

Few Presidents have had as much control over foreign policy as
Kissinger, a presidential retainer, exercised in the Watergate years
and immediately afterward. At Nixon's side, he had made a reputation, perhaps exaggerated, as a diplomatic wizard. He had negotiated an end to the Vietnam War, though on terms no more
favorable than were available four years earlier. He had reached
an understanding with the Russians, euphemistically called "détente," though without notably reducing the chances of war between East and West. He had negotiated an American opening to
China, though another decade of turbulence would pass before
the relationship would acquire real meaning. Whatever the level
of his achievements, Kissinger, serving as both secretary of state
and national security adviser, was at the pinnacle of his prestige.
And with Nixon fighting for survival, his hands were free.

It is interesting that, in his memoirs, Kissinger endorses advice
that Eisenhower, shortly before he died in 1969, offered to Nixon,
then embarking on the presidency. Though internationalist in
outlook, Eisenhower took pains not to involve his administration
in the various wars that seemed to be taking place at any given
moment around the world. He understood and regretted that his
own guarantee to Israel after the 1956 war had led, by 1967, to
American embroilment in the Middle East struggle. From it, the
United States has yet to extricate itself.

Kissinger recalled that Eisenhower, on the subject of peacemaking between Arabs and Israelis, stated, "if we became active, we

would be forced in the end to become an arbiter and then offer the parties our own guarantee of whatever final arrangements emerged. This would keep us involved in Middle East difficulties forever." In his memoirs, Kissinger cited the statement as support for his opposition to Rogers's Middle East initiatives. He did not cite it again in reviewing events four years later, when he was in a position to bring his own worldview to Middle East peacemaking.

Kissinger was aroused by the peacemaking challenge that Sadat had placed before him, but not because his mind turned to such mundane considerations as saving lives or promoting prosperity or opening borders, the natural consequences of an Arab-Israeli settlement. Global strategist that he was, Kissinger had grander ideas than that. It is true his immediate objectives were fixed by events —to stabilize the cease-fire on the battlefields and negotiate a prompt end to the oil embargo. But Kissinger's long-term aspiration, his transcendent vision, was to achieve in the Middle East a permanent strategic advantage over the Soviet Union, as a step to an American triumph in the cold war.

By the time Kissinger finished his peacemaking efforts in 1975, he had produced some Arab-Israeli rapprochement. Though modest in terms of an overall settlement, it was more than any negotiator had achieved before him. His work was also crucial in ending the oil embargo. But whether he had strengthened the strategic position of the United States—or advanced the cause of lasting peace between combatants in the Middle East—is another matter entirely. What he had surely done was to get the United States involved "in Middle East difficulties forever," which was precisely the trap he had praised Eisenhower for warning against.

7

Kissinger's Covenant

THE CEASE-FIRE AGREEMENT voted at the United Nations on October 22, 1973, to end the Yom Kippur War called for the belligerent parties to meet *immediately* to establish a "just and durable peace." It took three more days before the shooting actually stopped around the Suez Canal, after which quiet generally settled over the battlefields, but two months later soldiers of the contending armies still glowered at one another across fragile truce lines. The governments of the belligerents seemed uncertain how to move toward peace. Meanwhile, the proximity of heavily armed units, not just on the Suez front but on the Golan, seemed to invite a spark that would reignite the fighting.

Under the terms of the cease-fire, delegates of the Israeli and Egyptian military commands began meeting at Kilometer 101 on October 28, and they accomplished their mission expeditiously. Procedures were established for resupplying Egypt's encircled Third Army, thus defusing the most immediate danger. On November 15, the two sides marked another achievement with the first exchange of Egyptian and Israeli prisoners. The military delegations, in fact, got on so well in their talks that the two governments assigned them to negotiate the separation of the armies, the next step in liquidating the war's debris.

But disengagement, which on its most obvious level was a military problem, was in substance a political affair. Sadat had started the war to obtain territory with which to start bargaining for some sort of political settlement. What the armies held would be the point of departure for the negotiations. Their positions would influence the territorial provisions if the negotiations succeeded, and determine where the lines would remain if the negotiations failed. So disengagement, the opening step in political talks, had to be settled by the governments themselves.

At that point, Henry Kissinger stepped in. Kissinger had pledged to the Soviet Union during the cease-fire discussions in Moscow that as the first order of business the two superpowers would organize a peace conference in Geneva. To be sure, Kissinger disliked the prospect of the Russians joining the game on what he now considered his own playing field. But he had committed himself too deeply to them to go back on the promise. At the same time, however, he was determined to find a way to deprive them of real influence in the negotiating process.

Kissinger's notion was to convoke the conference ceremoniously at Geneva, with Israel facing the Arab negotiators across a table. He planned, once the speechmaking was over, to organize bilateral meetings between the belligerents, retaining the formality of superpower sponsorship while bypassing the Russians in the substantive talks. The principle of exchanging territory for peace, enshrined in Resolution 242, was to be the common commitment of all the participants. But the honest broker in working out its implementation would be the United States alone.

Egypt and Israel concurred in having Kissinger as intermediary. So, in fact, did Syria. The two Arab states welcomed Kissinger's involvement, reasoning that only he, representing the United States, had the power to exact concessions from Israel. They recognized at the same time that at the negotiating stage, Moscow had no real contribution to make to their cause.

Though the power behind the Arabs in the recent war, the Soviet Union had by its own doing cut itself off from a major role in the settlement talks. It had no diplomatic relations with Israel. It had shown neither skill nor interest in exploiting whatever potential leverage it had in Jerusalem, through control of the emigration of Soviet Jews, for example. The Soviet posture toward Israel was one of shrill, implacable, unproductive criticism. Though Israel's first choice was no negotiations at all, its fallback corresponded with the Arab position. Both preferred talks from which Moscow was excluded.

In his memoirs, Kissinger recalls Golda Meir's bitter observation that going to Geneva was the beginning of Israel's retreat. She had agreed to participate in the conference only because the bulk of Israel's forces were exposed and vulnerable west of the Suez Canal. Much as she disliked the idea, negotiation was the only way to get them out.

Mrs. Meir's reaction was characteristic of her. By reflex rather than deliberation, she had turned her back on Mainstream Zionism's own strategy, which held that Israel regarded occupied Arab territory, and particularly the Sinai, as simply an asset to be used in the bargaining for peace. Few Israelis ever really believed their armies were on the canal to stay. Almost all regarded the position as a bargaining ploy. But since the Six-Day War, Mrs. Meir had become so used to the occupation that she had lost all sense of its purpose. She could not see Geneva as an opportunity to enhance Israeli security by an arrangement that traded the territory to avoid further wars.

Israel's offer in the preliminary disengagement talks at Kilometer 101 had been to redeploy the respective armies to their pre-October stations on the Suez Canal. In the context of the positions of the armies on the battlefield, the offer was fair enough, but it would merely have restored the stalemate that existed before the fighting started. Sadat, who saw disengagement as the opening move in getting Israel out of the Sinai altogether, would not have that. In agreeing to make the journey to Geneva, Israel had acknowledged that some amount of territorial withdrawal was inevitable. But Mrs. Meir, skeptical of Sadat's proffers of peace for territory, planned to place obstacles at every step to his realizing his vision.

Kissinger had a vision of his own for the Geneva Conference, which was to create a system in which the United States would transcend the Soviet Union in influence throughout the Middle East. He had given up attaining the full peace settlement envisaged in Resolution 242 and, for tactical reasons, had come around to the course set by William Rogers, his erstwhile rival. Rogers had the year before advocated a series of partial Israeli withdrawals on the way to full peace. Without abandoning the goals of Resolution 242, Kissinger accepted the premise that Israel's departure from the occupied territories would be more easily accomplished in small bites. Though Israel had consented to the principle, however, its clear intention was to stop the process after step one. Kissinger thus needed to find a balance of pressure and blandishments, if Israel was not to thwart his grand design.

Kissinger's peace campaign opened theatrically in Geneva on December 21, 1973. That Israel, Egypt and Jordan were there was in itself a triumph. Though Syria boycotted the inaugural session, it left open the possibility of joining later. On the basis of Israel's veto, the Palestinians were absent, but in 1973, Jordan's King Hussein was still presumed to speak for them.

Before television cameras, the Israeli and Arab delegates opened the meeting with hard-line speeches, designed more for domestic than for international audiences. In private the next day, however, Kissinger accomplished what he had set out to do, when Israel and Egypt, by prearrangement, accepted the instructions of the conference to begin bilateral disengagement talks. Though these talks were not to take place at Geneva, it was agreed to keep the conference formally in session, as a gesture to the Russians and a sign of faith in the process. Then the show went on the road.

One of the paradoxes of Kissinger, as diplomatic technician, is that the traps he boasts in his memoirs of foreseeing so clearly are precisely those into which, without his acknowledging it, he later falls. This was particularly true in his dealings with the Israelis.

"Even when Israeli leaders accept a peace proposal," he wrote, "they first resist fiercely, which serves the purpose of showing that they are not pushovers and thereby discourages further demands for Israeli concessions. And their acceptance is usually accompanied by endless requests for reassurances, memoranda of under-

standing, and secret explanations—all designed to limit the freedom of action of a rather volatile ally five thousand miles away that
supplies its arms, sustains its economy, shelters its diplomacy, and
has a seemingly limitless compulsion to offer peace plans."

The quotation is worth remembering because Kissinger, in ac-
curately describing Israeli negotiating techniques, fails to note
that he, too, became their victim. Two years after the start of the
Geneva talks, when he had finished his diplomatic efforts, the
United States did indeed transcend the Soviet Union in the Middle
East. American influence was dominant not only in Israel but in
the Arab world. Yet Israel had succeeded so brilliantly in what
Kissinger called its design "to limit the freedom of action" of its
ally that the prospects for full peace were no brighter than when
he began. Israel, by then, had set the boundaries of American
policy objectives in the Middle East. The consequence—as the
coming pages will show—was that whatever Kissinger's diplomatic triumph over the Soviet Union, it contained in half-conceal-
ment the seeds of its own undoing.

At the same time that the diplomatic maneuvering over Geneva
was going on, the Israelis were conducting a belated election campaign at home. The voting had originally been scheduled for October 31, and the early campaigning had reflected Israel's content-
ment with its "Golden Age." Israelis, as a whole, felt wealthy and
impregnable. Public opinion was moving to the right and, under
Golda Meir, so was the Labor Party, adopting a platform that fell
barely short of the Revisionists' demand for territorial annexation.
With Mrs. Meir at the peak of her popularity, the Labor Party,
though fatigued and a bit tarnished after so many years in power,
was confident of being returned.

Begin, whose Herut Party had grown stronger in each succeeding election, had by now emerged as Mrs. Meir's chief rival. The
new Revisionist coalition had given him a mass base, but to get to
power, Begin saw the need to unite the diverse parties of the right
behind him. He made a pact, then, with the popular general Ariel
Sharon, who, having lost out in competition for nomination as

chief of staff, had recently resigned from active duty. A tenacious fighter, ruthless with Jews as well as Arabs, Sharon forged the right-wing parties into a new political front, called Likud, committed to Revisionist goals. The early betting held that Likud would put up a strong showing but would fall short of victory.

Sadat's Yom Kippur attack came in the midst of the campaign, forcing Mrs. Meir's cabinet to postpone the election. By the time campaigning resumed, Labor's commitment to a cease-fire based on Resolution 242, as well as to the disengagement process and to the Geneva conference, required it to defend a much more "dovish" program. The flamboyant Sharon, recalled to active duty during the campaign, returned from the war a hero of the drive across Suez. His charisma, put to the service of his "hawkish" convictions, was a major asset to Begin and to Likud.

According to opinion polls, a majority of the voters clearly favored Labor's program of exchanging territory for peace, but neither party felt confident of the popular mood. Some Israelis had vowed to punish the politicians who lulled the country into unpreparedness; others hesitated to change leadership during a period of crucial international negotiations. What alone seemed sure was that the electorate, sobered by the near disaster and aware that Israel's "golden age" was over, was far less complacent than before.

The election was held on December 31. A decisive victory for Labor would have presented Mainstream Zionism with a mandate for making peace. Instead, the election left the politicians confused. It was neither an endorsement of the Likud nor a repudiation of Labor's policies. Labor lost a few seats and Likud gained a few, confirming the trend of recent years, but the seats acquired by marginal parties of both the right and the left restored the former parliamentary balance, enabling Mrs. Meir to begin the political bargaining to re-form a government. The most that could be said of the results was that they were the authentic expression of an Israel deeply divided, loathing war but profoundly apprehensive of peace.

Ten days after the election, two weeks after the meeting at

Geneva, Kissinger flew to Egypt as the opening step in the process
that was promptly labeled "shuttle diplomacy." After a visit with
Sadat, he went off to Israel, and then flew back and forth, carrying
proposals and counterproposals, amendments and refinements,
maps newly drawn and redrawn. Though it was an airborne variation of Rogers's "proximity talks," its success must be credited
chiefly to the skill of the negotiator. Kissinger was willing to defy
the strict protocols of diplomacy. He was shrewd, patient and
charming, and however one may judge the consequences of his
work, it must be acknowledged that a man of lesser energy would
almost surely not have come away with a signed document. In
mid-January 1974, after a week on the "shuttle," Kissinger had the
long-awaited disengagement pact in hand.

The agreement met Sadat's demand in providing for much
more than the disengagement of armies. Israel consented to withdraw its forces from the western bank of the canal and to redeploy
behind a line in the Sinai some fifteen miles from the water. Egypt
agreed to establish new positions in a zone east of the canal which,
from the waterline, was only some six miles wide. A buffer running
the canal's length, patrolled by a U.N. force, was to separate the
two armies. The agreement provided for Israel's first evacuation
—and the Arabs' first reoccupation—of land seized in the Six-Day
War. It created a configuration along the canal that strongly
resembled the proposals that Sadat and Dayan, separately, had
made in 1972, well before the Yom Kippur War.

The agreement was also noteworthy for the supplementary letters written to the participants by the United States, providing for
permanent American involvement in its execution. In one of
them, Washington consented to monitor compliance through the
use of aircraft and satellites. Another conveyed to Israel an Egyptian pledge to reopen the Suez Canal and rebuild the canal cities.
In a third, Washington promised to provide financial help to both
countries. Though not a specific commitment to enforcement of
the agreement, the letters nonetheless seemed likely to make the
United States—in the terms in which Eisenhower conveyed his

apprehension to Nixon in 1968—"an arbiter involved in Middle East difficulties forever."

The Sinai disengagement agreement was signed on January 18, 1974, by the Israeli and Egyptian chiefs of staff. The ceremony took place not in Geneva but at Kilometer 101, as a way of excluding the Soviet Union. The signing meant, at least in symbolic terms, a giant step for Kissinger toward his goal of establishing Washington's preeminence throughout the Middle East.

Though I missed the ceremony at Kilometer 101, I was in Israel then, reading reports from the front describing an atmosphere so relaxed that soldiers from the two armies were casually crossing the old battle lines into each other's camps. Israelis and Egyptians alike seemed driven by an irresistible desire to make personal contact with one another, before the formations separated. At home, Israelis did not know what to make of it. These encounters provided me with one of the most moving moments I have experienced in the Middle East. This is what I wrote of it:

JERUSALEM—The most popular thing to appear on television screens in the postwar season in Israel were the shots of Egyptian and Israeli soldiers in face-to-face meeting just before the military disengagement on the Suez Canal.

I was sitting with friends in a small restaurant in a Tel-Aviv suburb when the film was shown as part of an evening news program. The noisy crowd, preoccupied with its dinner conversation, suddenly turned to a little television set in the corner of the room and watched with rapt attention.

Arabic-speaking Israeli soldiers were serving as intermediaries in the dialogue, which was translated into Hebrew in subtitles on the screen. One of my friends translated it into English for me.

The scene was of a dozen men in uniform, about equally divided between the two armies, standing around informally in the desert. The men laughed and joked, and traded cigarettes and souvenirs. I was reminded of similar scenes from our own Civil War, recounted in the colorful histories of Bruce Catton.

All this was commonplace enough, among soldiers, but then the

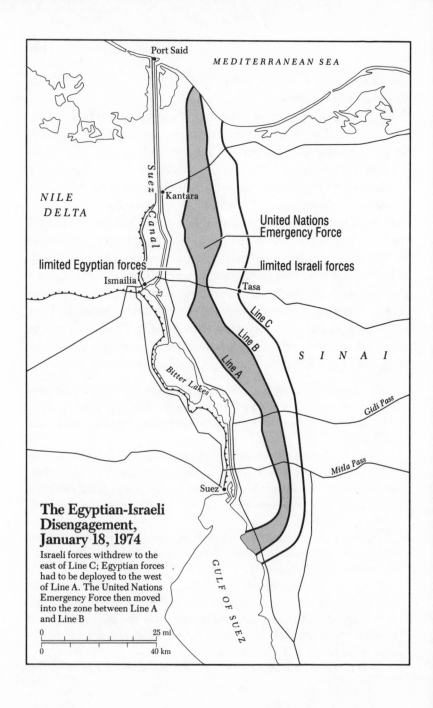

Port Said

MEDITERRANEAN SEA

*NILE
DELTA*

Kantara

United Nations
Emergency Force

limited Egyptian forces _____

limited Israeli forces

Ismailia

Tasa

Line C

Line B

S I N A I

Line A

Bitter Lakes

Gidi Pass

Mitla Pass

Suez

The Egyptian-Israeli
Disengagement,
January 18, 1974

Israeli forces withdrew to the
east of Line C; Egyptian forces
had to be deployed to the west
of Line A. The United Nations
Emergency Force then moved
into the zone between Line A
and Line B

Suez Canal

GULF OF SUEZ

| 0 | | | 25 mi |
| 0 | | | 40 km |

dialogue went a step further, when the Egyptians invited the Israelis to visit them in Cairo, and the Israelis asked the Egyptians to come see them in Tel-Aviv. The footage ended with the men exchanging addresses, shaking hands and clapping one another on the back.

The entire sequence took no more than a few minutes (and, for all we know, may have been staged). But the Israelis in the restaurant were stunned by it, and one of the women at my table wiped tears from her eyes. For days afterwards, Israelis everywhere seemed to talk of almost nothing else.

What touched Israelis so much was that the scene was so far removed from the hatred they had come to expect in Arab-Israeli relations. Here were Arabs and Jews actually being civil to one another, even warm. Though a fleeting incident, was it a meaningless interlude, or did it hold promise for the future?

Indeed, what has emerged from decades of uninterrupted warfare between Arabs and Jews in the Middle East is a kind of resignation, among Israelis, to undying hatred and perpetual conflict. This, in turn, has led to a pervasive intellectual sterility on the question of how Arabs and Jews might live together in peace.

What dominates Israeli thought today, in the contemplation of the Middle East's future, are strategic problems. How much of the territories won in 1967 can we afford to give back? Will the international community respond when our existence is threatened?

All of these questions are based on the assumption that the Arabs not only are implacably hostile but will continue to be, forever. They are based on the assumption that Israel must remain a fortress against those who would, at any opportunity, try to destroy it.

They are, moreover, based on the assumption that the Arab world is a monolith—that the rage of a Palestinian guerilla necessarily is the sentiment of a Beirut merchant, that the extremism in Damascus inevitably must triumph as overall Arab policy.

It is true that, given the current state of relations between Arab and Israeli governments, it would be premature to debate long-term questions of coexistence in the political arena. But neither are these questions being debated—even on a theoretical level—among intellectuals in the universities.

At best, a few old Zionists are still alive to remind contemporary

Israelis that the first settlers thought a great deal about living with the Arabs. And a handful of left-wing thinkers occasionally talk of it today.

But most Israelis regard the former as anachronisms and the latter as kooks—and if they think of Arabs at all, they think of them as a military, not a human concern.

But when the scene of the canal flashed on the television screen, large numbers of Israelis were reminded of what they had forgotten: how life could be with the Arabs as friends, and without the constant threat of annihilation.

Was the scene an omen of promise? One danger is that Israelis, conditioned for so long to be cynics, may be unable to relax long enough even to explore the possibility.

Kissinger, while engaged in the "shuttle," did not forget the oil crisis. The long lines in front of gasoline pumps in the United States, translating into political pressure on the Nixon administration, prodded him. So did the entreaties of America's allies, who felt more seriously squeezed by the shortages.

Sadat kept the promise he had made to Kissinger by appealing to Saudi Arabia, after the disengagement agreement was signed, to lift the oil embargo. Kissinger himself was in constant communication with the Saudis, complaining of the soaring prices, protesting even more vigorously the embargo itself. He even exhorted the Syrians to put pressure on the Saudis, threatening to abandon his plan to seek Israeli withdrawal on the Golan front, but his unfamiliarity with the murky labyrinth of inter-Arab politics was a handicap in playing one Arab state against another. Meanwhile, the Saudis seemed to have no clear policy, modifying their demands daily, so that he never quite knew where they stood. Thus, the embargo remained in force.

In his memoirs, Kissinger attributes to his own hard line the ultimate end of the embargo, contending that once the Arabs understood he could not be pressured, they gave up trying. It is true the United States, however harsh its criticism of the Meir government during the negotiations, at no point flinched in its basic support of Israel. The United States could afford this luxury, since its economy used relatively little oil from Arab producers. Its independence of Arab oil goes far to explain the contrast, then and since, between Washington's support of hard-line Israeli positions and the more balanced positions adopted by the Japanese and the Europeans. In fact, however, neither Kissinger's claims of potency nor America's oil independence reveal very much about why the embargo finally came to an end.

The answer lay in the inability of the Arab oil producers themselves to agree on an embargo policy. Their differences, basically, were the product of the conflicting interests of two broad categories of producers. One category consisted of producing countries such as Algeria and Iran, with large populations, heavily dependent on oil revenues not just for economic development but for daily bread. The other consisted of those with small populations, chiefly Kuwait and Saudi Arabia, which had surplus revenues, much of which was diverted into investment for future use. The latter group could afford a protracted interruption of income, while the former could not. This difference produced dramatic disagreements.

The underpopulated Gulf countries were rich enough to prolong the embargo, holding out for satisfaction of a range of Arab grievances; the poorer Arab producers, feeling the economic pain, wanted shipments resumed at once. The result created a paradox. Saudi Arabia, "moderate" among the Arabs, was concerned about the risks of the embargo to international stability, while "radical" Algeria was willing enough to see the global economic structure tumble down. But it was the Saudis, not the Algerians, who took the hard line. Meanwhile, Sadat, as his part of the disengagement deal, worked for the embargo's end. The Saudis were thus being criticized by the West for intransigence, and by other Arab states for defying Egypt, the chief donor of blood and money to the Arab cause. The pressure on the Saudi government was huge.

Notwithstanding, the Saudis did not yield easily, and the embargo dragged on for two months after the disengagement agreement was signed. Finally, Kissinger's announcement of a second "shuttle"—between Israel and Syria—settled the matter, permitting rich producers to claim that the embargo had served Arab interests. Their honor had been salvaged. With this announcement, the embargo ended, and by early March, oil was once more flowing into the world's markets.

The oil weapon was never used again. It seemed to stand in abeyance for some years, while OPEC effectively manipulated the international oil market to maintain prices at what consumers considered an exorbitant level. Meanwhile, the West was cutting consumption and finding new sources of energy. I recall a conversation I had with Rabin in 1979, in which he predicted that by the 1990s, the threat of an embargo would be deprived of political meaning. At the time of our talk, international oil supplies were already rising and demand was dropping, though it was not clear whether either trend was permanent, and I took Rabin's remark as the typical wishful thinking of a partisan Israeli. But in fact, market conditions were changing faster than either of us knew, and the power of oil as a political force collapsed a decade earlier than even Rabin had predicted.

Few outsiders recognized it, but the viability of the oil weapon may have begun to vanish well before the 1980s, in the councils of Arab governments that had come to depend too heavily on oil income. In the years after the Yom Kippur War, when oil was in scarce supply and prices were still rising, the Arab states chose to impose no more embargoes out of an unwillingness to defer their own spending. The good life was too much with them. It was not just the favored producers of the Persian Gulf who spent, but in generously spreading their wealth around the Arab world, they created a vested interest in oil income in almost every Arab capital. Arab governments managed this money, on the whole, with admirable competence, not only building new cities and industrial complexes but bringing popular standards of living in much of the Arab world to unprecedented levels. These governments also bought tanks and guns, airplanes and electronic warning systems. But military hardware had a paltry political impact compared to the potential of the oil weapon. Once the Arabs abandoned it, they lost their capacity to make the world tremble.

In recent years, with the oil market glutted and prices falling, the Arabs have been unable to regain this capacity. Though it is not clear how permanent the changes are, it is certain the market will not soon return to the conditions that existed during and after the Yom Kippur War. Since the embargo of 1973, the oil weapon has not been a factor in the Arab-Israeli struggle. Nor have the Arabs ever again been as strong.

The Israeli-Syrian "shuttle," which Kissinger launched at the end of April 1974, presented more complicated problems than the Sinai negotiations. In Syria's President Hafez al-Assad, Kissinger had no partner like Sadat, who took pride in being reasonable. History had made Syria a more implacable enemy of Israel than Egypt was. As the Syrians saw it, at the end of World War I the victorious Allies promised them Palestine and wound up instead giving it to the Jews. The loss made Syria's hostility toward Israel more direct than Egypt's. It fueled a permanent truculence which made Syria tougher and crueler. The Israelis, on their side, were not disposed to forget the years of Syrian shelling of their settlements from the Golan Heights. They took for granted the premise that the Syrians would never yield in their hatred, which made the prospect of concessions even harder to swallow. Compared to the Sinai, withdrawal on the Golan seemed to Israel a more painful defeat.

The Golan's proximity to centers of population and production in both Israel and Syria, though an incentive to agreement, also added to the two governments' wariness. So did the fact that the disputed ground, in contrast to the Sinai desert, was itself valuable. The cease-fire line of 1967 lay between fertile fields, which were home to Syrian farmers and town dwellers on the one side, to Israeli settlers and kibbutzim on the other. Compared with the Sinai, every square meter of the Golan Heights was precious. As a result, both Syrians and Israelis approached the negotiations with a sense of having little margin for what could mean fatal error.

The geography of the cease-fire provided a further burden. Starting much closer to Israel's heartland on Yom Kippur day, the

Syrians had provided a bigger scare than the Egyptians when they nearly broke through Israel's defenses. But Israel reoccupied all the land it had lost, then advanced to positions within fifteen miles of Damascus. Israel's victory had left Syria, unlike Egypt, with no territorial gain as bait for trade. The two armies, furthermore, were not entangled helter-skelter but separated by a straight line. They were easily resupplied, and closer to home than those straddling the Suez Canal, so the pressure on both governments to disengage was less intense. In this atmosphere, the two sides engaged in deadly, almost daily artillery duels long after the cease-fire went into effect.

Once the talks were under way, the Palestine Liberation Organization, fearful again that the Arab nations were selling out its interests, deliberately aggravated tensions with a string of killings in the development towns near the Lebanese border. In an attack in April, PLO *fedayeen* killed eighteen civilians in Kiryat Shmona and while Kissinger was shuttling between Jerusalem and Damascus in May, they killed twenty-four children and wounded many more in a school in Ma'alot. Israelis were beside themselves with rage, directed not just at the PLO but at Arabs generally. That Syria had long barred *fedayeen* from crossing the Golan into Israel, that the terrorists had come to the two towns not from Syria but from Lebanon, did not seem to matter. Israel felt more besieged than ever, which left accord with Syria more elusive than before.

As if these obstacles were not enough, Mrs. Meir's cabinet functioned with an extremely fragile mandate. During the negotiations to form a new cabinet, the plurality Labor had won in the December election, already thin, was undermined further by mounting criticism of its failure to prepare Israel for the Yom Kippur War. Time had made Israelis not more forgiving but more angry with their political leaders. Likud exploited these feelings both in parliament and in stormy street protests. In the bargaining over the new cabinet, the religious parties had demanded huge concessions, including strongly "hawkish" commitments. It took

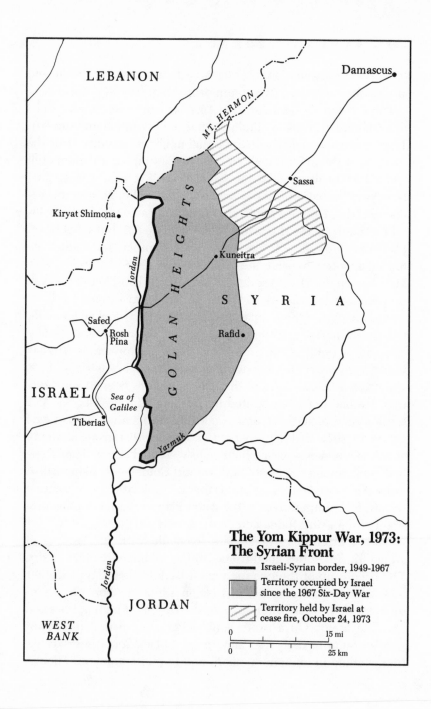

LEBANON

Damascus

MT. HERMON

Sassa

Kiryat Shimona

Kuneitra

S Y R I A

Safed
Rosh
Pina

Rafid

ISRAEL

Sea of
Galilee

Tiberias

Yarmuk

Jordan

Jordan

WEST
BANK

JORDAN

GOLAN HEIGHTS

**The Yom Kippur War, 1973:
The Syrian Front**

━━━ Israeli-Syrian border, 1949-1967

Territory occupied by Israel
since the 1967 Six-Day War

Territory held by Israel at
cease fire, October 24, 1973

0   15 mi

0   25 km

ten weeks of negotiations for Mrs. Meir to form a government, and at that she had only a weak, minority coalition.

Then, three weeks later, the Agranat Commission, an official body of inquiry, released findings on its investigation into the war. The commission held the general staff negligent in permitting the surprise at the Suez Canal, and the army's top commanders felt compelled to resign. On the issue of ministerial responsibility, however, the commission was less decisive. Public opinion demanded that Defense Minister Dayan, the cabinet's most powerful member, follow the lead of the general staff, but he refused. Dayan's stonewalling triggered a popular uproar, and Likud submitted a motion to bring the cabinet down. Fearful of losing, Mrs. Meir herself decided to resign in early April. Thus, in the midst of preparations for the Syrian talks, the Israeli government fell.

With no obvious heir apparent, the Labor Party looked about for two weeks before settling on a successor. By a narrow vote, and after bitter political infighting, the party electors chose Yitzhak Rabin, who was then a Knesset back-bencher. His was a fresh face, when it was widely agreed that Israeli politics needed rejuvenation. He had not been tainted in the Yom Kippur debacle. As a former chief of staff and ambassador to Washington, he had won his credentials outside party politics, which was a strong attribute at a time when established politicians were in disfavor. Though he had been among the hard-liners around Golda Meir, Rabin called himself a "dove," on the grounds that he preferred implementing the strategic imperatives of the Allon Plan to the Revisionist program of annexing Judea and Samaria outright.

Rabin's election turned out to coincide with the landing of Henry Kissinger, his good friend, in the middle of Israel's affairs. The friendship of the two men went back to their days together in Washington, during the first Nixon administration. On a personal level, they had often savored discussions of high politics and grand strategy. On a professional level, they had shaped joint policies on arms deliveries and, in the "Black September" crisis, they worked in tandem on coordinating military action. Though they sometimes quarreled over details of American-Israeli relations, Rabin and Kissinger saw eye-to-eye on the larger issues. Rabin had sided with Kissinger in the bureaucratic duel against William Rogers. He had supported Kissinger's controversial policies in Indochina. In 1972, in campaigning among American Jews for Nixon's reelection, he had subjected himself to considerable criticism for indiscretion. Now he had a sizable body of past favors for which he could command repayment.

But when the Syrian "shuttle" began, Rabin was still on his way in as prime minister, while Nixon was on his way out as President. It was happenstance that the governments in both Washington and Jerusalem were badly weakened by crisis. But it was lucky for Kissinger, because the two crises surely contributed to his success.

Nixon, convinced a triumph abroad could save him from the tightening vise of Watergate, repeatedly pressed Kissinger to go on at times when another President might have regarded the negotiations as hopeless. Mrs. Meir, required by Israeli law to stay in office until formation of a new cabinet, had been freed to make painful, highly divisive decisions, knowing herself no longer answerable to the Knesset. As prime minister, Rabin would prove to be far less dominating than she had been, but during the crucial weeks while Kissinger shuttled between Jerusalem and Damascus, he worked at forming his cabinet, involved in interparty rather than international negotiations. On Syrian issues, it was Mrs. Meir who took the opposition's wrath.

In his memoirs Kissinger wryly notes, talking of the Syrian-Israeli "shuttle," that he found Mrs. Meir and Syrian President Assad almost mirror images, and the direct opposite of Sadat. In their common insecurity, he wrote, both were suspicious, legalistic, tenacious, ungenerous. Strong as both were, neither had the power to deal with a proposal without consulting a passel of advisers, any one of whom might seek to exercise a veto, killing agreement on some point that had once seemed resolved.

Mrs. Meir also had to contend with the harm done by vicious Likud mobs, who greeted Kissinger on almost every visit to Jerusalem. They threw stones and reviled him with curses, some of them anti-Semitic. Once Kissinger, blocked by crowds, could not even get through the streets to a meeting at Mrs. Meir's house. Begin, meanwhile, assailed her relentlessly from the rostrum of the Knesset, accusing her of being too accommodating to the Arabs, and worse. Yet once embarked on the talks, she decided she did not want them to fail, and neither did Assad. Kissinger, having anticipated a week or so of negotiations, spent thirty-four grueling days on the road before he finally produced a deal.

Once more, however, to close the deal he had to commit the United States to crucial involvement in the outcome. At the final hour, with the beleaguered Nixon waiting in Washington to make an announcement that he hoped would turn the nation's attention from Watergate, the Israeli negotiators balked. Faced with a public outcry over the Ma'alot massacre, they demanded of Syria a pledge to forbid terrorists to cross the Golan into Israel. Without it, Mrs. Meir declared, the Knesset would never ratify the agreement. Though Assad has consistently denied the Golan to *fedayeen,* his sense of Arab honor prevented him from proclaiming a position that might be construed as truckling to Israel. Symbolic though it was, neither side was willing to budge on the issue, leaving Kissinger to salvage his thirty-four days of labor himself.

Kissinger filled the gap with a private letter promising America's approval of any response to terrorism that Israel might choose to make. The letter set no limits. Quoting from the text in the Knesset, Mrs. Meir stated the pledge as follows: "Raids by armed groups or individuals across the demarcation line are contrary to the cease-fire. Israel . . . may act to prevent such actions *by all available means.* The United States would not consider such actions by Israel as violations of the cease-fire, and will support them politically."

To Israel, the letter constituted a promise that no future President would withhold American economic or military assistance as punishment for antiterrorist reprisals. It committed Washington to support such attacks before the world, most notably at the United Nations. In effect, it imposed a serious new limitation on

America's ability to compel restraint within the cycle of violence that so often ran amok in the Arab-Israeli struggle.

The letter, however, cleared the way for the two sides to sign the agreement. Geographically, it followed the precedent of its Sinai counterpart. It provided for elongated zones of light armaments for each country, paralleling the two sides of a buffer patrolled by U.N. forces.

The line to which Israel withdrew lay to the west of the market town of Quneitra. Syria was presumably to rebuild the town, as Egypt was rebuilding the canal cities, to show confidence in the peace process. But the attitude in the Golan was more pernicious than in Sinai. In 1970, I had once visited Quneitra from the Israeli side. It was not beautiful but it was intact. Before turning it back to Syria, Israel bulldozed it to the ground, and the Syrians chose not to rebuild or repopulate it. When I visited Quneitra from the Syrian side in 1982, I imagined that it was as Carthage must have been after the Romans finished with it in the Punic Wars.

Whatever the similarities, however, the terms of the Golan agreement were dramatically different in one respect from the Sinai pact: The agreement was not based on a *trade* of territory. Israel, though victorious on the battlefield, evacuated ground held before the fighting had begun. When the Israelis withdrew from Syrian territory, they received no territory in return. In that sense, the agreement was closer to the spirit of Resolution 242 than the Sinai pact had been. Israel traded land for a promise of peace.

This outcome might be considered evidence either of Israel's *political* defeat in the Yom Kippur War or of its willingness, perhaps in spite of itself, to reach a Syrian settlement. In fairness, the agreement is probably evidence of both. Though Israel and Syria have since fought in Lebanon, the demarcation line separating them on the Golan Heights has been without warfare for more than a decade. Even Israelis admit, furthermore, that Syrian practice has been to allow no terrorists to cross the Golan frontier. Israel and Syria have, in this one place, kept the peace, which suggests that despite their unremitting antagonism, they may not yet have exhausted the possibility of further reconciliation.

On June 3, 1974, two days before the Israeli-Syrian disengagement agreement was signed at Geneva, Yitzhak Rabin was sworn in as Israel's prime minister. Fifty-one years old, native-born, he seemed to symbolize the end of the reign of the founding fathers, the accession of a new generation to power. The younger men who came into office with him, notably Shimon Peres as defense minister and Yigal Allon as foreign minister, suggested the prospect of a softer line in foreign policy. Rabin received from Mrs. Meir a legacy that was in sharp contrast to her years in office. Having saved him from the acrimony of the Syrian debate, she presented to him a signed agreement with Israel's bitterest enemy. Mrs. Meir, leaving behind a certain momentum for peace, had placed Rabin in a position to quicken it.

But, as Rabin states in his memoirs, the priority he assigned himself as prime minister, consistent with the definition he had given his role as ambassador, was not peace but acquisition of "a maximum of arms and military equipment from the United States in a minimum of time." Not long after he assumed office, Rabin told an Israeli journalist that he expected to engage in no negotiations until after the American presidential election of 1976, which as a practical matter meant a delay of nearly three years.

Israel did not, it should be noted, face any particular threat when Rabin took office in mid-1974. Though its victory was less decisive and its losses were heavier than in 1967, Israel had emerged from the Yom Kippur War less badly bruised than Syria and Egypt. Neither would be fit for battle for years to come. Furthermore, the Soviet Union was apparently in no hurry in 1974 to embark on a major rebuilding program. Moscow seemed to be reevaluating its Middle East role, and was keeping its military assistance to the Arabs well below the level of American assistance to Israel. Syria, Moscow's only reliable client in the region once Sadat tilted toward Washington, was hardly capable of taking on Israel alone.

Rabin, however, was not moved by the evidence of Arab weakness. He shocked even his Labor Party supporters by naming Ariel Sharon, the pugnacious ex-general and organizer of Likud, as his military adviser. The appointment was surely meant as a signal that he had a limited interest in talking peace.

Two weeks after Rabin's accession to office, Richard Nixon arrived from Washington on a grand tour of the Middle East, desperate to rescue his presidency in what were, by now, clearly its dying days. Nixon's fantasy was to establish himself in the public mind as indispensable to peacemaking in the region. He was greeted in Egypt with enthusiasm, in Saudi Arabia with respect, in Syria with cordiality. Only in Israel was he received in chilly fashion.

Though Rabin had often proclaimed indebtedness to Nixon for opening America's arms depots to Israel and coming to its rescue in two wars, he made clear to the American President his dissatisfaction with current policy. Rabin said candidly he did not want Kissinger to press Israel to make further concessions for peace. He much preferred the old relationship with the United States, Rabin said, in which Israel was supplied with all the arms it wanted, while sitting on the diplomatic status quo. Nixon, encouraged in the Arab capitals to intensify peacemaking efforts, received from Rabin's new government a sharp signal to slow them down.

Kissinger, however, was too elated by his recent successes to slow down. On the contrary, the "shuttle" had obviously generated its own momentum, which he was determined to seize. He had Cairo in his pocket and Damascus in his debt. He feared that any slowing down, at that point, would cost him his strategic objectives. Suspending the "shuttle" would become an invitation to both Egypt and Syria to gravitate back to the Soviet camp.

Kissinger saw the next logical step on his diplomatic agenda to be a "shuttle" to Jordan. He reasoned that unless a Jordanian presence, however symbolic, was reestablished on the West Bank, there could be no progress toward a Palestinian settlement, which he now considered fundamental to reaching his goal. He underestimated, however, Rabin's harsh reaction to the idea. Kissinger made a forceful argument to the Israelis—presciently, as it turned out—that a Jordanian agreement would forestall later demands from the Arabs for negotiations with the PLO, which was sure to prove a more intractable foe. But Rabin was not interested in Kissinger's logic, and he rejected the proposal.

Rabin had a range of reasons, not least of them that he simply did not see the Palestinian issue as central to the Arab-Israeli conflict. Rabin attached no particular importance to the rise of Palestinian nationalism. He considered the growing international appeal of the Palestinian cause as no more than a passing inconvenience. Though he saw terrorism as an irritant, he dismissed it as a threat to Israel's survival. A professional soldier, he measured danger by the size of the standing armies that the Arab nations could put into the field against Israel.

Rabin had no use for the hypothesis which held that Syria, Jordan and Egypt, having no direct interests in the Arab-Israeli conflict, would agree to peace once the Palestinian issue was resolved. He refused to believe the Arab nations were moved by any sense of solidarity with the Palestinians. This judgment is much disputed by Jews as well as Arabs. Though the Palestinian question does not cover all the outstanding differences between the two peoples, it is nonetheless centrally placed, and even most Israelis recognize that without addressing it there will be no peace. Rabin, however, dismissed the notion that Arabs feel a collective responsibility to one another. Indifferent to the Palestinians himself, he insisted they did not matter to Arabs, either.

Beyond that, Rabin had no interest in an Israeli-Jordanian deal because it contained no prospect of military advantage. Had Jordan joined in the surprise attack on Yom Kippur, its armies would surely have captured Israeli settlements on the West Bank, as they had in 1948. Their advance would have forced Israel to revise its strategy. It would have required a diversion of units from the Syrian front, where the watch was already close, to the Jordanian front. Fighting on another front would no doubt have left a different configuration on the field at the cease-fire, and might even have changed the war's outcome. But King Hussein had not attacked, and so there was no "disengagement" to arrange. The

Jordan River, the line of separation, was in fact the most stable of Israel's frontiers. Rabin's rejection of any talks was, ironically, his reward to Jordan for having kept the peace.

For Rabin, a deal with Jordan not only was without military advantage but contained the certainty of political penalty. Rabin was far from having Golda Meir's power to dominate the Labor Party, much less the Knesset. Having been "parachuted" into office by party kingpins, he had been a controversial choice, without a political base of his own. In bargaining for the support of the party's right wing, he had pledged to evacuate no part of the West Bank without prior elections. The Labor Party did not want elections and Rabin, notably lacking in charisma, had no reason to believe his own appeal to the voters was likely to improve the party's already narrow parliamentary margin. In fact, the loss of the few seats that stood between Labor and surrender of the government to the Likud seemed a more likely electoral outcome.

Rabin thus sensed himself squeezed between Kissinger and the Knesset. But while he understood that the United States was too important to Israel to defy outright, he was also astute enough to examine the prospect of turning peacemaking to his own purposes. Rabin was not against peace. He did not deny that political benefits might accrue from another agreement. He simply attached a higher priority to his goal of enlarging Israel's margin of military superiority. What Rabin found, hidden within Kissinger's agenda, was a channel to benefits which he considered grander than peace. He saw in peacemaking a way to fulfill his life's mission of providing Israel with permanent access to the weapons necessary to maintain the Middle East's mightiest army.

Rabin reasoned that Kissinger, itching to preside over an American-brokered peace, would pay heavily to get it. Any political concessions the Arabs might make as part of it, though useful, were barely relevant. What interested Rabin were arms and money, which were available not from the Arabs but from the United States. He knew from past experience that Kissinger was favorably disposed to the idea of a heavily armed Israel, available to serve American interests in the Middle East. Rabin saw the impending peace negotiations as Israel's opportunity to make an important deal not with its enemies but with its friends.

The actual costs of the Yom Kippur War had been astronomical. Economists calculated the total at nearly seven billion dollars, equal to more than a year of the country's gross national product. About a third of it consisted of the bill for equipment the United States had airlifted to the battlefield without consideration by either government of how it would be paid for. With a collective sigh of relief, Israelis greeted Nixon's decision to write off the entire amount for the airlifted supplies, but what remained was still a crushing burden. In 1974, the year after the war, Israel's service of its foreign debt approached one billion dollars, almost equal to its net exports.

"After the fighting in the Yom Kippur War, President Nixon came up with the special legislation to cover the expenses of the airlift," Rabin recalled. "Remember that before the War of Attrition, we received very little from the United States. In the early 1970s, after the War of Attrition, we got an increase, to about three or four hundred million a year, mostly loans. The cost of the airlift alone during the war was far beyond our capacity, about two and a half billion dollars. Nixon's action was the big financial breakthrough in our relations with the United States."

The expenses that the war generated, moreover, did not end with the cease-fire. Reviewing the early setbacks on the battlefield, Rabin and the Israeli general staff concluded that the performance of the armed forces had shown fundamental shortcomings. Israel had counted on superiority in intelligence to warn of attack, and it had been fooled. It believed its edge in technology and training would put the Arabs to rout, and on the battlefield it had found its preeminence perilously narrowed. Israel had long relied on a tough little standing army, backed by well-prepared reservists, but Rabin decided that was no longer enough. He wanted Israel to approach the Arabs quantitatively, both in levels of manpower and in weapons. Within months of the Yom Kippur

War, Israel's military spending exceeded that of Egypt, Syria and Jordan combined.

"The Yom Kippur War brought a new dimension to our defense problems," Rabin said. "Before, we could manage with what we produced and what we got from the Jewish people around the world, along with some limited loans from the United States. After, we had to look in a much greater way to American financial support. A new chapter was beginning in Israeli life."

Israel's official position has long been that its military budget soared after the Yom Kippur War in response to Arab arms expenditures, financed by the surge in oil revenues. In part, that is correct. Suddenly rich, the Arabs were able to buy what they liked, not what the Soviet Union or some Western power chose to ration to them. With almost limitless funds, the Arabs became compulsive shoppers in the international arms market.

Still, arms races take on a life of their own, and at a certain point it becomes impossible to distinguish who leads from who follows. Both camps in the Middle East made a deliberate decision after the Yom Kippur War to begin a military buildup, and once started, the race proved uncontainable. Israel under Rabin went to work on new, far more expensive strategic conceptions, based not only on qualitative but on numerical superiority. When it became apparent that the funds Israel had available were nowhere near equal to its ambitions, Rabin chose not to scale down the ambitions but, rather, to try to get the money from Washington.

"We started to elaborate on our ideas with the visit of Nixon in June of 1974," Rabin said. "I told him I believed the best way to approach peace was for Israel to reach a strategic and tactical understanding with the United States. I talked to him about our readiness to continue the negotiating process and the need for American commitments to Israel, above all in strengthening Israel's military power and her economy."

Shortly after his visit to the Middle East in the summer of 1974, Nixon, unable to keep Watergate at bay any longer, resigned from office. Gerald Ford, who succeeded him, retained Kissinger in the dual role as secretary of state and national security adviser. In terms of Middle East policy, the change in the presidency meant very little under Ford. Kissinger's commitment to negotiating a new agreement remained unchanged, and when he arrived in Jerusalem for his first visit in the service of the new President, he proposed a fresh round of "shuttle diplomacy." He found Rabin amenable but determined to press a new and major condition. Rabin said Israel would negotiate only with Egypt.

Rabin's decision was based on the perception of Egypt as the preeminent Arab power, the only one whose armies were strong enough to threaten Israel. Rabin's military mind calculated that there was still ground in the Sinai that Israel could safely evacuate. What he saw in return—as he acknowledged candidly in an interview with an Israeli journalist—was the prospect of separating Egypt from the rest of the Arab world. Convinced by now of Sadat's sincerity in seeking peace, Israel began contemplating maneuvers to achieve Egypt's isolation, an objective that in the years that followed became a cornerstone of its diplomacy. This objective emerged clearly in the Camp David talks in 1978. Kissinger, faced with choosing between negotiations on Rabin's terms or no negotiations at all, decided reluctantly to go along.

"When I came into office," Rabin said in one of his talks with me, "I had to decide on my priorities. I knew we had to start with Egypt. Whatever relationship existed between Israel and the Arab world had to start with Israel and Egypt. The disengagement agreement after the Yom Kippur War was a start, but I considered it only to be a consolidation of the cease-fire.

"What did I want to achieve? I believed there was no purpose in any more wars. That's why, after the disengagement agreement, I knew we had to continue the political process. But I knew that for the Arabs, the word 'peace' simply meant 'no more war.' They didn't want to make peace. The Arabs rejected the notion of peace in the real sense, normalizing relations. For me, peace without it was nothing. Still, we were willing to continue the process of disengagement. But we would continue it only through the good offices of the United States."

For Rabin, the concept of "normalizing relations" signified recognition by the Arabs of Israel's legitimacy. In itself, it was a leap beyond the substance of no-war into the formalities of peace, the crossing of a psychological barrier of vital importance. A few years later, Menachem Begin, as prime minister, was to dismiss the issue, asserting the Revisionist tenet that Israel's legitimacy, being *sui generis,* required no Arab confirmation. Whatever Rabin's objectives, however, in 1974 normalization was on no one's agenda. Not even Rogers had spoken of it, and U.N. Resolution 242 contained no reference to it. So Rabin was correct in saying that peace —so long as "normalization" was intrinsic to its definition—was far from being at hand.

Rabin was making the argument, in short, that waiting for a peace which was accompanied by normalization was better than rushing toward a peace which was not. He sounded in his talks with me very much like a man trying to reconcile a philosophical commitment to peace, based on Mainstream Zionist convictions, with the absence of any sense of urgency, based on his training as a soldier, about attaining it. But what he said next in our talk raised the question of whether he was interested in peace at all. Important as normalization may have been to him, the objective Rabin really considered worth waiting for was acceptance by the Arabs of changes in Israel's boundaries.

"I believed that the kind of peace I wanted—real peace, with normalization and security for Israel—could not be brought about in a single act. *Peace required bringing about changes; not dramatic changes, but changes in the boundaries of Israel.* We could move in this direction only gradually."

Boundaries reached much nearer than normalization to the heart of the debate between Arabs and Israelis. It was one thing for Rabin, a Mainstream Zionist, to say Israel would not agree to a settlement without "normalization." But Rabin was saying quite another in declaring that Israel would not consider any peace that required the full return of the territories. Israel could impose boundary revision, but no Arab regime would consent to normalization to accompany it. In dealing with Egypt at Camp David,

Israel obtained normalization but only by abandoning the condition of boundary revision. Rabin knew very well that the two
objectives were inherently contradictory. To attain them both,
Israel's wait for peace was likely to be long indeed.

In effect, Rabin was not so much arguing for moving slowly
toward peace as rationalizing the likelihood of not getting there
at all. In entering new "shuttle" talks with Kissinger, he made
clear that he was no readier to implement the territory-for-peace
principle insofar as "full peace" was concerned than Golda Meir
had been seven years earlier. This was the policy he followed
during his entire term as prime minister.

In February of 1975, Kissinger arrived in the Middle East to
begin the second Egyptian-Israeli "shuttle," only to find negotiating conditions had sharply deteriorated in the previous months.
Neither Rabin nor Sadat was as yet ready to extend to Gerald
Ford, whom they did not yet know, the confidence they had had
in Nixon. More important, in place of the common interests of
both sides in disengagement, there had been a retreat on both
sides toward positions conventionally taken before the Yom Kippur War. Sadat, apprehensive about getting too far out in front of
the Arab world, let it be known he wanted no agreement that did
not bring with it a substantial gain in territory. Rabin answered
that he preferred no agreement at all to giving away defensible
terrain.

Jordan and Syria had by now become extremely suspicious of
Sadat, and of the prospect of his making a separate deal that
overlooked their interests. The Arab oil producers were talking of
another embargo to put pressure on Israel for concessions, and it
was not clear whether they were bluffing. The Russians were waiting in the wings for the opportunity to cement together the pieces
of their old Middle East power base. Kissinger understood that the
United States would be much embarrassed if his peacemaking
program failed. Both Rabin and Sadat came away from visits with
him convinced that he was more anxious for a successful "shuttle"

than were either of them. That, of course, was precisely where they wanted him.

Sadat opened the bargaining with a demand that the demarcation line between the two countries be moved eastward beyond the Mitla and Gidi passes, the Sinai's most defensible barriers, and southward beyond Abu Rudeis, the oil fields from which Israel had been pumping since the Six-Day War. Rabin countered by calling for an Egyptian commitment to nonbelligerency, which would have meant Sadat's waiving war as an option for achieving the remaining items on the Arabs' list of differences with Israel. Though both retreated in the negotiations from their original terms, Sadat, in Kissinger's judgment, conceded more than Rabin did. Still, the gap between the two sides remained wide, and after two weeks of bargaining, Kissinger decided to suspend the "shuttle" and go home.

Back in Washington, Kissinger publicly blamed Israel for the breakdown. President Ford followed by announcing a "total reassessment" of American policy in the region and, in the ensuing weeks, he imposed limitations on arms shipments and economic assistance to Israel. It was as severe a blow as had been struck since Eisenhower's day. Rabin called the period "one of the worst in American-Israeli relations." But he stuck resolutely to his guns, while in Israel public opinion rallied to him, and in America the Jewish leadership urged the White House to soften its response.

Rabin did not expect Sadat to yield on the nonbelligerency issue, but he did not much care. On the other hand, he was confident that in time Kissinger would crack, which was the development that mattered to him. In May, pro-Israeli pressure persuaded seventy-six United States senators to sign a letter calling on Ford to loosen the screws. It was not just domestic pressures, however, that persuaded Rabin to wait. He understood that Kissinger could not bear to convey to the Soviet Union the image that American power in the Middle East was in disarray. Rabin bet that Kissinger, without other options, would return to Israel, bearing gifts not from Egypt but from the United States, which was the real prize he was after.

"Many people don't understand the interrelations between the superpowers and the countries of the region," Rabin replied when I asked how Israel could afford such defiance. "The superpowers do not give orders, either to the Arabs or to us.

"There is a realization on the part of the United States, as well as the Soviet Union, that you don't go in and say, 'You have to do what we say.' It just wouldn't work. The two superpowers have learned the delicacy of the interrelationships that exist between them and the countries of the region.

"Maybe the superpowers' relations with their allies in Europe are different. America's participation in Western European security is much more direct than its involvement with Israel. Moscow's relationship with Eastern Europe is more direct than it is with Syria. In Syria, Assad has to bear in mind the Russian interest and listen to advice from Russian advisers, but not do more than that. Though the Russians supply him with every bit of his military equipment, they cannot dictate to him. The same applies to relations between the United States and Israel."

Rabin emphasized that Russia's objectives were not always those of Syria, nor America's those of Israel. The relationships require mutual rather than one-way accommodation, he said. Since the superpower no less than the client is best served when the objectives of the two correspond, he argued, the incentive goes not in one direction but in both to avoid having policies that diverge.

"It is not in America's interest to convey the illusion that it can force Israel to agree to something that manifestly Israel cannot accept," Rabin said. "It wouldn't help the United States to give hope to the Arab countries that because of differences with us, they can get the upper hand through military means. The message of our joint policy must be clear, clear to the Arab world: Israel will not be weakened. Therefore, after the 'shuttle' broke down in early 1975, Kissinger could not allow the pieces to lie there. He had to choose another course of action."

Fortunately for Kissinger, Rabin and Sadat were in total agreement on an issue fundamental to the talks: They wanted not only to keep the Soviet Union *out* of the Middle East but to keep the United States *in.* Neither was interested in another war in the region, or more sessions in Geneva, if only because war and Geneva would have drawn the Russians back. Their common interest favored a peacekeeping structure that required the highest possible level of American participation. Though they were enemies, their shared vision established an alliance at the bargaining table that coaxed the United States ever deeper into the labyrinth of Israeli-Egyptian peace.

Sadat took the initiative to restore movement to the negotiations when he met with Ford and Kissinger in Austria in June. He volunteered there that if Israel moved as far back as the Sinai passes, Egypt would agree to the demilitarization of the evacuated area. Instead of moving into the passes, furthermore, it would allow Americans to man electronic warning stations within them to monitor compliance with the agreement. Ford and Kissinger, whatever their misgivings about American involvement, adopted the idea.

But the real breakthrough in talks occurred when Ford, shortly afterward, conveyed to the Israeli government the offer that Rabin had gambled on receiving. In return for Israeli evacuation of the passes and the oil fields, Ford said, the United States would assure to Israel permanent, large-scale military and financial support. It was a huge concession, which would transform not only American-Israeli relations but the entire structure of power in the Middle East. Rabin listened to the offer, then proceeded to organize task forces to formulate the commitments that Israel planned to elicit from the United States. In August 1975, after a few weeks of exchanges at the ambassadorial level, Kissinger returned to the Middle East.

Even with the groundwork laid in advance, it took Kissinger twelve days of shuttle diplomacy to negotiate the agreement known as Sinai II. This time, the United States acted as more than a simple broker, carrying bargaining points back and forth between Cairo and Jerusalem. These talks were triangular, with the United States as much a party to them as Israel and Egypt. In fact, so important were the demands made on the United States that it became clear the decisions of Washington would make or break the shuttle.

Israel and Egypt readily struck their bargain. Israel conceded a line of withdrawal behind the passes and the oil fields, and following the model of the earlier pacts, the two agreed upon a demilitarized buffer zone, along with zones of limited armaments, between the armies. In the passes themselves, the two countries were to establish electronic warning systems, both to be maintained by Americans. As "elements" of nonbelligerency, Egypt pledged not to use force to settle outstanding differences with Israel. Egypt also agreed to permit passage of nonmilitary cargo to Israel through the Suez Canal and to relax the boycott of companies dealing with Israel. Both governments also promised to work toward final peace under terms of U.N. Resolution 242.

In the context of the long struggle for Middle East peace, the Israeli-Egyptian segment of Sinai II was unquestionably a remarkable achievement. Israel, in giving up the passes, agreed to take undeniable risks with its security, and in giving up the oil fields, with its economy. Egypt made a psychological break from the Arab world, as well as from Arab history, to move away from the order of inexorable war that had defined its Israeli relations since 1948. Though Sinai II was not a definitive exchange of territory for peace, it was, in the jargon of the day, a "piece of territory for a piece of peace." In maintaining the momentum of negotiations, the agreement appeared to be a giant step toward an overall settlement of the Arab-Israeli conflict.

But it turned out there was less promise and, ultimately, more trouble than met the eye. The Israeli-American segment of the Sinai II agreement, the most painful to negotiate, emerged as a range of American commitments of extreme complexity. What this segment did was to carry American involvement in Israel's security, begun in Lyndon Johnson's day, into a new range. However brilliantly Rabin had planned, it is unlikely that even he foresaw the free hand the United States under Gerald Ford, with Kissinger as secretary of state, would be willing to grant to Israel in Middle East affairs. In the brief decade since Sinai II was written, history has largely established that the Israeli-American segment undid the promise of peace that the Israeli-Egyptian segment seemed on the point of realizing.

Kissinger, to get Israeli agreement to Sinai II, locked the United States into a rigid contractual arrangement, initially classified secret but subsequently leaked to the public. (See Appendix H.) It transformed the relationship between the two countries, all but excluding American judgment from Middle East issues. It attached Washington's endorsement to almost any military action an Israeli government might choose to take while, at the same time, it bound the United States to pick up the costs. In the end, what Kissinger handed over gratified not Israel's security requirements but its military fantasies. Sinai II served to spur not stability but an adventurism that carried an American stamp.

Sinai II's single most important provision lay in the sealing of the pledge that Ford had made earlier to Rabin. In it, the President accepted an obligation to "submit annually for approval by the US Congress a request for military and economic assistance in order to help meet Israel's economic and military needs." The accord contained a further obligation that the American government "make every effort to be fully responsive, within the limits of its resources and Congressional authorization and appropriation, on an on-going and long-term basis, to Israel's military equipment and other defense requirements, to its energy requirements and to its economic needs."

America's pledge, in effect, made it the custodian both of Israel's security and its economy. It overturned routine procedures of the American government for providing aid to foreign countries by extending to Israel the *right* to make claims on the federal budget. At the same time, it imposed a formal obligation on the United

States to pay those claims. The agreement was not quite an American "blank check" to Israel, but it came extremely close. On the one hand it legalized a patron-client relationship, while on the other it revoked virtually all of the patron's conventional powers of review over the client's policies. Kissinger's structure tied the United States to all decisions Israel made, while imposing on Israel no corresponding requirement to consider American interests in the making of them.

This structure created particularly dangerous possibilities in American-Soviet relations. A provision of Sinai II committed the United States to "view with particular gravity threats to Israel's security or sovereignty by a *world power.*" It promised explicitly that Washington would stand behind Israel with "support, diplomatic or otherwise," in the event of such a threat. In terms of the kind of cold war scenario that was dear to Kissinger, this promise may have been unexceptionable. But the reality of nuclear confrontation surely suggested more caution.

At least three times in its short history—in 1956, in 1967 and again in 1973—Israel provoked Moscow seriously enough to bring the superpowers to the brink of conflict. In each instance, Washington supported Israel, while taking serious exception to the substance of the Israeli position. In October 1973, the most recent instance, the military machinery of the two superpowers was actually mobilized after Israel, to America's consternation, violated the cease-fire at the Suez Canal. In each of the three instances, prudence ultimately prevailed. But under the language of Sinai II, America's control over such a dangerous situation was seriously impaired by a promise that appeared to rule out its own judgment over the unfolding of events.

Whatever America's misgivings, furthermore, many Israelis considered Sinai II risky for Israel, as well. The agreement institutionalized Israel's economic dependence. Though Washington asked for little in return for its generosity in the years that followed, a patron government by definition possesses vital powers to limit the sovereignty of a client. History offers ample evidence of client states that have lost their freedom. The possibility was a particularly sensitive issue for Israel, shaped as it was by the Zionist pledge to emancipate the Jews. Yet, in the name of security, Israel traded away vital elements of its independence, convinced that it could count forever on having in the United States a compliant patron.

Even more inexplicable than the military and economic vows that Kissinger made was his agreement in Sinai II to put an end to his beloved step-by-step diplomacy. Kissinger consented, first, to try for no further "interim agreement" with Egypt. Then, having cajoled and pleaded with Rabin for months to face the Palestinian issue by dealing with Jordan, and having lost face in Amman by failing to keep his own pledge of a shuttle, he proceeded to cross a Jordanian-Israeli "disengagement" accord off his agenda.

It was a strange reward for Kissinger to present to Rabin. Largely at Israel's behest, Kissinger in 1974 had substituted the step-by-step process for earlier efforts to implement U.N. Resolution 242 in a single transaction. Now, a year later, in scrapping the step-by-step strategy, he agreed to abandon the peace process altogether. Facing Rabin, Kissinger blinked. In the conference rooms of Sinai II, Rabin's vision of marching slowly toward peace —which, in effect, meant not marching at all—had triumphed.

Furthermore, having rewarded Rabin once for refusing to deal with Jordan, Kissinger proceeded bizarrely to reward him a second time. Kissinger had warned Israel in 1974 that refusal to come to terms with Amman would strengthen the PLO. Shortly afterward, his concern was vindicated when the Arab summit at Rabat transferred to the PLO all of Jordan's authority to speak for the Palestinians. Rabin naturally said he would have nothing to do with the PLO, and Kissinger said the United States would not either. In Sinai II, Kissinger made the now famous American pledge of self-denial, agreeing not to "recognize or negotiate" with the PLO. The pledge has made Washington as ineffectual in dealing with the Palestinian question as Moscow became, after breaking relations, in dealing with Israel. It has prevented any constructive American contribution to resolving the Palestinian dilemma. In effect, it has cut the United States off from the central issue of the Arab-Israeli conflict.

Kissinger's subsequent statements have never satisfactorily explained his willingness to give away the store to get an agreement at Sinai II. In testimony before the Senate Foreign Relations Committee on his return from the Middle East, he complained of the leak of the American pledges to the press but revealed little of why he made them. Certainly, his legendary ego was a factor. Kissinger did not want to go home bearing another failure, as he had the previous March. Rabin and Sadat had already agreed on terms for their segment of the pact, and he knew it was within his power to provide the American commitments to close the deal. But if ego was one factor in reaching the decision, Kissinger's personal *weltanschauung* was surely another.

Kissinger, whose objective in Arab-Israeli negotiations was to contain Soviet influence, saw no more powerful obstacle to the Russians in the Middle East than the Israeli army. Kissinger, after all, defined every encounter between Arabs and Israelis as either victory or defeat for the United States in the cold war. In Sinai II, he provided Israel with the means to prevail in America's behalf, if not against Moscow itself then at least against its clients.

Israel's official pronouncements justify Sinai II's generosity on the grounds that Israeli military power faithfully serves America's Middle East interests. Shortly after the invasion of Lebanon in 1982, Prime Minister Begin declared, "Israel gives the United States strategic assistance and contributes to the security of the United States more than the United States contributes to Israel." Israel's power in the "Black September" episode, when Soviet influence seemed about to explode throughout the region, was important, but how many other examples are there? American supporters tolerate poorly any questioning of the value of this power, even in insisting that the costs to the United States of Sinai II are a bargain.

Kissinger was too astute, of course, not to understand that what he bestowed also contained risks. In Sinai II, Israel acquired—to use Kissinger's own wry description of Israeli objectives—the power "to limit the freedom of action of a rather volatile ally five thousand miles away that supplies its arms, sustains its economy, shelters its diplomacy, and has a seemingly limitless compulsion to offer peace plans." In return for its signature on the Sinai II agreement, Kissinger granted to Israel a lien on American policy in the Middle East. Far from enhancing United States interests or promoting peace, this power has often served to undermine them both. Whatever the services Israel may render to American interests, it is still clear that in Sinai II Kissinger was badly outbargained.

When I asked Rabin whether Israel would have signed the Sinai II agreement with Egypt in the absence of the American concessions, he answered flatly that it would not. When I asked what the United States obtained in the bargain, he answered:

"The United States became the peacemaker in the region. I believe Kissinger realized that without the financial aid, there was no chance for Israel to manage its own defense budget, and without a strong Israel, there would have been no political solutions. When President Nixon decided to send arms to Israel during the Yom Kippur War, the clear message was 'We will not let Israel down.' It dispelled the illusion that by the use of military power the Arabs could force Israel to do something against its interest, either through war or through intimidation.

"The meaning was clear to the Arab world in a way it had never been. In simplest terms, what it meant to the Arabs was, 'If you want military action, go to Moscow,' but the American position showed them that Soviet assistance would not give them the upper hand. The Middle East problem could not be solved if you gave the Arab countries the slightest hope that they could win by military means. So what Sinai II said was, 'If you want political solutions, go to Washington.' For Kissinger, that was a tremendous achievement."

Yet, based on the same facts, it can also be argued that Kissinger made his real impact in the Middle East not as peacemaker but as architect of Israel's overwhelming military power, quite a different achievement. This power, in contributing to instability in the Middle East since Sinai II, is surely among the factors that has kept the Soviet Union in the region. Sadat's signal to Washington, before and after the Yom Kippur War, was that he would gladly finish with the Russians in return for a satisfactory deal with Israel. Syria's Assad, formally committed to Resolution 242, has periodically alluded to a similar willingness. Iraq, Moscow's other client, has made common cause with the moderate Arabs since its war with Iran, declaring a readiness to endorse a settlement of the Arab-Israeli conflict. The evidence is tantalizing that Russia would vanish entirely from the Arab world with the establishment of a stable peace in the region. The structure Kissinger built became a barrier to such a peace.

To accept Rabin's assertion that Sinai II had brought peace closer would require evidence that not only the Arabs but Israel stood ready to negotiate further. But in fact, there were no negotiations at all during the year that remained in Yitzhak Rabin's term as prime minister. By then, Kissinger was exhausted, and recognized the futility of pursuing a settlement any further. In fairness, it should be noted that in 1976 the Arabs were distracted by a civil war in Lebanon, the Israelis by the dramatic rescue of a hijacked airliner at Entebbe, the Americans by a presidential campaign. But as Rabin himself says, his government's preoccupation that year was with the integration of the huge flow of American arms promised in Sinai II. He was not much interested in talking peace.

Still, Rabin contends that without Sinai II Anwar Sadat would never have made his pilgrimage to Jerusalem in 1977. The visit, Rabin said, proved that his diplomacy had kept alive the momentum toward peace. If he were correct, it would seem logical that many Arab heads of government, not just Sadat, would be beating a path to Jerusalem. In fact, Sadat, the most committed of Middle East leaders to peace, went *in spite of* Sinai II. He took another

long chance in going to Jerusalem, of the nature of the Suez crossing on Yom Kippur 1973. Sadat made the trip not because the
momentum toward peace was alive but because it had become
moribund, the victim of Sinai II.

The Egyptian-Israeli-American agreement known as Sinai II
brought to a close the peacemaking season, the only one in the
decade that followed the Six-Day War. The seeds were dramatically sown by Sadat, the harvest skillfully reaped by Kissinger.
Rabin, who made up in shrewdness what he lacked in commitment to peace, knew well enough how to respond to an opportunity that he considered to be in Israel's interest. In Sinai II, he
provided so well for Israel that it never *had* to settle again. After
the agreement, Israel's position on the return of territory became
as rigid as it was before the Yom Kippur War.

Sinai II, by assuring its dominance in the region, took away
Israel's incentive to negotiate further. Far from promoting a new
taste for political accommodation, as Rabin suggests, the military
superiority bestowed by Sinai II generated in the region an atmosphere of intimidation. Israel thrived on it, while the Arabs
quailed. That was not peace, however, either by the Arabs' definition or by Rabin's. It was simply foreplay for more war.

Rabin succeeded in Sinai II in the illusory quest to bring Israel
absolute security. But as students of strategy recognize, *absolute*
security for one country, by creating permanent insecurity for its
neighbors, is no security for any of them. As prime minister, Rabin
conducted policy as if all Israel needed to be secure was the most
powerful army in the Middle East. He took no account of the
requirement that military power, to exceed the dangers it creates,
must function within a framework of stable relations among neighbors. This kind of stability would have required a political settlement—which, in Middle East terms, meant an exchange of territory for peace. That is precisely what Rabin wanted to avoid.

When I asked Rabin whether Sinai II did not give Israel a free
hand to do as it liked in strategic and political matters in the
region, he answered, "No doubt."

It was "absolute" security. Yet ironically, if it is proper to judge from the pervasive mood in Israel since the period of Sinai II, Israelis have never felt in greater jeopardy.

To make sure I had not misunderstood him, I asked Rabin a second time whether Israel had the military power to do in the Middle East much as it liked, he said, "Of course."

Rabin was confident that he himself would not upset the stability of the region by abusing the responsibility that went with armed might. He was, after all, a Mainstream Zionist, who asked of Israel's neighbors only to acknowledge the Jews' right to live in tranquillity. Rabin told me with satisfaction that as prime minister he repeatedly ordered the army to remove illegal Jewish settlements from the West Bank, "because I wanted to keep the occupied territory clear of Jewish people, because I was ready to give this territory back in the context of peace." Rabin maintained steadfastly that in his preoccupation with borders, his objective was to make not the *Greater* Israel for which the Revisionists yearned but only a more secure Israel.

Still, the mighty force Rabin had been so instrumental in creating was at the disposal of whatever ideology governed Israel. Mainstream Zionism, however benign its intentions, had no mandate to rule Israel forever. The next prime minister was free to use Israel's military forces as he judged best.

The next prime minister was Menachem Begin, a Zionist who did not hold to the Mainstream's dream. The next government was Revisionist in its ideology, and it was prepared to go beyond the mission of defense to assign to Israel's armed forces a far more contentious set of imperatives. The military power that Rabin had imparted to the Jewish state had acquired a dynamic of its own. Rabin's triumph was put to Revisionism's purposes.

8

Revisionism's Triumph

MENACHEM BEGIN AND HIS ALLIES, at first, did not understand the significance of the Sinai II agreement. On the eve of ratification, Likud and the religious parties rallied some twenty-five thousand demonstrators for tumultuous street protests. Gush Emunim, Rabbi Levinger's organization of zealots dedicated to settling the West Bank, confronted Kissinger in Jerusalem with placards and banners, many vilifying him with anti-Semitic epithets, others accusing him of betraying the Jews. Rabbi Kook, the oracle of religious Zionism, proclaimed his distrust of Sinai II on grounds that Kissinger was married to a non-Jewish woman. After a tempestuous debate in the Knesset, Begin rounded up forty-three members, more than a third of the total body, to vote against the agreement.

Geula Cohen was in the front rank in the opposition, leading demonstrators in the streets. When I asked her to explain her objections, she said they were based on military security but she added that the Jews also had historical claims, had they chosen to assert them, strong enough to justify their keeping the Sinai. By giving up the mountain passes, Israel put itself in military jeopardy, she said, and by surrendering the oil fields, in economic jeopardy. Cohen dismissed as insignificant the concessions Israel received from Sadat in return for the territory. As for the political and economic commitments made to Israel by the United States, she had given them little thought. As a practical exchange, Cohen said, Sinai II was a "silly bargain."

Mainly, however, Geula Cohen was offended by the principle of territorial withdrawal. She considered the retreat from territory as contrary in itself to the purposes of Zionism.

"The Jews did not come back to Israel to make peace or even to be safe," she declared, "but to build a nation on the lands given to us by the Bible."

To dramatize her dissent, Geula Cohen placed herself one day at the head of a protesting crowd in Jerusalem and was arrested. It was her first arrest, she told me with some satisfaction, since her days in the underground. In the years that followed, she continued to place herself at the head of protests, energetically contesting every territorial concession that Israel proposed to make.

After the War of Independence, Geula Cohen enrolled as a student at the Hebrew University in Jerusalem and received a master's degree in Jewish philosophy. Having married during the war, in a thrilling secret ceremony which took place under the noses of the British police, she gave birth in the 1950s to a son, but she admitted it was not easy for her to adjust to family requirements, or to peacetime life. For a few years, she worked with a group of former colleagues from the underground on a small magazine promoting Revisionist ideas. Later she wrote a memoir of her underground days, heavily ideological but almost poetic in its personal passion. In 1960, she took a job with the conservative newspaper *Ma'ariv*, one of Israel's popular dailies, in the columns of which she kept up the struggle for Revisionism's unrequited goals.

"I was very much worried about the problem of the borders before 1967," she said, "and I wrote in *Ma'ariv* that now is the time to talk about Hebron and Bethlehem. Everybody said I was dreaming and I am so unrealistic. And I said, 'Okay, maybe so, but these are our places, and to go there is not to go as occupiers but as liberators, even if there is not now any chance.'

"Once I interviewed Ben-Gurion, two weeks before the Six-Day War—you can read it in *Ma'ariv*—and I asked him, 'What will you say to your grandchild if he wants to write a song of longing about East Jerusalem?' and he answered, 'If he wants to write, let him write, but I'll advise him not to.' I could not understand Ben-Gurion, or why no one wanted to think about the territory beforehand."

In those days, when there seemed to be no place in Israel for Revisionist activism, Geula Cohen thought of herself as an educational missionary. In addition to writing, she traveled around Israel's schools, offering philosophical lectures to students, conveying to them what she believed Zionism and Judaism really were. She was also among the first in Israel to promote aggressively the cause of Jewish emigration from the Soviet Union. Most Israelis acknowledged the integrity of Geula Cohen's political commitment. Young or old, almost all admired this fiery, dark-eyed woman, legendary heroine of the underground wars. But few, in those days, followed her lead.

It was not until 1970, when Begin resigned from the cabinet over Golda Meir's acceptance of Resolution 242, that Geula Cohen quit the newspaper for politics. A decade later, after she had broken with Begin over his signature on a peace treaty with Egypt, she said to me that she had always had reservations about his resolve. During Israel's war for independence, she had quit the Irgun, Begin's underground group, to join Lehi, a band that was politically more radical and tactically more audacious. She said she always believed Ben-Gurion had taken the threat of Begin too seriously in firing on the *Altalena.* "Begin jumps to attention and sings *Hatikvah,* but he does nothing," she said condescendingly. For years, she had refused membership in his Herut Party, though she shared its ideology, because Begin seemed more interested in controlling the party's machinery than in advancing its goals. It was only when he quit the Meir cabinet rather than acquiesce in the principle of territorial withdrawal, she said, that she announced, "I am coming to help you."

The first assignment Begin gave her, she recalled, was to establish a school of Zionist thought for Herut members and followers. It was, in a sense, a mission of propaganda, an extension of her educational work in Israeli schools and at *Ma'ariv*. Even in the underground she had been in propaganda, behind a microphone rather than a gun. But as Begin quickly learned, she was no one's mouthpiece. Geula Cohen had gone into politics to serve not a party but a cause, the one to which she had dedicated her life since the days of the British. It was not an idle boast when she said, "I'm still wearing khaki under my clothes. Since I joined the underground, I never really returned home." In time for the election of December 1973, Begin's party made her the highest woman on its electoral list, and she won a seat as a member of the Knesset.

Four years later, she was elected again, when Likud won a narrow victory over Labor and, for the first time, had enough seats in the Knesset to lead a government. The Sephardim, along with the Orthodox Jews, provided the margin of difference in the 1977 election. Begin became Israel's prime minister, the first to wear a *kipa,* which identified him as practicing Jew as much as Israeli. The election was a watershed in Israel's history, a major shift to the right, though its full significance was not at first appreciated.

The initial interpretation was that the voters had simply tired of the old faces. Labor, tarnished by scandals which touched even Rabin, had lost nineteen seats in the 120-member body, but most were not taken by Likud, which gained only four. They were won by a newly organized reformist party, which promptly disappeared. The swing in power took place within the Knesset itself, when the religious parties, Labor's historic supporters, decided to change partners to form a coalition with Likud. Only in retrospect was it clear that the election had signaled much more than a switch by a handful of Knesset members. It marked a decisive turn by Sephardim and Orthodox Jews, both leaders and voters, to more nationalistic, more militant, more populist government. But at the time, few Israelis saw it as more than a temporary digression from Labor's rule.

Menachem Begin, after nearly three decades in opposition, had finally carried Revisionism to the center of power, but he was a man not yet tested at governing. Nor was Revisionism, which offered little beyond the pledge to annex the West Bank, an ideology ready to be transformed into a political program. While thrashing about to find a governing theme, Begin maneuvered to form a cabinet. He did not find it easy, nor did the results promise Revisionism much reward.

Geula Cohen had been slated to become minister of education, but in the course of the give-and-take of bargaining, Begin assigned it to a Religious Party leader. The decision left her a disappointed backbencher, but freer than a minister to speak her mind.

The most controversial of Begin's appointments was Moshe Dayan, the former general and veteran Labor Party politician, whom he named foreign minister. Dayan, long frustrated in his ambition to become prime minister, later humbled while serving as defense minister during the Yom Kippur War, had in recent years adopted an increasingly hard line in external affairs. In violation of Labor Party rules, he had even voted against ratification of the Sinai II agreement. But notwithstanding his move toward the "hawks," Dayan was, by outlook and upbringing, a Mainstream Zionist. His appointment seemed to be Begin's way of telling the world that he would show restraint in carrying out Revisionism's expansionist imperatives.

"It was unbelievable that Begin would give the foreign ministry to Dayan," said Geula Cohen. "I think Begin's many years of being in opposition in the Knesset brought him to power with a feeling that he could not achieve what he had always preached. It is true the people of Israel did not want another war, and Begin had the reputation of a man of war. He didn't like it that everyone said the second he is in power he will declare war. I think it damaged Begin's self-confidence and made him weak.

"But don't misunderstand me. Though he made an agreement with Egypt that I didn't like, I know Begin really loves Eretz Yisrael. He was willing to give up the Sinai because, I think, he just did not believe the Sinai was part of Eretz Yisrael. And I don't think the Golan was on the Revisionists' map. That was not true of Judea and Samaria, of course. They were in Begin's blood. He believed that by giving the Sinai to Egypt, he could defend Judea and Samaria better.

"Begin wound up saying, 'Because I am a hawk, I can give away everything.' So he took Dayan and the Labor Party's compromising mentality, and he decided to make the peace with Egypt."

Like Golda Meir a decade earlier, Begin started his term in office on a fresh footing with the United States. When he became prime minister in May 1977, he faced in Washington a President who had arrived only a few months before him.

Jimmy Carter's position on the Middle East, within the framework of Washington's political struggles, was much closer to William Rogers's than to Henry Kissinger's. Though he assumed the same formal commitment as his predecessors to Israel's security, Carter did not see the Middle East as necessarily an arena of superpower rivalry, where Israel, wearing American colors, had to win every contest. In Carter's view, the Arab-Israeli conflict stood on its own, and peace in itself was in America's national interest. Carter placed the Middle East high on his list of diplomatic priorities. Even before Begin's term began, Carter came into sharp disagreement with Israel in announcing that Resolution 242, with its insistence on return to the 1967 borders, was the best available formula for a settlement.

No more than the Israelis themselves had Carter foreseen that the elections in Israel would transform the government. He initiated his peacemaking efforts while Rabin was still prime minister, and the proceedings were not auspicious. In meetings in early 1977, Carter took an instant dislike to the blunt ex-soldier, who was willing to compromise on nearly nothing. Carter greeted Begin's election almost with relief, but the feeling was short-lived. The President found Begin more congenial as a person, at least for a time, though by no means more conciliatory as a politician.

The trouble with Begin started early. Among Begin's first moves as prime minister was the initiation of policies to promote Jewish settlement in the occupied territories, a departure from Mainstream practice. Carter considered the move more provocative than anything Rabin had done. He was upset by Begin's reference to the West Bank not just as Judea and Samaria but as "liberated" rather than "occupied" land. When the two finally met in July, Begin lectured an impatient Carter on how Jewish rights on the West Bank derived from the Holocaust. The meeting was not successful.

But by the fall of his first year, Carter thought he saw an opening. He perceived that while Rabin did not have the Revisionist's designs on the West Bank, Begin did not have the soldier's strategic concerns in the Sinai. From that Carter concluded that Begin might be more generous than Rabin in trading territory for a peace with Egypt. In search of some defining political purpose for his regime, Begin repeatedly offered in his early months to return to a Geneva conference. In Geula Cohen's words, Begin, a conventional Revisionist thinker, "did not believe the Sinai was part of Eretz Yisrael." His readiness to bargain over the Sinai was the wedge that led, ultimately, to Camp David.

Still, the Sinai was not the only issue on the Middle East agenda, and it was far from the most difficult. Indeed, the differences separating Begin and Sadat over the Sinai were to prove readily negotiable. When the two finally met, they would argue long and hard over how much territory Israel was to cede in return for how much recognition from Egypt, but there was never real doubt the gap would be bridged. The crucial obstacle was Sadat's concern with the West Bank, along with the fate of the Palestinians who claimed it. The Arab-Israeli conflict began with the Palestinians, and over decades the problem had grown only worse.

In November of 1977, while Carter was floundering in maneuvers to organize peace talks, Sadat made his dramatic pilgrimage to Jerusalem. The sudden decision to make the visit was the product of his prolonged frustration during the Kissinger years over the failure of the peace process. Now Kissinger was gone, and Sadat convinced himself that an end to the Arab-Israeli conflict was within reach. What he saw were "psychological barriers" standing in the way of a stable, tranquil Middle East. His grand vision was for Egypt and Israel to move beyond a Sinai settlement to a *comprehensive* peace, sweeping clean the agenda of Arab-Israeli differences.

Sadat's visit was itself a public acknowledgment of Israeli legitimacy. For a settlement to go with it, Sadat was prepared not only to adopt the structure of Resolution 242 but to adorn it with the ornaments Israel wanted. Sadat's offer was full peace, according to Israel's understanding of the term. It embraced "normalization," as Rabin had defined it. What he asked in return was full restoration of the captured territories, the goal of the Arabs since 1967. In innocence, he believed he could make Begin see the logic, as well as the generosity, of his offer. He was convinced that by bringing his case directly to the Israeli capital, he could sweep away Israel's reservations and anxieties about peace.

I was in Israel when Sadat arrived and, of course, I will never forget the moment. Sadat, stepping from his plane, enveloped Golda Meir in smiles, made jokes with Ariel Sharon, told Dayan he need wait no longer for his phone call. Jews danced in the streets when Sadat's car reached Jerusalem, and I found it incredible, the following morning, to be talking with Egyptian journalists in the coffee shop of the King David Hotel. Sadat made a candid speech in English to the Knesset, setting out his terms, and at that moment the psychological barrier did indeed totter. In the ensuing days, Israel floated on a cloud of disbelief.

The one sour note I recall during those otherwise euphoric days was the anger of some young Arab men I encountered in the market in Jerusalem's Old City. They were convinced Sadat had come to Israel to sell them out. In Damascus, I learned later, rioting mobs protested Sadat's visit. Then and since, I have believed that Sadat made the journey in the conviction that he was serving the Arab cause, but the cynicism of the young Arabs in the Old City was ultimately to be justified. Whatever promise the visit held for the Palestinians, the reality came crashing down a few months later. The Palestinian issue, core of the Arab-Israeli conflict, remained unresolved, leaving peace a distant dream.

When Israel emerged from the intoxication of Sadat's visit, it was apparent no miracle of psychological metamorphosis had taken place. Sadat had been unequivocal in stating to the Israelis that he considered the Palestinians a moral responsibility that Egypt, the strongest of the Arab nations, owed to the Arab world. He declared that, much as he wanted a reconciliation with Israel, Egypt's honor would not permit the abandonment of responsibility. He would not make a separate Sinai peace. But Israel, though ready to negotiate, was not prepared to be reborn. Israelis did not shed their uncertainties and mistrust, and the differences between Arabs and Jews over the West Bank, Sadat's visit notwithstanding, did not vanish.

For Begin, as for Geula Cohen, the West Bank was more important than peace. Rabbi Levinger, the Gush Emunim leader, sneered at the entire negotiating process, blaming it on the "virus of peace." For all three, Judea and Samaria defined the ideology that governed their lives. Begin would not consider any compromise of Israel's claim to the West Bank, much less a Palestinian state there or an agreement that would legitimize the PLO. Begin's objective in seeking a peace with Egypt was precisely to relieve the international pressure imposed on Israel to give up Judea and Samaria. For Cohen and Rabbi Levinger, peace with Egypt was in itself conceding too much.

Dayan's vision was somewhat different from Begin's. Dayan argued, within the context of Mainstream Zionism, that making peace with Egypt would remove the biggest Arab army from the field. Far from caring about Egyptian honor or Sadat's duty, Dayan schemed to obtain peace terms that would isolate Egypt from the Arab world. For Begin, the loss of the Sinai was a reasonable price to pay for the realization of Revisionism's territorial doctrine. Dayan's interest in peace with Egypt was the enhancement of Israel's security.

After Sadat's visit to Jerusalem, reaching an agreement took nearly two years. Meetings were held all over the world, at summit, ministerial and technical levels. All of them were contentious. The climax came at President Carter's retreat at Camp David in the fall of 1978. Sadat fought tenaciously for Palestinian rights throughout the talks there, and without Dayan's prodding, it is likely Begin would have given up on the negotiations. Faced with deadlock, Dayan suggested a plan of "autonomy" for the Arabs of the occupied territories, a program he had himself promoted when he was defense minister in successive Labor governments. Largely to avert Carter's wrath, Begin consented. Under its terms (see Appendix I), a decision on the sovereignty of the West Bank and the Gaza Strip was to be deferred for five years. Meanwhile, the Israeli army was to withdraw from the territories, leaving the Palestinians under the direction of an "elected self-governing authority." The compromise saved the negotiations, and a formal peace treaty was signed the following year. But the psychological breakthrough on which Sadat had counted never took place and a "Camp David spirit," implying an attitude of conciliation among the participants, never existed.

Though he had accepted "full autonomy" to save face, Sadat in fact yielded on the issue which he had claimed was the *sine qua non* of peace. In the Camp David agreement, Israel met his demand for the full return of the Sinai, while he in turn pledged the "normalization" of relations that was so important to Rabin and the Mainstream Zionists. Egypt also agreed to the Sinai's demilitarization. But Sadat did not get a homeland for the Palestinians, much less a state, and after the documents were signed even "autonomy" turned out to be a sham.

Begin placed such narrow limits on what "autonomy" meant that, shortly afterward, Dayan himself resigned in indignation. Months of bargaining after the treaty was signed yielded no agreement on implementation on that provision of the Camp David accords. "Autonomy," having begun as a sop to Carter, ended as ashes for Sadat. The peace Israel and Egypt finally made was precisely what Sadat had said he would not accept. It was an Egyptian peace.

Yet, notwithstanding its shortcomings, the Egyptian-Israeli treaty was a triumph for peacemaking. It set a precedent, in proving there *could* be a formal settlement, with mutual recognition, between Israel and the Arabs. It demonstrated to Israelis that relations with Arabs need not inevitably be hostile, to Arabs that they could swallow the concept of a sovereign Jewish state without choking. It not only broke the cycle of war that existed between Arabs and Jews in the Middle East in the twentieth century but transformed the pattern of relations that had existed between them for a millennium. Future peacemaking was made easier by establishment of the principle that Arabs and Jews *could* coexist in sovereign nations.

But the treaty was not, as many believed, a step in a process marching inevitably toward full Arab-Israeli peace. President Carter and his company seemed certain that, whatever the deficiencies in the machinery, the *momentum* given peace by the treaty was strong enough to overcome resistance from whatever quarter. Sadat left Camp David with a vested interest in believing the same. He understood the survival of his authority depended on his demonstrating that the peace process contained a dynamism which, within some reasonable time, would bring a resolution of Israel's disputes with all of the Arab world.

Begin and his Revisionist followers, however, made no secret of their determination to use the treaty's machinery to attain precisely the opposite result. They wanted the treaty to lead nowhere. That is where Rabin, Dayan and much of Mainstream Zionism also wanted it to go. The treaty satisfied the concerns of the Revisionists/Mainstream over territory, of the other over security. In terms of advancing peace in the Middle East, both achieved their objectives. Important as it is in itself, the treaty has *led* nowhere.

Geula Cohen, however, did not share Begin's conviction that Camp David strengthened Israel's hold on the West Bank. She was outraged at the provision of the treaty that required dismantling

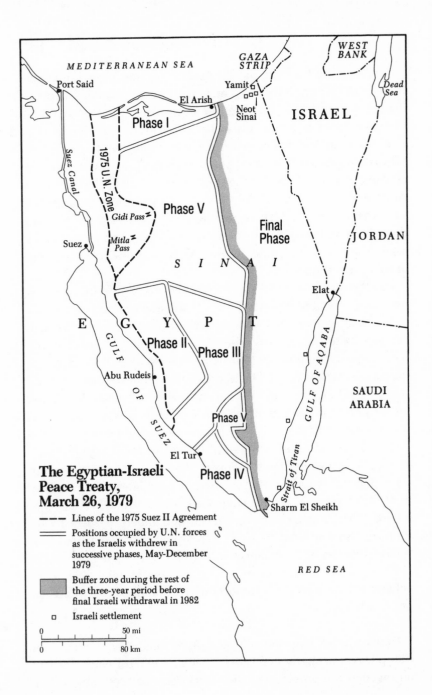

MEDITERRANEAN SEA

Port Said

El Arish

Phase I

1975 U.N. Zone

Gidi Pass

Mitla Pass

Suez

Suez Canal

GAZA STRIP

Yamit

Neot Sinai

ISRAEL

WEST BANK

Dead Sea

Phase V

S I N A I

Final Phase

JORDAN

Elat

E G Y P T

Phase II

Phase III

Abu Rudeis

GULF OF SUEZ

Phase V

El Tur

Phase IV

GULF OF AQABA

SAUDI ARABIA

Strait of Tiran

Sharm El Sheikh

The Egyptian-Israeli Peace Treaty, March 26, 1979

‑‑‑‑ Lines of the 1975 Suez II Agreement

═══ Positions occupied by U.N. forces as the Israelis withdrew in successive phases, May–December 1979

▨ Buffer zone during the rest of the three-year period before final Israeli withdrawal in 1982

□ Israeli settlement

RED SEA

0 ———————— 50 mi

0 ———————— 80 km

of settlements that Jews had set up in the Sinai. She insisted that, whatever Begin's rationalization, such a provision foreshadowed Israel's eventual surrender of the West Bank.

"I don't want peace," she said, "if I cannot have Judea and Samaria." To Cohen, the principle of exchanging land for peace, especially land where Jews had settled, was in itself objectionable. Settlements were more vital to Zionism than peace, she declared, and if the two were in conflict, she would not hesitate to choose the settlements.

Begin did not deny that at Camp David he had retreated from old vows. Geula Cohen taunted him in the Knesset, proclaiming that he, chief of the Revisionists, heir to Jabotinsky, should be ashamed to be Israel's first leader to dismantle Jewish settlements. Begin suffered the blows, acknowledging the pain.

Cohen and the diehard Revisionists were not the only critics of the Camp David agreement. Yigal Allon led a contingent of Labor Party members, Rabin among them, who protested bitterly that abandonment of the Sinai settlements put Israel's security in jeopardy. In fact, Begin had tried tenaciously at Camp David to hold on to them, but Sadat made clear that his own breaking point lay in his demand to get back every inch of his lost land. Ironically, Dayan, who as Labor's minister of defense had forcefully advocated moving Jews into the Sinai for security reasons, became at Camp David the chief advocate for moving them out. Reluctantly, Begin had deferred to Dayan's judgment. But he told the Knesset that if it wanted peace, it would have to share responsibility. By a margin of 84 to 19, the Knesset endorsed the agreement. In the end, the Labor contingent supported Begin. Geula Cohen, however, voted no.

In September 1978, when the text of the Camp David accord was formally placed on the Knesset's agenda, Cohen took the floor that Begin resign. During the debate, she created such a rumpus that, after repeated calls to order, she was forcibly evicted. It was the first of her many evictions. "It's not that I can't control myself," she said later. "It's that I don't want to." Camp David transformed Cohen from a Likud backbencher to an internationally celebrated troublemaker.

To celebrate the signing of the formal peace treaty (see Appendix J) six months later, Carter himself came before the Israeli parliament. Cohen was quiet while he spoke, but her dignified silence gave way when Begin mounted the podium to talk. She screamed "traitor" at him and heckled his every word. Once more, she was bodily removed. After her departure, Begin smiled weakly at Carter and said, "You see how beautiful is our democracy, Mr. President," and Carter smiled weakly back.

A few months afterward, Geula Cohen joined a band of three hundred settlers, led by militants from Gush Emunim, in standing against evacuation of the Sinai village of Neot Sinai. The village had been founded by Begin's own party. Begin even said at one time that he would retire there. But Neot Sinai was included in the first of succeeding segments of territory scheduled under the peace treaty for return to Egypt. As the day of the transfer approached, the settlers encircled the property with barbed wire and armed themselves with pipes and stones, torches and gasoline, and even with some guns, announcing that whoever sought to evict them would have to risk the consequences. Two cabinet ministers who later arrived as mediators were shoved, spat upon and driven away. When an army unit approached the barbed-wire perimeter, the settlers threw torches and stones, injuring seven soldiers.

Finally Begin himself, abroad at the time, pledged to make one last plea to Sadat—predictably, with no results—to stay. Only then did the settlers agree to withdraw, though as part of the deal, they extracted from Begin a promise, which many Israelis considered extortion, to have the state pay a large indemnity to the dispossessed. Neot Sinai forced Israelis to take note of the kind of violence, practiced in the name of Zionism, which had started in the West Bank soon after Begin took office. Benefiting from the government's tacit acquiescence, it had become part of the routine of life for West Bank Arabs. At Neot Sinai, the settlers were saying it would spread through all Israel if the government tried to return more of the occupied territories.

It was just after the Neot Sinai episode that I met Geula Cohen for the first time. She received me in her small apartment, decorated with Arab artifacts, above a supermarket in a working-class district of Tel Aviv. By then, she had passed over into the Knesset opposition, and was in the process of forming her own party, to be known as Tehiya (Renaissance), which would stand to the right of Likud. She was much gentler in her speech, and much more forthright about her political tactics, than I had anticipated. It was the eve of *shabbat,* and she was preparing supper for her son, who was returning for the weekend from the army.

"Begin has failed in every way," she told me. "He is a liar when he says he is bringing peace. Anyone can be a great leader if he agrees to give everything away. That's not statesmanship. It's not even peace. What's the big deal?

"I went to Neot Sinai to identify with the resistance. I believe that the first millimeter of land we give back represents every kilometer of the land of Israel. I went there, as a member of the Knesset and a Jew, because I think that's where Israel's integrity begins, and that's where my own home begins. I was not elected for the purpose of expelling Jews from the land but for the contrary. The tragedy is that the government—a government formed by my own Likud Party—decided to expel these people. Our government gave the order to do the work of Sadat, and it was my duty to resist."

Three years later, in the spring of 1982, Geula Cohen stood arm in arm with Rabbi Levinger and another contingent from Gush Emunim, vowing to prevent the army from evacuating Yamit, the chief town in what was then Israel's last remaining sector in the Sinai. For a few weeks, a new *Altalena* affair seemed to threaten, with the ironic difference that this time Begin and the Revisionists were not insurgents but in power. Finally, the Begin cabinet made major financial concessions to the Yamit settlers, as it had to the settlers at Neot Sinai. Begin also repeated his vows that Israel would never abandon the West Bank.

"Tomorrow they'll decide to give Jerusalem back," Geula Cohen said sardonically at that time, "and they'll do it with an orchestra and a ceremony. And everyone will tell me, 'Shh! Don't interrupt.' In Yamit, Gush Emunim's policy was to use only passive resistance, and never put a hand on a Jewish soldier. But in Judea and Samaria and the Golan Heights, they will not stick to passive resistance. I am sure—I am *afraid*—they will use guns. For myself, though I identify morally with resistance, I stop at violence against Jews. I think Israelis will draw the same line, and a civil war can be avoided. But the line between passive resistance and armed violence is very thin."

While Begin struggled with Jewish opposition on one side of the line, Sadat had to confront the Arabs on the other. Carter had anticipated that Egypt, after Camp David, would serve as a bridge to the Arab world, promoting the virtues of the peace process. But far from perceiving virtues in Camp David, the Arab world was unforgiving of a treaty that gave Egypt back the Sinai while leaving the remainder of the occupied territories in Israeli hands.

It is reasonable to ask whether Sadat could have left Camp David with any agreement at all of which the Arab world would have approved. From the start, Syria made clear it would not cooperate with Egypt in negotiating with Israel, much less show sympathy with Egypt for negotiating alone. So did the PLO. One can argue whether, as "rejectionists," they were uninterested in any peace whatever, or only in peace on terms to which Israel would agree. Whichever was the case, by the time the Camp David negotiations opened, the "rejectionists" had succeeded in turning upon Sadat the Arab world's chronic penchant for suspicion. By the time Camp David was over, Egypt was an outcast.

In battling at Camp David for a settlement that would resolve the Palestinian issue, Sadat had warned of precisely this outcome.

He tried to persuade the United States and Israel that it was to their advantage for Egypt to remain the dominant power among the Arabs, and he pointed to the dangers that would accompany a seizure by the "rejectionists" of Arab leadership. Carter, in the interest of an ongoing peace process, joined Sadat in pleading the case to the Israelis. He failed, however, because Begin's attention was fixed on Israeli rule of the West Bank, and Dayan had in mind a totally different view from Sadat's of the kind of relationship with Egypt that would best serve Israel's interests.

As Dayan makes clear in his memoirs, the Israelis had gone to Camp David with the clear objective of isolating Egypt from the Arab world, in order to breach the unity of the enemy's military front. In formulating Israel's plan, Dayan was not thinking of a Middle East at peace, as Carter was, but of a Middle East at war. Egypt had long-standing security commitments to the Arab states. Dayan's goal was to unhinge these commitments, so that the Israeli army would not again have to fight a war on more than one front.

Israel demanded that Egypt pledge expressly, as a provision of a peace agreement, to remain uninvolved in the event of a war on its northern front. The demand presented a terrible dilemma for Sadat, who recognized that acquiescence would leave the Arabs without a military option for regaining the West Bank and the Golan Heights. But that was precisely what Dayan wanted. When the Israeli delegation threatened to leave Camp David over this issue, Sadat saw his vision of regaining the Sinai vanishing before him. He swallowed, and took the pledge.

Sadat was thus in a fragile position when the "autonomy" plan was presented to the Arabs. Jordan, asked to participate in negotiating its implementation, refused outright. The Arabs disputed Carter's view of "autonomy" as an opening to Palestinian rule, if not to Arab sovereignty. They saw it, instead, as Egypt's legitimation of Israeli occupation. Reflecting the Arab position in boycotting the "autonomy" talks, the Jordanians argued that negotiating with Begin would not have produced favorable results under any circumstances. They may have been correct. But they missed an opportunity to weaken Israeli control over the West Bank and Gaza by waiving any influence in advance. Their move compounded the Arab world's disarray and played into Begin's hands.

Amid charges of betrayal, the Arab governments drove Sadat from their counsels, burning the bridge Carter hoped to build to Arab participation in an ever-expanding peace process. As head of the most powerful Arab nation, Sadat had once been persuaded that his leadership of the Arab world would permit him to be the peacemaker for the entire Middle East. He realized only at Camp David that neither Arabs nor Israelis would let him be both. The Israelis, making clear that the Sinai was the only territory they intended to return, had nullified his promise to the Arabs of a *comprehensive* peace. Jordan and Syria, with no prospect of regaining their lost territory, concluded that to follow Sadat's lead offered nothing to them. Thus, to Carter's chagrin, Camp David left Sadat neither a leader nor a peacemaker. In fact, it left him with no further role at all to play in the complex politics of peacemaking in the Middle East.

The "rejectionists" had triumphed, in making a pariah of Sadat, but it was a pyrrhic victory. In depriving him of his natural friends, their revenge forced him to rely increasingly on the goodwill of his former enemy. Their decision played into Dayan's strategy. However justified they believed it to be, isolating Egypt would prove costly to them in battles yet unfought. Playing its traditional role as leader in the Arab world, Egypt might have served as a restraining influence on Israel, most notably in Lebanon. Its isolation, which made the Arabs weaker, also left the Middle East a more volatile, more dangerous place than before.

The full military implications of Egypt's neutralization may not have figured in the calculations of Begin and his team at Camp David. The discussions there dwelt upon the threat that Arab armies posed to the security of Israel. There is no evidence of discussion on the contrary hypothesis: that Israel, in the absence of Egyptian constraint, might be a danger to the security of the Arabs. Such a risk had not occurred to Carter, and it seems likely that it had not occurred to Sadat either. If the "rejectionists" had considered it, they surely reacted unwisely, for in pushing Egypt away, they were left alone to face an Israel that was to become increasingly adventurous.

Soon after the Camp David treaty was signed, Dayan passed from the scene, along with Ezer Weizman, the defense minister, the principal proponents of peace in Begin's cabinet. They were succeeded by Ariel Sharon as defense minister and Yitzhak Shamir as foreign minister, both doctrinaire Revisionists. Sharon and Shamir would understand clearly the potential of Egypt's neutralization. For them, it presented not so much the prospect of greater security for Israel as an opportunity to satisfy Revisionist ambitions. Egypt's departure from military calculations was an opportunity which they, with Begin's endorsement, were soon to exploit.

Yitzhak Rabin had not intended to be sardonic in commenting on Likud's stormy objections in 1975 to ratification of the Sinai II agreement, his own chief contribution to Middle East diplomacy.

"That our policy provoked the anger of the Likud opposition," he has written, " . . . has not prevented Mr. Begin's government from reaping the fruits of our labors."

Bitter fruits.

Seven years after Sinai II, three years after signing the treaty of peace with Egypt, Begin sent the Israeli army into Lebanon. What was initially described as a limited incursion quickly revealed itself as a full-scale invasion. Rabin bitterly opposed the operation, which took six hundred fifty Israeli lives, for no ostensible gain. Three years after the war began, serving as defense minister under the successor government, Rabin found himself cleaning up the debris. Whatever the strategic or political justification, or the provocations to which it responded, the invasion would surely not have taken place if the military power of Israel had not been swelled by Sinai II, and if the armed forces of Egypt had not been neutralized by the Camp David treaty.

So convinced had Carter been at Camp David of improvement

in Middle East stability that he expressed, in a conversation with Dayan, a hope that the American government would soon be able to reduce the financial contributions pledged to Israel under the Sinai II accord. Dayan, asserting that Israel's interest lay in limiting its dependence on the United States, replied to Carter that he shared the hope.

The actual outcome was quite different. The Camp David treaty had presumably enhanced Israel's military security by removing the most powerful Arab state from the list of its enemies. The treaty further required that the Sinai, once returned to Egypt's control, be demilitarized, providing Israel with no less "strategic depth" than it had before. Yet at no time were there actual discussions between Carter and the Israelis, at Camp David or later, on reducing the military, financial or diplomatic commitments that Kissinger had made in 1975. In execution, in fact, the treaty imposed on the United States even further financial burdens than before.

One might construct a syllogism of American-Israeli relations composed of the following parts: If the objective of the American financial contributions under Sinai II was to promote Israeli security, and if Israel became more secure still under the provisions of the Camp David treaty, then the requirement for American financial contributions should have declined.

The corollary that suggests itself is that if American contributions did not decline, the reason must have been that Israel, with American approval, put the money to some other use. Few observers would contend that, by any reasonable definition, Israel's military policy in the eight years that followed Camp David was focused on security. It was, rather, put to the realization of Revisionist political doctrine. One of its exercises was the invasion of Lebanon. Indeed, the corollary explains why much of the world has held the United States responsible for the militarization of Israel's foreign relations, as well as Israel's indifference to making peace.

Ronald Reagan took over from Jimmy Carter as President of the United States in January 1981. In Israel in the same year, Begin was elected to a new term as prime minister. Begin was delighted with the election of Reagan, who endeared himself from the start by withdrawing American opposition to Israel's West Bank settlement policy, which Carter had bitterly opposed.

Begin's reelection campaign in the summer of 1981 had prefigured major changes in the policies of the Israeli government. It was a campaign characterized by blatant ethnic appeals, stirring up latent anti-Ashkenazi animosities in Sephardi voters. Begin made no protest when gangs of Sephardi youths viciously disrupted Labor Party rallies, shouting "Begin, Begin, King of Israel." The campaign was the most disruptive in Israel's history. It suggested—correctly, as it turned out—that Begin's first term would be looked upon as tame by comparison.

Begin found sympathetic souls among Reagan's men, particularly Alexander Haig, the new secretary of state. In contrast to Carter's views, their attitude was reminiscent of the Nixon-Kissinger vision of the Middle East. Haig had actually worked under Kissinger in the White House and, like Reagan himself, shared Kissinger's conviction that the world was an arena of immutable antagonism between Communism and Freedom. Haig was also a general, former commander of NATO, and he sympathized with the Israeli leadership's ready disposition to rely on military power.

Begin first signaled his new aggressiveness in June, when he dispatched the Israeli air force to bomb a nuclear reactor in Baghdad. Though some within the Reagan administration were livid, Secretary of State Haig came to Begin's defense. Haig acknowledged in his memoirs that "there were obvious dangers for the United States in this action. American equipment, delivered to the Israelis for defensive purposes only, had been used in the attack." But then, echoing the arguments of Henry Kissinger, his mentor, Haig concluded that "our strategic interests would not be served by policies that humiliated and weakened Israel." In the end, the American chastisement was limited to a brief delay in the shipment to Israel of four F-16 aircraft.

At the same time, Israel involved itself more publicly on the

Phalangist side in the Lebanese civil war, bombing Palestinian refugee camps and, on one occasion, coming close to war by shooting down two Syrian helicopters. In July, Israeli planes bombed downtown Beirut, in a "surgical strike" that was directed against PLO offices but left some three hundred civilians dead.

Washington conveyed public disapproval of the Beirut bombing. A few weeks later, however, Reagan received the Israeli prime minister in what Begin described as "the warmest atmosphere I ever enjoyed in Washington." PLO forces in Lebanon retaliated against the Beirut bombing by shelling the depressed development towns of northern Israel. Begin's campaign promise to the largely Sephardi population there was contained in the slogan "No more Katyushas," a reference to the Soviet-made weapon associated with the PLO. Washington, no less than Begin's local audience, understood the slogan as a pledge to invade Lebanon to destroy the PLO.

The social disorder that accompanied the electoral campaign in the summer of 1981 hardly surprised Begin. He had courted it, as a means of wooing his constituency. In the balloting, 70 percent of Likud's votes came from Sephardim, while 70 percent of Labor's vote came from Ashkenazim. The margin that separated the two blocs on election day added up to only a single Knesset seat, barely enough for Begin to form a new cabinet. But the campaign demonstrated that Israel's right wing, far from being the transient majority it had seemed to many in 1977, had become the dominant force in Israeli politics. At the same time, it conveyed a willingness to sanction violence throughout the society.

Begin's second cabinet was far more Revisionist than the first. The stalwarts of Camp David—Foreign Minister Dayan and Defense Minister Weizman—were gone. Yitzhak Shamir, the new foreign minister, had come to politics from the Stern Gang, where he had been one of Geula Cohen's commanders. Ariel Sharon, the new defense minister, arrived from the officers' corps where, even among hard-liners, he was considered extreme. Far from favoring "autonomy" in the territories, these two urged Palestinians to migrate across the river to Jordan. Sharon, particularly, advocated to the Palestinians that they overthrow King Hussein and establish their own state there.

In the Knesset, Geula Cohen's recently formed Tehiya Party had won three seats in the election and, in opposition, goaded Begin relentlessly. Cohen saw herself as Begin's conscience, tormenting him with reminders of what he had been before he gave in to the expectations of high office. She persistently mocked him on the Knesset floor for observing a cease-fire with the PLO on the Lebanese border, negotiated by the Americans in the summer of 1981 after the shelling of the development towns. In December, she announced her plans to force a Knesset vote on a bill to annex the Golan Heights, which Begin forestalled by abruptly rushing through a bill of his own.

Passage of the Golan annexation law was a challenge to the United States and to Egypt, as well as to Syria. Among them, however, Washington alone had means to redress the situation. The annexation clearly violated international law, and confirmed Syria's contention that only war could dislodge Israel from the territories. Sadat, who had been assassinated in Cairo a few weeks before, looked foolish in retrospect for the confidence he had placed in Israel's goodwill. The annexation, coming not long after the bombing of the Iraqi reactor, signaled unambiguously how Begin intended to exploit Egypt's self-imposed impotence. As for the Reagan administration, it complained of not being notified in advance of the measure, and announced the suspension of a recently negotiated American-Israeli agreement on strategic cooperation. The feebleness of the gesture, however, made clear Washington's indulgence of the annexation itself.

Reagan's White House said very early that it had no intention of interfering with Israel's exercise of its military power. Reagan admired tough little anti-Communist Israel. Secretary Haig even tried resurrecting Dulles's old dream of uniting a Middle East alliance against Communism, with the difference that he would have had the Israeli army serve as its hinge. It did not occur to

Haig that a precondition of his plan was peace between Israel and the Arabs, a goal in which the Reagan administration showed little interest. Not surprisingly, Haig's concept died quickly in the Arab capitals, and Israel's army resumed its posture as guardian of America's Middle East interests.

In his brief career as secretary of state, Haig got along particularly well with Israeli Defense Minister Sharon. The two communicated regularly on a common anti-Communist policy and, in November 1981, drafted the document known as the Memorandum of Understanding (see Appendix K), in which the United States and Israel pledged "to act cooperatively and in a timely manner" to meet any Soviet threat. It was a symbolic statement, leaving contractual obligations unclear, but it brought the two countries closer than ever before to formalizing their military relationship. Though execution of the Memorandum was suspended in protest of Israel's annexation of the Golan Heights, Washington did not repudiate it. The Memorandum was the Reagan administration's proclamation that, whatever their differences, the United States valued its alliance with Israel more than ever before.

Two weeks after the signature of the Memorandum of Understanding, Sharon delivered a remarkably candid speech to Tel Aviv's Institute of Strategic Studies. In it, he outlined his concept of Israel's preeminence in the Middle East. It was an audacious warning to the Soviet Union, as well as to the Arabs, that Israel would tolerate no challenge to its own dominance in the region.

Sharon began by charging Washington with "strategic passivity," in permitting "Soviet advances in the region . . . during the 1970's." The remark was obviously directed at the Carter administration, and its disposition to have Israel return the occupied territories. It was Sharon's way of placing on the record, for Washington to see, his vow that Israel would withdraw no further.

In stating that "the PLO poses a *political* threat to the very existence of the State of Israel," Sharon was acknowledging the insignificance of the PLO's *military* arm. Retrospectively, the words became justification for the military assault on Lebanon, which was directed at the PLO's political infrastructure.

Sharon's most revealing assertion, however, was in his claim of boundaries for an Israeli sphere of influence. "Israel's national security interests," he stated, "are influenced by developments and events far beyond the direct confrontation area where Israel had focused its attention in the past. . . . Israel's sphere of strategic and security interest must be broadened to include in the 1980s countries such as Turkey, Iran and Pakistan and regions such as the Persian Gulf and Africa, particularly the countries of North and Central Africa."

No matter how sympathetically the assertion is examined, it emerges as fantasy, except that as minister of defense, Sharon was stating *policy.* The fantasy was that Israel, a tiny country of barely three and a half million citizens, would exercise strategic dominance over an area covering five thousand miles end to end and containing hundreds of millions of inhabitants, nearly all of them Muslim. It seemed no less audacious that of the countries he cited by name as being in Israel's sphere, the United States was formally allied in NATO with one, Turkey, and had close military ties with another, Pakistan.

Sharon ended the speech with the assertion: "The Memorandum of Understanding on Strategic Cooperation just signed between the United States and Israel constitutes a new starting line for a fruitful and mutually beneficial security relationship . . . consistent with the defense policy I have just described." It is not implausible to read into these words the implication that Washington was familiar with the ideas Sharon expressed. If the Reagan administration did not give them its formal endorsement, neither did it ever express any protest of the speech.

Sharon's strategic conception was surely the high-water mark of militant Zionism, a declaration of the triumph of Revisionism that transcended Jabotinsky's wildest dreams. Israel had by far the strongest army in the Middle East. With Egypt's departure, the Arabs were in disarray, weaker than they had ever been. Israel's security was guaranteed by the greatest of the superpowers, which bestowed upon it a huge annual subsidy and all the arms it needed, while imposing on it no political limitations. In his speech, Sharon was extolling the power of an irresistible military machine which had gone out of control. Successive Labor Party governments, proclaiming the humane values of Mainstream Zionism and relying on the decent intentions of the United States, had built this juggernaut. But it was now Revisionism's to use.

Six months later, in June of 1982, Begin and Sharon sent the Israeli army into Lebanon. Its first objective was to destroy the PLO as the political organization of the Palestinian movement, so that no cohesive opposition would be left to Israel's absorption of the West Bank. Its second goal was to replace Syria as the arbiter of the chaotic communal conflict in Lebanon, building from the rubble of civil war there a government dominated by Christians who would be sympathetic to Israel.

The army achieved neither objective. Instead, it counted 650 dead and 3,800 wounded. It suffered the shame of the massacres at Sabra and Shatila and the humiliation of retreat before bands of Shiite irregulars. Its morale was shattered and, according to Israeli critics, its fighting capacity severely impaired. Three years later, it stumbled out of Lebanon, badly wounded, its reputation of invincibility shattered.

For the United States, the invasion of Lebanon was also a serious defeat. The reason was not that Israel, its Middle East outpost, was ultimately forced to withdraw from the battlefield without a clear victory, though that would have been Kissinger's measure. The reason was that America's client chose in the first place to invade an Arab country with which it was not actively engaged in hostilities. The invasion—if not endorsed then surely tolerated by the White House—caused a rift in American relations with the Arab world that has not yet been repaired.

Though Sharon alone knew how large the assault was to be, the intention of the Begin government to invade had for months been an open secret. I visited Israel and Lebanon late in 1981, and wrote that war was simply waiting to happen. It was not speculation. The Israelis were saying as much. Certainly, the Reagan administration was as aware as I that the invasion was pending.

Haig writes in his memoirs that he warned Begin repeatedly the United States would not support Israeli action in Lebanon without an "internationally recognized provocation." This was an invitation to find one, which Israel had no trouble doing. When a prominent Israeli diplomat was shot in London, Israel blamed the PLO and its waiting army moved. Though subsequent investigation established that the PLO had not been responsible for the shooting, it hardly mattered. The Begin government concluded quite reasonably that it had met Washington's terms.

Though most of the world knew nothing, of course, of Haig's double message, America's involvement was established to the satisfaction of the Arabs by the American label on nearly every weapon of the invading army. Among the powers, furthermore, the United States alone supported Israel's action at the United Nations. It took several months of heavy casualties and few achievements for most Israelis to acknowledge that the invasion had been detrimental to Israel's interest. From the start, it was hard to establish what the Reagan administration thought the interest of the United States in the invasion might have been.

The invasion of Lebanon was, in the eyes of the Arab world, America's consummate act of contempt. As if to underline this contempt, the White House chose that moment to announce reinstatement of the Memorandum of Understanding, negotiated between Haig and Sharon the previous fall but kept in suspense in protest of Begin's annexation of the Golan Heights. Shortly after the invasion, a binational strategic body, organized under the terms of the Memorandum to exchange military information, met with some fanfare. Reagan's action showed that he still attached a far higher priority to military relations with Israel than to any relations at all with the Arab world.

The Arab world, for the most part, reacted with disbelief at the indulgence Washington showed to the Lebanon invasion. Arabs rarely think of America as a colonial power, or identify it with injuries inflicted on them by the West during the colonial era. When they argue that Israel is a product of Western imperialism, they blame Britain and France. Arabs are attracted to Americans personally, in contrast to the reservations they have about Britons and Frenchmen, and the innate suspicion that they feel toward Russians. When Kissinger came to them in 1973 with the claim that Washington could persuade Israel to exchange territory for peace, they took his words as a pledge. They also breathed a collective sigh of relief at the opportunity to distance themselves not just from the Soviet Union but from the Russians as individuals.

Since then, the United States has been the preeminent foreign influence in the Arab world, while the Soviet Union has held on by its fingertips. If Moscow has remained paramount in Syria and within the PLO, it is because Washington has supported Israel's refusal to strike a bargain with them. Hostile to a status quo that stands between them and the occupied territories, Syrians and Palestinians have no interest in the regional stability that Washington promotes. Moscow, on the other hand, has consistently been willing to promote *instability*, knowing that resolution of the Arab-Israeli struggle may end its influence in the region altogether. As long as the issue of the occupied territories remains unresolved, the opening beckons for Moscow's exercise of power. Yet whatever their disappointments, Arabs turn reflexively to the United States for help in promoting a Middle East settlement.

In some measure, their disposition to turn to the United States for help is self-defeating. Characteristically, Arab governments, instead of shaping intiatives of their own, have expected outsiders to deliver benefits to them. By refusing to engage in the "autonomy" talks, for example, they lost an opening to challenge Begin's view of the Camp David agreement and Israel's control of the West Bank and Gaza. By giving up the oil weapon when they had it, they lost the chance to wield significant power. This inability to take responsibility for themselves—to devise systems of punishment and reward for dealing with the outside world—has given Arab interests a secondary place in America's calculations of policy. It has created an irresistible temptation to the United States, with its cold war priorities, to opt routinely for Israel's military resolve.

To Arabs, the invasion of Lebanon was unmistakable evidence that Washington, whatever Kissinger's claim, had no restraining influence over Israel. What the Arabs saw was not American concern about Israel's security but American indulgence of a client that held Arab lands, kept Arabs in bondage, bombed Arab cities with impunity, and could, as Sharon seemed to be suggesting, march its army all the way to the Euphrates. It hardly mattered to the Arab world whether the United States gave its client these options out of helplessness or choice. Arabs usually single out the "Jewish lobby" in Washington as the explanation, attributing virtual omnipotence to it. But whatever the explanation, Lebanon proved to them that America was powerless not just to persuade Israel to return the occupied territories, which had been Kissinger's promise, but to keep Israel from reaching for dominion over the entire region.

As most Israelis saw it, the deterioration in American-Arab relations that accompanied the Lebanon invasion was reason to rejoice. It has long been a premise of Israel's foreign policy that its security is jeopardized in ratio to America's friendliness with the Arab world. Begin and Sharon were not unaware, in invading Lebanon, of the prospect of weakening American influence in the Arab world.

But did their success make Israel more secure? In 1975, Kissinger had boasted of his Sinai II negotiations that "We have maintained our special relationship with Israel, while at the same time dramatically improving our relations with the Arab world. It is the United States alone among the world's nations that both Israel and the Arab nations have been prepared to trust." A plausible argument can surely be made that the Lebanon invasion, in severely undermining the Arabs' trust, jeopardized Israel's security in the long run by impairing American capacity to restrain Arab adventurism.

The invasion of Lebanon was, furthermore, Israel's invitation to the Arab world to turn again to Moscow. It was a call for a repolarization. The invasion was the long-ripening fruit of an American policy that began prudently enough, even laudably, when President Johnson agreed after the Six-Day War to play a positive role in maintaining Israel's security. But the policy leaped out of control after Kissinger, whatever his claim, squandered in Sinai II the ability of the United States to contain events. Carter tried to regain control and largely failed. Reagan, bowing to Begin's Revisionist designs, did not try at all.

The invasion of Lebanon reversed the trend toward American preeminence in the region and ended the rich hopes for peace— for a *pax americana*—with which the 1970s began. Whatever the Arabs' instinctive attraction to the United States, since Lebanon all talk of a settlement among them has been accompanied by the demand that the Soviet Union serve as a negotiating party to watch over their interests. Kissinger's goal of making the United States the sole arbiter between Israel and the Arabs has been turned upside down. His peace efforts, within only a few years, have not only made the Middle East a more dangerous place than before. They have also weakened the United States in the Middle East arena in its contest with the Soviet Union.

"I was against that war," said Yitzhak Rabin, angrily. "It was a war of choice, and I long ago gave up believing we could achieve the far-reaching political goal which is the only justification of a war of choice. Begin became intoxicated by our military strength, but the war in Lebanon had to fail. We cannot impose peace on our neighbors through the force of arms."

Indeed, as Rabin learned in his studies of Clausewitz, Israel is not the Soviet Union, whose armies exercise a military dominion —which they call peace—over Eastern Europe. Nor is Israel the United States, whose power is great enough to safeguard the stability of the Western Hemisphere. Far from imposing peace in Lebanon, Israel succeeded only in aggravating disarray, weakening its own security.

Lebanon transformed the promise of the Camp David treaty into a deep and prolonged Egyptian-Israeli crisis. It seriously worsened the always volatile relationship with Syria. It produced a new and intensified reign of terrorism from Palestinians in the occupied territories, within Israel itself, and internationally. It created dangers on Israel's border with Lebanon, from Lebanese who had never been actively hostile to a Jewish state.

Rabin's objection to the invasion of Lebanon, however, had little to do with its disastrous effect on Israel's relations with its neighbors, much less the pursuit of peace. He found the full-scale invasion too ambitious, strategically misconceived. Like many Labor members of the Knesset, he had favored conducting a limited strike at the PLO in Lebanon, for which the model was a 1978 operation in which Israeli army units struck quickly and departed, leaving military installations behind them in ruins. Rabin was suggesting only a different military tactic—not an Israeli search for peace—as an alternative to Begin's war.

Once I asked Rabin whether even limited attacks, such as he proposed, did not actually help to perpetuate the conflict in the Middle East. He acknowledged to me that they did. Absent from our conversation was any suggestion from Rabin that the Arab problem might be ended altogether by Israel's sitting down with its remaining adversaries—most notably, with the Palestinians—with the aim of negotiating a permanent peace.

How, then, in practical terms, does Yitzhak Rabin's Mainstream Zionism differ from Geula Cohen's Revisionism, as a guide for conducting Israel's relations with its Arab neighbors?

Rabin says firmly that, unlike Cohen, he has no ideological dedication to the occupied territory, though he would give back only that part of it which was superfluous to Israel's security. Cohen, in contrast, has such a deep ideological commitment to the territory that she would stop at nothing, not foreign war, not civil war, to keep from giving back any at all.

Stated another way, Rabin insists he cares for peace and would give up some of the territory for it, though in fact he cannot get peace by giving up only some. Cohen says she will give up none of the territory, and is indifferent to peace. So Israel is in a dilemma. If it goes the way of Cohen, seeking to keep all the territory, it faces war, sooner or later, with its neighbors. If it goes the way of Rabin, seeking to keep only part, it faces war not only with its neighbors but with itself.

Keeping the dilemma at arm's length is Israel's powerful army, Rabin's progeny. The army preserves not only the territory Rabin would keep but that which Cohen would keep, as well. The two, then, have a common interest in Israel's armed might, the instrument for keeping Israel safe while not at peace. As long as Israel is willing to live without peace, Mainstream and Revisionist Zionists need not renew the animosities of the *Altalena*. Rabin and Cohen can continue to argue but they need not fight. Together, they share an interest in not making peace.

Starting, then, from different premises, Rabin and Cohen end by responding with the same answer to the territorial question. Cohen applauded the invasion of Lebanon, Rabin criticized it on tactical grounds, but the two agreed that invasion of an adjoining state was a legitimate way for Israel to deal with the problem of the Palestinians. Neither has called for a political solution.

In reliance on the army, the pragmatism of Mainstream Zionism converges with the zealotry of Revisionism. Building military impregnability is easier for Israelis than building the political consensus needed for a government to reach out to negotiate a settlement with Israel's neighbors.

Without an exit from this dilemma, Israel remains destined to endless war, no peace.

9

The Bar Kokhba Road

As late as 1977, a decade after the Six-Day War, only five thousand Jews lived in the West Bank. The policy of the Labor government during this period often appeared uncertain, even bumbling, but it was unmistakably averse to generalized Jewish settlement. The prospect of repartitioning, along one set of lines or another, was more or less taken for granted. Though the army was stern in maintaining order among the Arabs, the relative absence of Jews in the territories also muted tensions, permitting a minimum of intrusion in the daily life of the local inhabitants. With no clear design for the territories, the government improvised in its dealings with the Arabs, in the aim of avoiding painful incidents.

Free to enter the Israeli labor market, the Palestinians in the territories enjoyed more prosperity than they had under Jordan and Egypt. They acquired a third of Israel's jobs in construction, a substantial proportion in industry and farming, and a majority in the menial work of municipal sanitation, hospital and hotel service, gardening and dishwashing. Meanwhile, money crossed into the territories from the oil-producing countries of the Gulf, where Palestinians held well-paying jobs. What followed the influx of wealth into most Arab homes was, first, electricity, then refrigerators and television sets. Automobiles soon became common. Diet improved, infant mortality dropped and literacy rose. Though the West Bank and Gaza economies in themselves remained stagnant, the gap between Israeli and Arab living standards narrowed significantly during these years.

What shocked Israelis was that the rise of prosperity, guided by an administration they regarded as benign, did not produce a decline in Palestinian nationalism. On the contrary, nationalist feelings intensified under military rule. Nearly every Palestinian I encountered in the territories during those years spoke openly of a personal allegiance to Yassir Arafat and the Palestine Liberation Organization. Public opinion polls consistently confirmed these loyalties. In 1976, in the one free municipal election held in the West Bank, candidates identified openly with the PLO won overwhelmingly. Though no real resistance movement ever arose, Israeli authorities had ample indication from recurring demonstrations and occasional outbreaks of violence that opposition to the occupation was not likely to abate.

The one course the Labor government did pursue single-mindedly in these years was execution of the Allon Plan, the West Bank's strategic security program. It provided for the establishment of a double line of defense that would guard against an attack by Arab armies from the east. With Israel itself to the west, this double line left the heavy Arab population of the West Bank surrounded by Jews. One string of Jewish settlements was founded along the Jordan River, another parallel to it on the mountain ridges above the Jordan valley. These settlements, faithful to the Mainstream's pioneering philosophy, performed both agricultural and military functions. The boundaries around them signaled the limits of the Mainstream's concept of "territorial compromise" that presumably was available to the Arabs whenever they were prepared to make peace.

Interestingly, the Joint Chiefs of Staff in Washington had reservations about the Allon Plan's strategic foundations. In a secret study,* since declassified, the Joint Chiefs went beyond the Allon Plan to point to the advantage of straightening Israel's eastern border, in order to shorten defensive lines. They seconded the Allon Plan's provision for military emplacements in the mountains overlooking the Jordan valley. But they saw no justification for the Allon Plan's establishment of settlements along the Jordan River. Lightly populated, these settlements would be permanently vulnerable to Arab attack, much like the ill-fated Bar-Lev line at Suez, but without its firepower. The Joint Chiefs, while focusing on military concerns, also laid stress on their conviction that Israel's political relations with its neighbors could not be ignored in any real evaluation of its national security.

After the election of Menachem Begin as prime minister in 1977, the emphasis in the territories shifted from the Allon Plan and security to settlement and absorption. Only under Begin did a government commit itself unequivocally to incorporating both the West Bank and Gaza into Israel. Practices that had been improvised under Labor became policy under Likud. The water, electricity, telephone and transportation systems of the occupied territories were integrated with those of Israel, and their economies were made increasingly dependent on Israel's economy. In Rabin's last years as prime minister, when Labor rule was at its weakest, Gush Emunim consistently manipulated the government to found settlements in the West Bank. When Begin arrived, he actively encouraged Gush Emunim, and the rush to the West Bank began.

Not long thereafter, press reports made apparent that the level of violence in the territory had significantly risen. With these reports in mind, I spent the summer of 1979 preparing an extended article on the confrontation between Palestinians and Is-

---

*Memorandum for the Secretary of Defense. Subject: Middle East Boundaries, 29 June 1967. Signed by Earle G. Wheeler, Chairman, Joint Chiefs of Staff. Document #JCSM-373-67. Acquired under the Freedom of Information Act. Graciously supplied to me by Richard I. Brody of PanHeuristics, Marina del Rey, California.

raelis in the West Bank. The opening segment of it conveys the atmosphere of what I found:

In the early morning of Israeli independence day last May, in the Arab village of Birzeit on the West Bank of the Jordan River, several dozen high school students, singing Palestinian songs and waving flags, marched in one of their periodic protests against Israel's twelve-year military rule.

Some of them rolled rocks onto the road, blocking traffic through the village, but they were expected to tire by noon and return to classes, as they had in many demonstrations before. The occupation authorities would then have written off the episode as one more harmless release by young Arabs of anti-Israeli emotions. But independence day of 1979 was unlike any before it in Birzeit, for a Jewish settlement had recently established itself on a hilltop a few miles up the road.

From the Six-Day War of 1967, when Israel drove a Jordanian army from the West Bank, until the Yom Kippur War of 1973, when Arab arms gave Israel a serious scare, the military occupation of this territory had been rather uneventful. Israeli jeeps patrolled the roads, but the army scarcely intruded upon daily life. Though would-be terrorists were treated severely, only a small minority seemed disposed to terror. Committed as Arabs remained to the principle of recovering Palestine from the Jews, the West Bankers, more humiliated than oppressed by the occupation, put up virtually no resistance to it.

But after the Yom Kippur War, tensions began to grow. Israelis became more conscious of security, and embarked on a major self-analysis over the national purpose. The war, at the same time, seemed to have given the Arabs a new sense of strength, and of reality, and they talked less of destroying Israel and more of establishing a Palestinian state in the West Bank and the Gaza Strip, where Arabs predominate. Over persistent Israeli objections, in fact, the Arabs—largely through the Palestine Liberation Organization—succeeded in winning sympathy for their cause from public opinion around the world. The two trends collided after Menachem Begin was elected to office in 1977 on a promise of restoring the boundaries of Biblical Israel, and Jews in substantial numbers began arriving in the West Bank, planning to stay.

Near Birzeit, the settlers moved into a fortress built for British forces during the Mandate, before World War II. They were members of

Gush Emunim, which means "faith bloc," and they drew their zeal from the duty they feel to repossess the land of the Biblical Jews. Under the protection of the Israeli army, they quickly built pre-fabricated homes, along with a school and a synagogue, and they surrounded themselves with barbed wire. They called their settlement Neve Tsuf —"Oasis of Nectar"—and they pledged to make it the beachhead of a Jewish presence that would radiate throughout the region.

With the arrival of the Gush Emunim settlements on the West Bank, the tranquillity of the early years of the occupation was shattered. The trouble was inevitable. The settlers proclaimed that their purpose was to establish the principle of Jewish dominance on the West Bank, at the same time as the Arabs began to have real hope that the military occupation would end. Since they hammered their first stake into the hilltop, the men of Neve Tsuf have driven daily through Birzeit, bristling for a confrontation. Watching them, young Arabs no longer felt content to cower in the shade.

Last independence day, some Neve Tsuf settlers were headed for Tapuach, a Gush Emunim settlement near the Arab city of Nablus, where a rally was scheduled in favor of West Bank annexation. The first car which drew to a stop at the roadblock, put up by the Arab high school students, contained five adults and two children. When the driver got out to clear the way, he was pelted with stones. Then a second settlers' car arrived, and a stone smashed into the windshield. The two drivers, exercising a power granted to Jewish settlers by the military government, took the guns they carried in their cars and fired a series of rounds into the air. Apparently by ricochet, a student was struck in the chest, and only by a narrow margin escaped a mortal wound.

The student who was wounded was enrolled not in the high school but in Birzeit University, and was among twenty or thirty who, after a mid-morning break in classes, had made their way to the village center to look into the excitement. Birzeit, the best known of three small Arab universities on the West Bank, is regarded by Palestinians as the intellectual hub of their society, and by the Israeli government as a hotbed of extremism. Birzeit people generally scoff at the notion of extremism, though they unhesitatingly declare Palestinian patriotism. Birzeit students occasionally throw stones, they say, but it is hardly an act of rebellion. It is, rather, a gesture of self-assertion, within the context of the shame they feel as subjects of foreign rule.

Because of the university, and its proximity to several secondary schools, the village of Birzeit is considered by the military government to be one of the most troublesome on the West Bank. After a student demonstration in 1974 Dr. Hanna Nasir, the university's American-educated president, was charged with subversion and deported. When the Camp David agreement was announced last fall, the Israelis lifted restrictions on political assembly only long enough for a thousand students to rally on the campus against what they called a sell-out of Palestinian rights. Immediately afterwards the Israelis clamped down on all political discussion. Then, last March, during a tumultuous protest over the signing of the Egyptian-Israeli peace treaty, a university student and three townspeople were shot by Israeli soldiers.

The military government has taken each disturbance as evidence of the university's extremism. The university answers by saying that students are not robots who can be sealed off from the great political issues that affect their lives. As the university sees it, demonstrations are not subversion. A military government spokesman told me, in fact, that in its many searches at Birzeit it had discovered no revolutionary cells, no weapons or explosives, not even serious revolutionary literature. It is not a terrorist base. Yet, since the military government's job is to keep the peace, it regards the university as a threat to public order.

Shortly after the shooting that day, Israeli soldiers arrived in the village, fired tear gas at the remaining stone-throwers and imposed a curfew on the campus. They seized the identity papers of more than one hundred university students, and detained about half of them for interrogation. The Neve Tsuf settlers promptly made a public announcement that they had been within their rights to fire, and that the students alone were to blame for the incident. They said they would stand for no investigation into their own conduct—and there was none —and that Birzeit would have to be severely punished. A day after their statement, the military government shut down the university indefinitely.

Since those days, the level of violence between Jews and Arabs in the occupied territories, particularly in the West Bank, has risen precipitously. In the first decade after the Six-Day War, the number of lethal acts—gunfire, grenades, Molotov cocktails, bombs, mines—averaged about one a week. In the succeeding five years, when Begin served as prime minister, the frequency more than doubled. From mid-1983 to mid-1984, the last period for which figures were available, lethal acts occurred almost daily. As for "violations of law and order," the designation given illegal demonstrations and rock throwing by Palestinians, the number rose tenfold from 1977 to 1984.

The violence has originated among both Jews and Arabs. The PLO and other Palestinian guerilla groups, their leaders acting from abroad, have been responsible for much of it. Some has also been organized by independent Arab resistance units within the West Bank and Gaza, and some by free-lance activists. Since the late 1970s, however, much of the violence has also been initiated by Jews.

Jewish settlers, particularly in the West Bank, have justified this violence as retaliation, but in practice, their main goals have been to intimidate Arabs, demonstrate their own power and warn other Jews that under no circumstances will they withdraw from the territories. In 1985, Israeli authorities broke up a ring of Jewish terrorists and brought twenty-seven of its members to trial— among them Israeli army officers and prominent settlement leaders—for crimes that included attempts on the lives of Arab mayors, the bombing of buses, an attack on a college and a conspiracy to bomb the Dome of the Rock on the Temple Mount. Sentences for those convicted ranged from a few months to life in prison.

These militant new settlers, who doubled the Jewish population of the West Bank in the first two years of Likud rule, claimed to be the heirs of the pioneering tradition of Zionism, but they were unlike the Zionist pioneers of old. They showed no interest in cultivating the land, though they ceaselessly proclaimed their love for it. Almost all held jobs in the cities. Though support for their cause was strong in Israel, they were themselves only a small minority of zealots. Even with Begin's encouragement and Gush

Emunim's recruitment, it soon became apparent that there were not nearly enough of them to fill the territories.

The Revisionist breakthrough came when international Zionist organizations, donors of funds for land development since the early pioneering days, decided to make annual allotments for settlements in the occupied territories. These contributions, along with the elimination of many restrictions on private commercial development, led to the "suburbanization" of the West Bank. Out of those changes came a redefinition of Zionist pioneering. Most of the newcomers did not even pretend to any interest in the land. Quite simply, they were commuters between middle-class bedroom communities that happened to be in the West Bank and jobs in Tel Aviv and Jerusalem. They chose the occupied territories not as a Zionist affirmation but because government subsidies and lower land values made living accommodations there cheaper. By 1985, the West Bank's Jewish population had increased to more than fifty thousand, tenfold over 1977.

Israel's chief expert on the occupied territories and their impact on Israeli society is Meron Benvenisti, a native-born scholar and former deputy mayor of Jerusalem. As administrator of the Old City, Benvenisti was influential in the years after the Six-Day War in seeking to bridge differences between Jerusalem's Jews and Arabs. Since then, he has studied the West Bank's demography, land and water resources, investment patterns, transportation and utilities, and administration.

In a recent report on his work, Benvenisti predicted that Likud, though it had fallen short of its goal of 100,000 settlers by 1986, would reach that figure around 1990. This will mean a "critical mass" of supporters, ready to vote, perhaps even to fight, to preserve the personal and financial interests they have acquired. In fact, there are signs the "critical mass" may already have been reached. Benvenisti points out that in the 1984 Knesset elections, only 14 percent of the settlers voted for Labor, while 86 percent voted either for Likud or for parties to its right—including Geula

Cohen's Tehiya, Rabbi Kahane's Kach and the Orthodox religious parties. Labor's leadership heard the message, he contends, and promptly undertook an effort to lure back the votes of the settlers with promises that their interests would be served.

Based on his findings, Benvenisti has concluded regretfully that Israeli colonization of the territories has proceeded so far that it has become *irreversible*.

His conclusion has been the source of much controversy, both in Israel and abroad. Jews and Arabs who aspire to a Middle East peace, as well as Zionists nostalgic for the more innocent era of their ideal, find his evaluation a cause for despair. Ironically, it has been most applauded by Israel's Revisionists, on the one hand, and "rejectionist" Arabs, on the other. For the Revisionists, Benvenisti confirms the success to date of their policy to absorb the territories and the promise of its full realization in the future. To supporters of the PLO, he offers naked proof of Israeli expansionism and violation of international law.

My own view is that while Benvenisti's scholarship is unassailable, his conclusion is wrong. The transfer of the sovereignty of territory is a political act. No such transfer is intrinsically permanent, much less irreversible.

Benvenisti bases his conclusion on two grounds: administrative integration and "critical mass." In refutation, I cite the examples of the American South, which changed flags twice from 1861 to 1865 in its struggle with the North, and the province of Alsace, which went back and forth four times in wars between France and Germany from 1870 to 1945. In none of these transfers were the administrative complexities a serious problem. As for "critical mass," it was an argument cited in behalf of the million Frenchmen who vowed in the 1950s to keep Algeria's ties with Paris, but de Gaulle succeeded in transferring sovereignty to an independent Algeria in spite of them. These examples leave no doubt that the transfer of authority is itself attainable. The question is whether the political commitment exists to achieve it without brutal war.

In the Israeli context, the more crucial issue is "critical mass." In the settler movement, Israel is confronted by a strong and determined minority. De Gaulle, by personal will, enjoying national support, overcame a similarly strong and determined minority in Algeria. Is any Israeli leader self-confident enough to take on such a minority and is the support strong enough in the nation to sustain him? The answer, at present in the negative, will in the long run determine whether Israel and the Arab states can reach agreement on a change in the status of the occupied territories without further war.

The conclusion we might rightly draw from Benvenisti's work is not that Israel's hold on the territories is irreversible but that Israel currently has the power to keep the Arabs from reversing it. Successive Israeli governments have encountered no serious barriers—neither Arab nor American—in their pursuit of absorption of the occupied territories. Thus, no prospect of upsetting the status quo is apparent. Still, the status quo in human affairs, far from being permanent, is likely to be as transitory as all of human existence. The current power relationship between Israel and the Arabs is not immutable. The status quo can certainly be changed by war. But it can also be changed by voluntary agreement whenever Israelis conclude that there is advantage to negotiation with the Arabs over the conditions of transfer.

The Israeli election in the summer of 1984 ended in a tie. Labor and Likud emerged with equal power in the Knesset, and the distribution of seats among the smaller parties left each with a veto over any cabinet formed by the other. After weeks of bargaining, Labor and Likud, historical and ideological enemies, agreed to establish a "national unity" government, in which they would share authority. In September of 1984, Labor Party leader Shimon Peres became prime minister and Likud Party leader Yitzhak Shamir became foreign minister. Their understanding was that they would exchange their offices two years thereafter. Predictably, the government in the next two years functioned in a permanent state of uncertainty, dependent upon a willingness of its members to ignore the hammer-and-tongs traditions of Israeli politics and to lay long-standing grievances aside to work together.

Early in 1985, Prime Minister Peres was confronted with a peace proposal, presented to him at the initiative of Jordan's King Hussein. Presumably, it had Washington's endorsement. The king, to find a detour around Israel's long-standing refusal to deal with the PLO, had signed an agreement on February 11 with Yassir Arafat. The agreement provided for establishment of a joint Jordanian-Palestinian delegation, whose membership would be subject to Israeli approval, to represent Palestinian interests in an international conference, the chief sponsor of which would be the United States. Peres declared himself favorably disposed to the idea, and even indicated endorsement of two Palestinian nominees to the joint delegation.

What Peres liked about Hussein's offer was the prospect he saw in it for realizing a "Jordanian solution" to the problem of the West Bank and Gaza. To Labor, a "Jordanian solution" meant the Jordanian monarchy and not some Palestinian authority would rule in the territories. Labor has long been persuaded not only that Hussein's regime would be more reliable than the Palestinians but, against all evidence, that it would be willing to limit its rule to the segment of the West Bank that Israel was prepared to relinquish. How much territory, if any, Peres was willing to return was not clear but the evidence suggested that he remained bound by the concept of the Allon Plan. Likud, though opposed to any solution at all, chose not to upset the "national unity" arrangement by rejecting Hussein's proposal outright.

Despite the Hussein-Arafat agreement, the proceedings foundered over the PLO's objection to Resolution 242. In addition to the celebrated territory-for-peace principle, Resolution 242 contains no provision for a settlement of the Palestinian question except as "the refugee problem." Arafat announced his acceptance of the territory-for-peace principle. He also agreed to an American condition that he publicly condemn terrorism. But, refusing to be guided by the limitation in the wording of Resolution 242, he insisted that the talks include negotiation over the right of the Palestinians to self-determination.

Arafat's published proposal stated as follows:*

> The Palestine Liberation Organization (PLO), the sole legitimate representative of the Palestinian people, holds the strong belief that the peace process should lead to a just, comprehensive and durable peace in the Middle East and should secure the legitimate rights of the Palestinian people, including their right of self-determination within the context of a Jordanian-Palestinian confederation.
>
> On the basis of the Jordanian-PLO accord of the 11th of February [1985], and in view of our genuine desire for peace, we are ready to negotiate within the context of an international conference with the participation of the permanent members of the Security Council, with the participation of all concerned Arab parties and the Israeli government, a peaceful settlement of the Palestinian problem on the basis of the pertinent United Nations resolutions, including Security Council resolutions 242 and 338.
>
> The PLO declares its rejection and denunciation of terrorism, which had been assured in the Cairo Declaration of November, 1983.

A careful reading of the PLO statement leaves little doubt that if the State Department's purpose was to elicit a clear commitment to the territory-for-peace principle, it had obtained what it wanted in the endorsement of Resolutions 242 and 338. If the State Department was determined to require PLO acknowledgment of Israel's existence, it succeeded by getting explicit reference to "the Israeli government." If it insisted on limiting the definition of "self-determination," the statement made clear that the PLO was resigned to a "Jordanian-Palestinian confederation" —which Arafat has defined as power-sharing between a sovereign Jordan and a sovereign Palestine—as a possible outcome of negotiations.

*A complete text of the PLO's proposals, along with the accompanying statements of the Department of State, appears in the Congressional Record of June 5, 1986, pp. 1967–1969.

The statement also contained a renunciation of terrorism, though, in citing the Cairo declaration, the PLO limited its application to territory outside Israel. In doing so, it did not renounce "armed struggle" against Israel itself. The PLO's statement, however, addressed only the *pre*conditions for negotiations. It was not meant as a negotiating offer itself. Had the PLO surrendered the principle of "armed struggle" in advance, in effect acknowledging surrender to Israel, there would have been little left for its delegates to bargain about. What more the PLO could have done before negotiations opened is hard to imagine. Yet the State Department rejected the proposal, insisting it was inadequate.

In response to questions raised by the House Foreign Affairs Committee, the Department explained its rejection on the following grounds:

> The U.S. expects a clear PLO acceptance of 242, not one conditioned on simultaneous U.S. acceptance of self-determination for the Palestinians. . . . The term 'self-determination' has in the Middle East context come to connote the establishment of a Palestinian state. (Reference to a 'Jordanian/Palestinian confederation' in no way changes this fact, given that the February 11 agreement between Jordan and the PLO refers to a confederation of two states.) The United States does not support the establishment of a Palestinian state. Therefore, such a reference is not consistent with U.S. policy.

Had the United States accepted the principle of Palestinian self-determination, of course, it would have totally changed Peres's expectations for the talks. Peres was willing to consider a local deal between Israel and Jordan, exchanging peace for whatever territory was not required for realization of the Allon Plan. He gave no indication of an openness to discuss further issues of territory or sovereignty, and the United States backed him unequivocally. The PLO's refusal to accept this limitation led in turn to quarreling between Arafat and Hussein, and in due course to a breakdown of the February 11 agreement. Thus ended the hope for peace talks in 1985.

Abba Eban, Israel's senior diplomat and a confirmed "dove," was frustrated by the failure and contemptuous of America's negative participation. These were some of his remarks:*

> I have no hesitation in saying that if the Americans had not behaved as they did in 1973 and in 1977, we would not have had disengagement agreements, partial agreements, the Camp David agreements or the peace treaty with Egypt. These were simply not feasible without a very sophisticated, assertive and assiduous mediation at a very high level. Their absence is one of the great obstacles to progress.
>
> The initial positions of the parties over disengagement following the Yom Kippur War in 1973 were totally different, but Henry Kissinger went twenty-six times to Damascus, twenty-one times to Jerusalem and thirty-two times to Cairo. . . . In 1977, the U.S. President himself got involved after Sadat's visit to Jerusalem. He would go into a room with a pencil and draft things with rather junior people from our side. They spent thirteen days and nights at Camp David, and when things went wrong the President himself rushed out to the Middle East, sweating all over the place and running around.
>
> This time, the peace process broke down over semantics, and if some words were wrong, there are others. No other international dispute has been so overladen with symbolic semantic considerations of legitimacy, recognition and what I call "diplomacy by incantation." My own feeling is that there is too much docility in accepting the situation.
>
> Now, the [American] secretary of state wants success to be guaranteed in advance. He wants to come out to celebrate, not to mediate. We have a deputy assistant under secretary from Washington who travels six thousand miles every six weeks to make a few communications between the various capitals. How crazy can you be?

If polls are to be trusted, the Palestinians were more disappointed by the failure of the peace effort than the Israelis. According to the survey of an Arab newspaper in Jerusalem, 70 percent of Palestinians were willing to back Arafat on negotiations based on Resolution 242, provided self-determination was on the agenda. A similar poll by a Tel Aviv newspaper showed Israelis

*Reprinted in *The Washington Jewish Week*, July 24, 1986.

evenly divided on the territory-for-peace principle, but only 15 percent were willing to apply it to *complete* withdrawal. Whatever the meaning of these findings, once it was clear the maneuvering would not produce negotiations, all the parties tried to shift the blame elsewhere.

In fact, the prospect of peace talks in 1985 collapsed because none of the parties was willing to concede—and, as Eban points out, no outsider was available to bring about concessions—on the substance of its positions:

• Peres, faithful to the Allon Plan, was not prepared for talks that might have led to full withdrawal from the territories. It is doubtful, furthermore, whether he could have delivered a delegation, given the fragility of his domestic support, to talks limited even to *partial* withdrawal. As for Palestinian self-determination, the Israeli government did not even bother to take up the issue.

• Arafat, representing Palestinian nationalism, considered self-determination more important than territory. Had he succeeded in getting it on the conference agenda, his prospects were good for overcoming the forces within the PLO that opposed any territorial concessions. Without it, opposition inside the PLO was intractable, whatever the promise of Israel's territorial withdrawal.

• The Reagan administration, conscious as always of the political power of the American-Jewish community, was unwilling to support the Palestinians on the issue of self-determination.

• Hussein, sensitive to the power of the Palestinians in his realm, was unable to enter talks without authorization from the PLO. Without self-determination on the agenda, such authorization was inconceivable.

On these differences the prospect of talks collapsed.

Certainly, Peres had had little room for political maneuver in the proceedings. Israel's profound economic problems were the coalition's first priority. Peace negotiations, a disruptive issue with small promise of success, seemed to him worth only minimum risk. During the discussions over Hussein's plan, settler organizations, supported by Likud, issued ominous warnings against territorial concessions. Politically pressed, Peres decided to show his hard-line side. In June 1985, he sent Israel's air force on a retaliatory raid against PLO installations in Tunisia, a longtime innocent among Arab countries. The raid, endorsed by President Reagan, served as the coup de grace to negotiating prospects, though, in fact, the differences over preconditions had already doomed them.

Whatever Israel's role, Washington found it politically useful to blame the collapse of the talks on King Hussein, who of all the parties had most consistently championed them. Had not Peres, after all, said he was ready to talk? Had not the PLO, Jordan's client, rejected Resolution 242? In its own diplomatic efforts, the Reagan administration pressed Hussein hard to abandon the PLO and go it alone. This Hussein was unable to do. In contrast, Washington asked Israel to yield only on procedural points.

Congress totally ignored the substantive issues in demanding late in 1985 that Hussein end Jordan's formal state of war with Israel. When Hussein pleaded an inability to accept without resolution of the status of the Palestinians and the territories, Congress vetoed a commitment the White House had made to sell Jordan military equipment. Congress's punishment won the applause of Israel's hard-liner backers. But it persuaded Hussein to move to improve relations with Syria, Moscow's closest Middle East ally, and to announce his intention to buy Soviet weapons. For the first time, it seemed possible that Russian technicians would be based on Israel's eastern border. Congress, its political judgment swayed by pressure from the American-Jewish community, thus undermined the interests not only of the United States but of Israel, too.

The collapse of Hussein's initiative demonstrated once more that the heart of the Arab-Israeli conflict was the Palestinian issue. Though the route to peace clearly passes through the PLO, Israel has been relentless in refusing to allow the PLO into settlement deliberations. To be sure, Israeli anger at the PLO is understandable. Though PLO terror during the past two decades has weakened Israeli security very little, it has disrupted the equilibrium of Israeli life very much. Terror may be the only way for the weak to wage war against the strong, but as a tactic, it concedes the moral high ground to the other side. Israelis insist the PLO is morally contemptible. Whether it is or not, the PLO remains central to the resolution of the Palestinian issue, and thus to the making of peace. The fate of Hussein's peace initiative reaffirmed that reality anew.

In fact, it can be argued that if there is to be peace in the Middle East, Israel needs the PLO as much as the PLO needs Israel. With whom else can Israel settle the complex Palestinian issue?

The PLO has demonstrated repeatedly—despite the hostility not just of Israel but, at times, of Jordan, Syria and other Arab governments—that it is the one organization in which the Palestinian people has confidence. Since 1974, it has been recognized as the Palestinians' official negotiating authority by the Arab world and by most non-Arab countries as well. Even the Israeli government does not dispute its preeminence among the Arabs under its rule. Most Palestinians to whom I have spoken over the years have lamented the PLO's factionalism and its tactical ineptness, and some have even quarreled with the brutality to which it has often lent its name. But few have denied it their allegiance. Arab governments have many priorities, of which Palestinians are only one. But the PLO, Palestinians say, is faithful to a single cause: the Palestinian people.

What this means is that the PLO alone—not Jordan's King Hussein—has the power to remove the long-standing grievances of the Palestinians from the agenda of the Middle East conflict. Israel's dispute, it must be recalled, is not just with the 1.2 million who live in the occupied territories but with the Palestinians as a people. A "West Bank peace" would not be peace enough. Peace must settle, once and for all, Israel's differences with the two million Palestinians who are still classified as refugees, a majority of them outside the occupied territories. Palestinians would surely feel an obligation to repudiate a peace negotiated for them by non-Palestinians. Sadat learned as much too late. For Israel to make a real peace, the Palestinians must sign the contract. Only the PLO can do it in their behalf.

One hears the argument, of course, that the PLO's signature on a peace treaty would be of dubious value. It is said the organization, badly divided, speaks with more than one voice. But could the same description not apply to a variety of governments, including the United States itself? The PLO has been forged in the same contentious fire as other revolutionary regimes, which means it must constantly validate its claims to legitimacy. Still, it has kept agreements it has made, not least of them the cease-fire with Israel negotiated by the United States in 1981, which the Begin government broke by invading Lebanon. It is also backed not just by a Palestinian consensus but by the collective authority of the Arab nations. If the PLO did not exist, it would be in Israel's interest, in entering peace talks, to invent it.

Could the PLO, by agreement with Israel, actually end the long struggle over the land between Zionism and the Palestinians? As measured by ideals, surely not. Palestinians can no more be deprived of their dreams than Jews, who prayed for return to the land of their forefathers for two thousand years. But if peace were contingent upon dreams alone, it would exist virtually nowhere. In practice, both Palestinians and Jews can tailor their dreams to the reality of territorial compromise. That is the message of Resolution 242.

Still, a territorial solution would not be enough, without resolving the problem of the refugees. Officially, the terms of an Arab-Israeli agreement on the refugees are governed by a U.N. resolution that promises them repatriation but that also hints at compensation as an alternative remedy. Israel, realistically, cannot contemplate the repatriation of two million Palestinians, but it has over the years expressed a willingness to provide compensation for the loss of property. No doubt the United States and other governments would offer help in defraying the costs of such an agreement. But whatever the final terms, any agreement would require the Palestinians to waive future claims on Israel, and only the PLO could sign such a waiver in the Palestinians' behalf.

Some Israelis dismiss as pointless any agreement with the PLO, on the grounds that it would not put an end to terrorism. It is true that even with peace, terrorism would probably continue. The question is, however, how much.

Not even Israeli officials accept the currently fashionable notion that there is a widespread "culture of terrorism," independent of political concerns. Most terrorism is a response to political discontent and related to specific grievances. Since 1948, terror—called "armed struggle" by Palestinian organizations—has been socially sanctioned by Palestinians, even by those who would not think of practicing it themselves. Most Palestinians see it as their only available instrument of liberation. Under the terms of a peace settlement, the PLO would of course be required to call off the "armed struggle." Few Palestinians would object. Most would direct their energies into building a homeland. In the absence of popular sanction, the reservoir from which young fighters have been drawn would dry up, leaving terror to hard-core fringe elements.

A plausible case can also be made that the PLO's demands on Israel would be more moderate than Hussein's. The king has said consistently that the only settlement over which he could preside would require Israel to withdraw from the entire territory taken in 1967. He has pointed out that whatever the Arab objections to the Camp David agreement, Sadat set a standard on the land issue by getting back every inch of the Sinai. No Arab leader can now do less. Hussein says, furthermore, that the territory of the West Bank and the Gaza Strip is not his to give away. Few Arabs disagree. If there are concessions to be made, it is acknowledged that the Palestinians must make them.

Arafat, in contrast to Hussein, has repeatedly stated a willingness to consider a range of concessions, including territory, in return for an end to the occupation. He has also spoken of providing Israel with security guarantees along the lines of those that accompanied the Sinai agreement. He has withdrawn his condition that a sovereign Palestinian state be established in the territory that Israel evacuates, and said he would agree to a "confederation" of the West Bank and Gaza with Jordan. But his minimum condition is self-determination, the requirement that the Palestinians themselves make the decision about the land.

It is true that Arafat's line on these issues has often wavered, depending on his platform and on the political pressures to which he is exposed at a given time. It is not even clear whether he can get formal PLO approval for a peace agreement. But until now, he has been measured, especially by the United States, only in terms of the unilateral concessions demanded of him—recognition of Israel's right to exist, acceptance of Resolution 242, renunciation of "armed struggle." His assertion that the PLO is ready to make peace with Israel has never been *tested*.

Some years ago, a dissident group within the Israeli Labor Party devised the "Yariv-Shemtov formula," which provides that Israel will recognize and negotiate with any authority willing to recognize and negotiate with Israel. Though directed at the PLO, no Israeli government has been willing to invite the PLO to subscribe to it. The result is that no one knows how the PLO would respond, any more than anyone knows what it would demand at the negotiating table or what it would be able to deliver. No one will *ever* know, if the two sides cannot be brought to sit down and talk.

But one thing is clear: In any negotiation, Israel would now enter with the upper hand. It has the territories, which it need relinquish only when satisfied that its security requirements have been met. The Sinai agreement is the precedent. Israel can insist upon demilitarization. It can demand electronic early-warning stations on the peaks of the mountain ranges, which the United States would no doubt be willing to staff. An American contingent would, in itself, be a security asset. It can require guarantees, already provided tacitly by Jordan and Syria, to keep terrorists from crossing the border. As for hostile armies, it can demand the right to occupy the high ground in the West Bank in the event of attack. It can also demand on a routine basis satellite photos of the entire region. Since any Arab army would have to cross miles of open desert to reach Israel, the likelihood of surprise attack from the east would be extremely remote.

With ample security arrangements, it would seem hardly to matter whether the West Bank and Gaza became an independent state, which is the Palestinian preference, or was joined in federation with Jordan. Israelis seem all but unanimous in ruling out a Palestinian state. Some suggest it would quickly become a Soviet puppet, though it is hard to find supporting evidence for such foreboding. I suspect the explanation for Israel's deep objection to a Palestinian state has more to do with the Jewish state's psychological than security problems. Most Israelis find it easier to deny Palestinians any right at all to a state than to contemplate the implications of even limited statehood.

In my judgment, creation of an independent state on the West Bank and Gaza is not only the fairest way of resolving the Palestinian problem but holds out the best prospect of neutralizing the Palestinians as a threat to Israel. For the first time, it would give Palestinians something worth preserving, some stake in Middle East stability, something to be careful about. A Palestinian state would be squeezed between a suspicious Jordan to the east and a suspicious Israel to the west. Its geography would be reason for it not to provoke either neighbor by a cavalier attitude to terrorism. Demilitarized, it would present far less risk to Israel than a Jordanian-Palestinian federation, which the Palestinians, outnumbering Jordanians two to one, would ultimately dominate.

I come now to the issue of Jerusalem, generally said to be the most difficult to resolve in the conflict between Arabs and Jews. Jordan erred seriously after 1948 in dividing the city, barring Jews from the Old City, offending everyone. All parties to the Arab-Israeli conflict now seem to agree that Jerusalem must never be divided again. In fact, all parties seem to recognize that a peace which places rigid barriers not just between East and West Jerusalem but between the West Bank and Gaza on the one hand and Israel on the other is likely to be doomed. Unless there are open borders, permitting free circulation from the Mediterranean to the Jordan River, the historical antagonism of Arabs and Jews is liable to rise again to unmanageable levels.

While recognizing Jerusalem's importance as a symbol to both Jews and Arabs, I would cite a distinction in the way the two peoples perceive the city. For both, Jerusalem is a religious shrine. The Arabs feel the same attachment to the Dome of the Rock that the Jews feel to the Wailing Wall. For the Jews, however, Jerusalem has also been their historic political capital, while for the Arabs it has played little of a political role.

Jerusalem was never a great Arab capital, like Damascus or Baghdad. In the Turkish centuries, it was a provincial backwater. Jerusalem's political importance was restored only under the Mandate, when the British and the Jews made the city their administrative seat and, for convenience, the Arabs followed suit. Significantly, King Hussein's grandfather chose not to move his throne from Amman to Jerusalem after he took the eastern part of the city in 1948. His action provides a precedent for establishing a Palestinian capital elsewhere, in Ramallah or Nablus, for instance, important Arab cities on the West Bank. Such a move would reduce the frictions that the presence of two capitals in Jerusalem would almost surely produce.

Having said that, however, I must emphasize that tranquillity in the Holy City demands some sharing of its symbols of sovereignty. The Arabs are particularly fearful of Israeli designs on the Temple Mount, site of two of Islam's holiest mosques. In 1985, Jewish terrorists attempted to blow up these shrines. In 1986, Geula Cohen—who does not pretend to be devout—led a group of right-wing Knesset members in prayer there, provoking a riot. Recently, Orthodox Jews have taken to demanding that Arabs surrender the site for the construction of the Third Temple, though not even under Begin has any government treated the proposal seriously. Most Israelis remain unwilling to outrage world opinion and to provide Moslems with a cause for permanent holy war. But most Arabs are unlikely to be satisfied until an Arab flag, even symbolically, flies over the Temple Mount.

Many proposals for Jerusalem's rule have been written with the objective of overcoming fears that one group will dominate another. The fears are exchanged not just between Jews and Arabs, but between religious and secular Jews. They are felt by the tiny religious and ethnic groups, mostly Christians, that inhabit the city as well. The most prominent proposal is the borough plan, identified with Jerusalem's longtime mayor, Teddy Kollek. It would combine elements of London's administrative system, offering a measure of neighborhood self-rule, with elements of the Turkish *millet* system, providing each group with a maximum of religious and ethnic autonomy. It is a complex plan, as the others all are, reflecting the complexities of the city itself. But none will succeed as long as one group living in Jerusalem dismisses the sensibilities of the others, or seeks to use the city as a symbol of political dominance.

Though the West Bank and the Palestinians remain the key to a resolution of the Arab-Israeli conflict, real peace in the Middle East will also require an Israeli accommodation with Syria. Syria is both the strongest and the most hostile of Israel's Arab neighbors. That it expects to be treated as a major power in the region —which it is—is beyond question. Conventional wisdom has long held that Syria will be the last of Israel's neighbors to agree to peace. Though it has endorsed Resolution 242, Syria has consistently sought to block initiatives toward a settlement. Most Israelis insist the explanation lies in Syria's persistent unwillingness to live with them in peace. But another explanation lies in Syria's hostility to any peace initiative that gives its attention to the West Bank without taking equal account of its own occupied territory, the Golan Heights.

Alone among the territories captured in 1967, the Golan Heights has been formally annexed by Israel. Though the United States has not officially recognized the annexation, neither has it held out to Syria any prospect of the Golan's return. President Reagan's peace proposal of September 1, 1982, made no mention of the Golan Heights. As for the Israelis, they ignore the issue and treat the peace with Syria as unattainable. Yet Syria's stubborn resistance to a separate Israeli deal with Jordan and the PLO is understandable. Such a deal would leave Syria to face Israel alone in the campaign to get the Golan back.

For more than a decade, Syria's policy has been to achieve military parity with Israel, an objective strongly supported by the Soviet Union. Its purpose, Syria says, is not to annihilate Israel but to persuade the Israeli government to negotiate. It has hinted it would agree in negotiations to the Golan's demilitarization and to other security guarantees, and it has been scrupulously faithful to the commitments it made in the disengagement agreement on the Golan in 1974. Yitzhak Rabin, in one of our talks, assured me that the military problems presented by the return of the Golan Heights could be solved far more easily than those involving the West Bank. But as Syria sees the situation, Israel will not negotiate over the territory unless it faces an enemy whose power is equal to its own, presenting it with the prospect of military defeat. Sadat's reasoning, it is worth remembering, was much the same when he crossed the Suez Canal to wage the Yom Kippur War. With Israel convinced of its military superiority, the political situation in 1973 was paralyzed. It was only after Egypt bloodied the Israelis at the Bar-Lev line that they agreed to talk. Indeed, history since 1967 seems to confirm the Arabs' belief that military conflict is the only way to persuade Israel to start a peace process.

Since its withdrawal from Lebanon in 1984, Israel has grown increasingly alarmed over the buildup of Syrian military power, not only on the Golan Heights but in Lebanon itself. One of the measures of Israel's strategic defeat in Lebanon is the fact that Syria has since posed a more serious threat on its northern frontier than the PLO ever did. Major infusions of modern Soviet arms have bolstered Syria's geographic advantages in Lebanon, substantially narrowing its margin of strategic inferiority. Among the new weapons, according to reports, are missiles capable of striking distant Israeli cities. Israeli strategists, as well as some Syrians, clearly believe parity may be at hand, and that war—in the absence of political settlement—inevitably must follow.

Syria's political intentions are not clear. Though its forces occupy northern Lebanon, maintaining a measure of stability in the area adjacent to its border, Syria has made no effort to annex Lebanese territory. My own judgment, based on talks in Damascus, is that the Syrian government, while anxious to maintain the preponderance of Syrian influence in Lebanon, has no desire to import Lebanon's troubles into Syria to inflame its own serious domestic problems. Some Syrian circles talk occasionally of a settlement with Israel based not just on the return and demilitarization of the Golan Heights but on the neutralization of Lebanon. Both countries surely have an interest in Lebanon's standing between them as a buffer zone, leaving the unfortunate Lebanese to wage their civil war to their heart's content.

Israel, I believe, is faced with a choice. It can go to war, with some reasonable expectation of winning a victory sufficient to eliminate Syria as a threat for a decade or so. Or it can accept the prospect of its own withdrawal from the Golan Heights, then meet with the Syrians at the negotiating table. "Hawks" on both sides appear primed for a showdown and, without a significant try for peace, few observers doubt that in time the war will come. It is likely to be far costlier in human lives, to both sides, than any of the Syrian-Israeli conflicts that have preceded it.

On May 11, 1982, a few weeks before Israel's invasion of Lebanon, Prime Minister Begin presided over a solemn burial in the Judean desert. In a nearby cave some twenty years before, searchers had found human bones which, upon examination, were said to be remains of the followers of Bar Kokhba, a celebrated Jewish hero. In the second century A.D., Bar Kokhba had led a fierce but foredoomed rebellion against the Romans, finishing in catastrophic defeat and exile for the Jewish people. Historians say the rebellion ended the history of the Jews as a nation, until its resumption by Israel eighteen hundred years later. Notwithstanding the catastrophe, Jabotinsky venerated Bar Kokhba for his martial ardor, and even named Betar,* the Revisionist youth movement, after the site of the hero's last stand. As prime minister, Begin later sought Bar Kokhba's sanctification, which troubled many Israelis, who contend that his heritage for the Jews is one of chivalrous ruination. Begin's funeral rites in the desert served to fuel the controversy.

Yehoshafat Harkabi was among those convinced that Bar Kokhba's admirers were sending a grotesque message to Israelis. Born in Israel, Harkabi had been a general, serving as chief of military intelligence. On his retirement, he became a professor at Jerusalem's Hebrew University, specializing in Arab affairs. I had read several of his books, including *Arab Attitudes to Israel,* published in 1972, and I found his positions to be extremely hard-line. Some years later, I visited with Harkabi, and he told me he was still a hard-liner, but convinced now that Israel's survival depended on its reaching an accommodation with its Arab neighbors. Accommodation was the message of a book he wrote in 1983 on the Bar Kokhba controversy, called *The Bar Kokhba Syndrome.*

Harkabi sees in some Israelis' glorification of Bar Kokhba the exaltation of fantasy over reality. He argues that Israelis have been dizzied by the notion of the miraculous—the miracle of Zionism, the miracle of Jewish independence, the miracle of the Six-Day War. It has deprived them of respect for the limitations of a small country and distorted the sense of their own responsibility for their actions.

Ideology and zealotry, Harkabi says, have become a substitute

*Betar is also the initials in Hebrew of Brith Joseph Trumpeldor (Joseph Trumpeldor League), named for an early Zionist thinker and pioneer—and associate of Jabotinsky—who was killed in 1919 defending his kibbutz against Arab attackers.

for reason. Bar Kokhba was indeed heroic, but his rebellion was a disaster. A wrongheaded reading by Israelis of Bar Kokhba's role in history, he argues, has become rationalization for a "policy of vainglory," characterized by contempt for obstacles, underestimation of the adversary, blind faith in the power of will. It indulges a quest for goals beyond Israel's reach.

"Having chosen statehood," Harkabi has written, "our destiny is, to a considerable degree, in our hands, more than at any time since Bar Kokhba. This new situation demands not myths, but sobriety, much self-criticism, and severe critiques of the historical circumstances in which we find ourselves. . . .

"The problem is not how Bar Kokhba committed a mistake—that can be explained—but rather how we have come to admire his mistake, and how it influences our national thinking. By admiring the Bar Kokhba rebellion, we Israelis enmesh ourselves in the predicament of reverencing our people's destruction and rejoicing at an act of national suicide."

As Harkabi suggests, Bar Kokhba's era does not necessarily prefigure our own, but to ignore the warning it offers is irresponsible. Reason tells us that Israel can survive only by being prepared to defend itself; but it tells us as compellingly that Israel cannot survive in a state of perpetual war. In any age, there is surely a limit to miracles. Israel's friends, Jewish and non-Jewish, do it no service by indulging, even by silence, a disposition to self-aggrandizement, to what Harkabi calls a "policy of vainglory."

At best, to create a structure in which Israel can live at peace with its neighbors will be difficult. But the difficulty lies not with the neighbors alone. The lesson of the years since 1967 is that Israel must achieve a sense of proportion that is appropriate to its place in the Middle East. As a goal, the situation of no war, no peace makes little sense. As Harkabi suggests, Israel's security requires the acquisition by Israelis of a recognition of its limitations as a nation. After that, Israel can join its neighbors in search of a stability with which they all can live. That is Israel's best hope for a secure future.

Postscript

THE EDITOR of a prominent Israeli daily, a man who had been in newspapers since the days of the Mandate, once said to me, "We're such a little country, barely three million people, and look how often we're on page one all around the world." The delight he conveyed reflected, admittedly, a newspaperman's peculiar perspective on events. I have some of that perspective myself. But I seriously doubt whether such prominence is good for Israel. The editor might have questioned whether Israel would do better to stay off page one and attend to the business of developing the nation in a less dramatic manner. I was reminded of his comment as this book went to press, because Israel had been on page one without interruption for weeks, and it was not clear what the outcome of the story was going to be.

The events that have dominated the news concern Israel's role as the clandestine conduit for the United States of arms to Iran. For years, reports had circulated that Israel was secretly sending weapons to the Khomeini regime for use in its war against Iraq. Washington's policy throughout these years was officially to embargo sale of its arms to Iran, which meant that any such delivery would have been a violation of U.S. law. Israeli officials routinely denied the reports, and American officials routinely took the position that it had no confirmation of them. During a visit to Washington last September, Prime Minister Peres said, "We do not sell arms to Iran. It would be highly imaginative to believe that Israel looks to Khomeini as the promise of the future or as the promise for Jewish destiny. Let's not exaggerate. . . . [The reports are] completely unfounded." A few weeks later, however, admissions from the White House, in response to a leak of information from Teheran, made clear that Israel, working with agents of the President, had indeed been sending Iran arms. It was further disclosed that payments had been deposited into a secret Swiss bank account and were then illegally used to support Contra forces seeking to overthrow the government of Nicaragua.

As this is written, the story's ramifications have been growing wider from day to day, seriously eroding President Reagan's leadership. Where the ramifications will stop is not predictable. It is known that Israel was the White House's willing collaborator in the shipping of the arms. It seems possible, from the information available, that Israel even initiated the idea. What is unresolved is whether Israel conspired knowingly to make the proceeds from the sales available to the Contras—a violation of American law that may well run it afoul of Congress, and even of law-enforcement agencies. Israel denies it knew where the money was going, and we have seen no evidence to the contrary. Yet, whatever remains to be revealed, many Israelis are deeply troubled by the incident. It raises questions that go directly to the issue of peace with the Arabs, and no less to the issue of the independence of the Jewish state.

That the Israeli government should choose to aid and abet the cause of the Ayatollah Khomeini seems almost to defy belief. In his statement above, Prime Minister Peres conveyed his awareness that Khomeini was no friend of Israel. It is true that in geopolitical terms, Iran is important to Israel. The two countries stand at opposite flanks of the Arab heartland, against which both have fought many wars. But, as Lord Palmerston once said, countries have neither eternal allies nor perpetual enemies, only permanent interests. Though Israel and Iran share a wariness of the Arab world, that is not enough to make them even temporary allies. It made sense for Israel to maintain cordial relations, even a quasi-alliance, with a friendly Shah, but it is quite another thing for Israel to cultivate Khomeini's Iran. The Shah and Khomeini regimes are hardly interchangeable. Khomeini, in the name of militant Islam, has sworn to destroy Israel, and those who take his vow lightly may be making the same mistake as the Jews who in the 1930s chose to dismiss Hitler's *Mein Kampf.*

Remember that Iran has more population in proximity to Israel than all of the Arab states (except Egypt)—Iraq, Syria, Jordan, Lebanon, Libya, Saudi Arabia—*combined.* It is driven by deep religious fanaticism. It sits on one of the world's largest reservoirs of oil and, if it defeats Iraq, it will readily incorporate the nearby sheikhdoms of the Persian Gulf into its orbit, providing it with access to their oil as well. Such control will guarantee Iran as much money as any conceivable military mobilization program requires. Anti-rational, anti-humanist, anti-modern, the Khomeini regime has designs that cannot be contained within the borders of Iran. In Shi'a and Sunni fundamentalists, it has the potential for gathering huge support within the Arab world for a drive against secular Arab regimes and against Zionism. Make no mistake: in Iraq, and through its followers on Israel's Lebanese frontier, it has already begun a campaign of conquest.

Israel has chosen to ignore this threat. It has preferred to treat the Iran-Iraq conflict as an opportunity for weakening the Arabs' potential to make war, rather than as an opportunity for exploring the Arabs' potential to make peace. Ideologically, Israel has far more in common with Iraq, Jordan and even Syria, secular states with a commitment to a better life for their people, than with Iran, a religious state with messianic aims. Strategically, with Arab alliances in disarray, Israel has never had a more favorable time to examine settlement terms. Syria, the strongest of Israel's neighbors, has sided against Iraq in the war, leaving it isolated from most of the Arab world. Jordan, having taken Iraq's side, has been on tense terms with Syria. Iraq has necessarily moved the Arab-Israeli conflict down on its priority list, announcing it will endorse any peace agreement to which the Palestinians subscribe. All of the countries of the region, furthermore, are in a state of economic stress. A decade from now, with the Iran-Iraq war over and oil prices on the rise, Israel might well again be facing a rich, united Arab front.

The reverberating debate over the arms shipments has also exposed strains within the Israeli-American relationship. President Reagan has tried to lay off on Israel some of the blame for what turned out to be a disastrous decision. Congress, long the popular base for Israeli influence in the American government, will not take well to any disclosure that Israel knowingly conspired with the White House to evade the prohibition it established against arming the Contras. If Israel becomes the subject of contention, either between the White House and Congress or within them, the annual American subsidy to the Israeli treasury could fall victim. So far, nothing we have learned about the Iran shipments seems to place the American-Israeli relationship itself in jeopardy. But the incident is surely a warning that American domestic politics, long Israel's source of support, cannot be taken for granted. Israel may wake up some morning to find that it has fallen from favor with a President or with Congress, while all prospect of reconciliation with its neighbors in the region is foreclosed. At that point, it will be in deep trouble indeed.

The Israeli leadership's explanation for sending arms to the Khomeini regime raises a further fundamental question. Peres, serving now as foreign minister under Israel's "rotation" agreement, has continued to be defensive. "We did not sell arms," he told the Knesset. "We received arms and we delivered arms. . . . This is not an Israeli operation. This is a matter for the United States, not for Israel. . . . Israel was asked to help and we did it." If his words suggest that Israel submitted to an American request against its better judgment, it would not be the first time. In 1985, Israel consented to the installation on its territory of a Voice of America transmitter to beam propaganda broadcasts to the Soviet

Union. Some Israelis expressed concern that the decision would provide Moscow with further reason to deny the emigration of Soviet Jews, long an objective of Israeli foreign policy, indeed of Zionism itself. It is no doubt appropriate for Israel to take an extra step to accommodate the United States. A client owes as much to a generous patron. But to accommodate the United States, how often has Israel been asked to violate its better judgment, even its national interests; and what is likely to be asked of it in the future? The arms incident, following on the heels of the transmitter decision, raises the question of whether Israel, in tying itself so closely to American policy, has grown accustomed to compromising its independence.

Washington, D.C.
December 8, 1986

Appendix A

Balfour Declaration (November 2, 1917)

Dear Lord Rothschild,

I have much pleasure in conveying to you, on behalf of His Majesty's Government, the following declaration of sympathy with Jewish Zionist aspirations which has been submitted to, and approved by, the Cabinet.

"His Majesty's Government view with favour the establishment in Palestine of a national home for the Jewish people, and will use their best endeavours to facilitate the achievement of this object, it being clearly understood that nothing shall be done which may prejudice the civil and religious rights of existing non-Jewish communities in Palestine, or the rights and political status enjoyed by Jews in any other country."

I should be grateful if you would bring this declaration to the knowledge of the Zionist Federation.

Yours sincerely,
ARTHUR JAMES BALFOUR.

Appendix B

Israel's Declaration of Independence (May 14, 1948)

Eretz-Israel* was the birthplace of the Jewish people. Here their spiritual, religious and political identity was shaped. Here they first attained to statehood, created cultural values of national and universal significance and gave to the world the eternal Book of Books.

After being forcibly exiled from their land, the people kept faith with it throughout their Dispersion and never ceased to pray and hope for their return to it and for the restoration in it of their political freedom.

Impelled by this historic and traditional attachment, Jews strove in every successive generation to re-establish themselves in their ancient homeland. In recent decades they returned in their masses. Pioneers, *ma'pilim* † and defenders, they made deserts bloom, revived the Hebrew language, built villages and towns, and created a thriving community, controlling its own economy and culture, loving peace but knowing how to defend itself, bringing the blessings of progress to all the country's inhabitants, and aspiring towards independent nationhood.

In the year 5657 (1897), at the summons of the spiritual father of the Jewish State, Theodore Herzl, the First Zionist Congress convened and proclaimed the right of the Jewish people to national rebirth in its own country.

This right was recognised in the Balfour Declaration of the 2nd November, 1917, and re-affirmed in the Mandate of the League of Nations which, in particular, gave international sanction to the historic connection be-

Eretz-Israel (Hebrew)—the Land of Israel, Palestine.

†*Ma'pilim* (Hebrew)—immigrants coming to Eretz-Israel in defiance of restrictive legislation.

tween the Jewish people and Eretz-Israel and to the right of the Jewish people to rebuild its National Home.

The catastrophe which recently befell the Jewish people—the massacre of millions of Jews in Europe—was another clear demonstration of the urgency of solving the problem of its homelessness by re-establishing in Eretz-Israel the Jewish State, which would open the gates of the homeland wide to every Jew and confer upon the Jewish people the status of a fully-privileged member of the comity of nations.

Survivors of the Nazi holocaust in Europe, as well as Jews from other parts of the world, continued to migrate to Eretz-Israel, undaunted by difficulties, restrictions and dangers, and never ceased to assert their right to a life of dignity, freedom and honest toil in their national homeland.

In the Second World War, the Jewish community of this country contributed its full share to the struggle of the freedom and peace-loving nations against the forces of Nazi wickedness and, by the blood of its soldiers and its war effort, gained the right to be reckoned among the peoples who founded the United Nations.

On the 29th November, 1947, the United Nations General Assembly passed a resolution calling for the establishment of a Jewish State in Eretz-Israel; the General Assembly required the inhabitants of Eretz-Israel to take such steps as were necessary on their part for the implementation of that resolution. This recognition by the United Nations of the right of the Jewish people to establish their State is irrevocable.

This right is the natural right of the Jewish people to be masters of their own fate, like all other nations, in their own sovereign State.

ACCORDINGLY WE, MEMBERS OF THE PEOPLE'S COUNCIL, REPRESENTATIVE OF THE JEWISH COMMUNITY OF ERETZ-ISRAEL AND OF THE ZIONIST MOVEMENT, ARE HERE ASSEMBLED ON THE DAY OF THE TERMINATION OF THE BRITISH MANDATE OVER ERETZ-ISRAEL AND, BY VIRTUE OF OUR NATURAL AND HISTORIC RIGHT AND ON THE STRENGTH OF THE RESOLUTION OF THE UNITED NATIONS GENERAL ASSEMBLY, HEREBY DECLARE THE ESTABLISHMENT OF A JEWISH STATE IN ERETZ-ISRAEL, TO BE KNOWN AS THE STATE OF ISRAEL.

WE DECLARE that, with effect from the moment of the termination of the Mandate, being tonight, the eve of Sabbath, the 6th Iyar, 5708 (15th May, 1948), until the establishment of the elected, regular authorities of the State in accordance with the Constitution which shall be adopted by the Elected Constituent Assembly not later than the 1st October 1948, the People's Council shall act as a Provisional Council of State, and its executive organ, the People's Administration, shall be the Provisional Government of the Jewish State, to be called "Israel."

THE STATE OF ISRAEL will be open for Jewish immigration and for the Ingathering of the Exiles; it will foster the development of the country for the benefit of all its inhabitants; it will be based on freedom, justice and peace as envisaged by the prophets of Israel; it will ensure complete equality of social and political rights to all its inhabitants irrespective of religion, race or sex; it will guarantee freedom of religion, conscience, language, education and culture; it will safeguard the Holy Places of all religions; and it will be faithful to the principles of the Charter of the United Nations.

THE STATE OF ISRAEL is prepared to cooperate with the agencies and representatives of the United Nations in implementing the resolution of the General Assembly of the 29th November, 1947, and will take steps to bring about the economic union of the whole of Eretz-Israel.

WE APPEAL to the United Nations to assist the Jewish people in the building-up of its State and to receive the State of Israel into the comity of nations.

WE APPEAL—in the very midst of the onslaught launched against us now for months—to the Arab inhabitants of the State of Israel to preserve peace and participate in the upbuilding of the State on the basis of full and equal citizenship and due representation in all its provisional and permanent institutions.

WE EXTEND our hand to all neighbouring states and their peoples in an offer of peace and good neighbourliness, and appeal to them to establish bonds of cooperation and mutual help with the sovereign Jewish people settled in its own land. The State of Israel is prepared to do its share in a common effort for the advancement of the entire Middle East.

WE APPEAL to the Jewish people throughout the Diaspora to rally round the Jews of Eretz-Israel in the tasks of immigration and upbuilding and to stand by them in the great struggle for the realization of the age-old dream—the redemption of Israel.

PLACING OUR TRUST IN THE ALMIGHTY, WE AFFIX OUR SIGNATURES TO THIS PROCLAMATION AT THIS SESSION OF THE PROVISIONAL COUNCIL OF STATE, ON THE SOIL OF THE HOMELAND, IN THE CITY OF TEL-AVIV, ON THIS SABBATH EVE, THE 5TH DAY OF IYAR, 5708 (14TH MAY, 1948).

David Ben-Gurion

Daniel Auster	Rachel Cohen	David Zvi Pinkas
Mordekhai Bentov	Rabbi Kalman	Aharon Zisling
Yitzchak Ben Zvi	Kahana	Moshe Kolodny

Eliyahu Berligne
Fritz Bernstein
Rabbi Wolf Gold
Meir Grabovsky
Yitzchak Gruenbaum
Dr. Abraham
    Granovsky
Eliyahu Dobkin
Meir Wilner-Kovner
Zerach Wahrhaftig
Herzl Vardi

Saadia Kobashi
Rabbi Yitzchak
    Meir Levin
Meir David
    Loewenstein
Zvi Luria
Golda Myerson
Nachum Nir
Zvi Segal
Rabbi Yehuda Leib
    Hacohen Fishman

Eliezer Kaplan
Abraham Katznelson
Felix Rosenblueth
David Remez
Berl Repetur
Mordekhai Shattner
Ben Zion Sternberg
Bekhor Shitreet
Moshe Shapira
Moshe Shertok

Appendix C

Law of the Return (1950)*

1. Every Jew has the right to immigrate to this country.

2. (a) Immigration shall be by immigrant's visa.

(b) An immigrant's visa shall be given to every Jew who has expressed his desire to settle in Israel, unless the Minister of the Interior is satisfied that the applicant—

    (1) is engaged in an activity directed against the Jewish people; or

    (2) is liable to endanger public health or the security of the State; or

    (3) is a person with a criminal past liable to endanger public welfare.

3. (a) A Jew who comes to Israel and subsequently expresses his desire to settle may, whilst still in Israel, receive an immigrant's certificate.

(b) The exceptions set out in section 2(b) shall also apply to the grant of an immigrant's certificate, provided that a person shall not be considered as endangering public health on account of an illness contracted after his arrival in Israel.

4. Every Jew who immigrated to this country before the commencement of this Law and every Jew born in the country, whether before or after the commencement of this Law, is in the same position as one who immigrated under this Law.

4A. (a) The rights of a Jew under this Law, the rights of an immigrant under the Nationality Law, 1952 and the rights of an immigrant under any other legislation are also granted to the child and grandchild of a Jew,

*As amended in 1954 and 1970.

to the spouse of a Jew and to the spouse of the child and grandchild of a Jew—with the exception of a person who was a Jew and willingly changed his religion.

(b) It makes no difference whether or not the Jew through whom a right is claimed under sub-section (a) is still alive or whether or not he has immigrated to this country.

(c) The exceptions and conditions appertaining to a Jew or an immigrant under or by virtue of this Law or the legislation referred to in sub-section (a) shall also apply to a person claiming any right under sub-section (a).

4B. For the purpose of this Law, "a Jew" means a person born to a Jewish mother or converted to Judaism and who is not a member of another religion.

5. The Minister of the Interior is charged with the implementation of this Law and may make regulations as to any matter relating to its implementation and as to the grant of immigrants' visas and certificates to minors up to the age of 18.

Regulations regarding sections 4A and 4B require the approval of the Constitution, Law and Justice Committee of the Knesset.

Appendix D

Aide-Mémoire of U.S. Secretary of State Dulles (February 11, 1957)

The United Nations General Assembly has sought specifically, vigorously, and almost unanimously, the prompt withdrawal from Egypt of the armed forces of Britain, France and Israel. Britain and France have complied unconditionally. The forces of Israel have been withdrawn to a considerable extent but still hold Egyptian territory at Sharm el Sheikh at the entrance to the Gulf of Aqaba. They also occupy the Gaza Strip which is territory specified by the Armistice arrangements to be occupied by Egypt.

We understand that it is the position of Israel that (1) it will evacuate its military forces from the Gaza Strip provided Israel retains the civil administration and police in some relationship to the United Nations; and (2) it will withdraw from Sharm el Sheikh if continued freedom of passage through the Straits is assured.

With respect to (1) the Gaza Strip—it is the view of the United States that the United Nations General Assembly has no authority to require of either Egypt or Israel a substantial modification of the Armistice Agreement, which, as noted, now gives Egypt the right and responsibility of occupation. Accordingly, we believe that Israeli withdrawal from Gaza should be prompt and unconditional, leaving the future of the Gaza Strip to be worked out through the efforts and good offices of the United Nations.

We recognize that the area has been a source of armed infiltration and reprisals back and forth contrary to the Armistice Agreement and is a source of great potential danger because of the presence there of so large a number of Arab refugees—about 200,000. Accordingly, we believe that the United Nations General Assembly and the Secretary General should seek that the United Nations Emergency Force, in the exercise of its mission, move into this area and be on the boundary between Israel and the Gaza Strip.

The United States will use its best efforts to help to assure this result, which we believe is contemplated by the Second Resolution of February 2, 1957.

With respect to (2) the Gulf of Aqaba and access thereto—the United States believes that the Gulf comprehends international waters and that no nation has the right to prevent free and innocent passage in the Gulf and through the Straits giving access thereto. We have in mind not only commercial usage, but the passage of pilgrims on religious missions, which should be fully respected.

The United States recalls that on January 28, 1950, the Egyptian Ministry of Foreign Affairs informed the United States that the Egyptian occupation of the two islands of Tiran and Senafir at the entrance of the Gulf of Aqaba was only to protect the islands themselves against possible damage or violation and that "this occupation being in no way conceived in a spirit of obstructing in any way innocent passage through the stretch of water separating these two islands from the Egyptian coast of Sinai, it follows that this passage, the only practicable one, will remain free as in the past, in conformity with international practice and recognized principles of the law of nations."

In the absence of some overriding decision to the contrary, as by the International Court of Justice, the United States, on behalf of vessels of United States registry, is prepared to exercise the right of free and innocent passage and to join with others to secure general recognition of this right.

It is of course clear that the enjoyment of a right of free and innocent passage by Israel would depend upon its prior withdrawal in accordance with the United Nations Resolutions. The United States has no reason to assume that any littoral state would under these circumstances obstruct the right of free and innocent passage.

The United States believes that the United Nations General Assembly and the Secretary General should, as a precautionary measure, seek that the United Nations Emergency Force move into the Straits area as the Israeli forces are withdrawn. This again we believe to be within the contemplation of the Second Resolution of February 2, 1957.

(3) The United States observes that the recent resolutions of the United Nations General Assembly call not only for the prompt and unconditional

withdrawal of Israel behind the Armistice lines but call for other measures.

We believe, however, that the United Nations has properly established an order of events and an order of urgency and that the first requirement is that forces of invasion and occupation should withdraw.

The United States is prepared publicly to declare that it will use its influence, in concert with other United Nations members, to the end that, following Israel's withdrawal, these other measures will be implemented.

We believe that our views and purposes in this respect are shared by many other nations and that a tranquil future for Israel is best assured by reliance upon that fact, rather than by an occupation in defiance of the overwhelming judgment of the world community.

Appendix E

Khartoum Declaration (September 1, 1967)

The eight Arab Heads of State who attended the Conference were from the UAR, Saudi Arabia, Sudan, Jordan, Lebanon, Kuwait, Iraq and Yemen. Morocco, Libya, Tunisia and Algeria were represented by their Prime Ministers. Syria, who did not attend, was represented by her Foreign Minister, Dr. Ibrahim Makhous, at the Foreign Ministers' Conference which preceded the Summit and drew up its agenda.

First, the Conference affirmed Arab solidarity and the unification of Arab joint action in a cordial atmosphere of coordination and conciliation.

The Heads of State reaffirmed their commitment to the Charter of Arab Solidarity issued at the Third Arab Summit Conference in Casablanca.

Second, the Conference affirmed the necessity of concerted joint efforts in the elimination of all traces of aggression on the basis that the recovery of all occupied Arab territory is the joint responsibility of all Arab countries.

Third, the Arab Heads of State agreed on unifying their efforts in joint political and diplomatic action at the international level to ensure the withdrawal of Israeli forces from the occupied Arab territory. This is within the framework of the basic Arab commitment, which entails non-recognition of Israel, no conciliation nor negotiation with her and the upholding of the rights of the Palestinian people to their land.

Fourth, the Ministers of Finance, Economy and Oil recommended the possibility of using oil as a weapon in the struggle. The Summit Conference, after careful study, sees that oil export could be used as a positive weapon which would be directed toward the strengthening of the economies of the Arab countries that suffered directly from the aggression.

Fifth, the Conference approved the proposal submitted by Kuwait to establish an Arab Economic and Social Development Bank in accordance with the recommendations of the Arab Finance, Economy and Oil Ministers' Conference which met in Baghdad.

Sixth, the Conference decided that it is necessary to take all steps to consolidate military preparedness to face the consequences of the situation.

Seventh, the Conference decided to speed up the liquidation of foreign bases in the Arab countries.

Appendix F

Security Council Resolution 242 (November 22, 1967)

The Security Council,

Expressing its continuing concern with the grave situation in the Middle East,

Emphasizing the inadmissibility of the acquisition of territory by war and the need to work for a just and lasting peace in which every State in the area can live in security,

Emphasizing further that all Member States in their acceptance of the Charter of the United Nations have undertaken a commitment to act in accordance with Article 2 of the Charter,

1. *Affirms* that the fulfilment of Charter principles requires the establishment of a just and lasting peace in the Middle East which should include the application of both the following principles:

(i) Withdrawal of Israel armed forces from territories occupied in the recent conflict;**

(ii) Termination of all claims or states of belligerency and respect for and acknowledgement of the sovereignty, territorial integrity and political independence of every State in the area and their right to live in peace within secure and recognized boundaries free from threats or acts of force;

2. *Affirms further* the necessity

(a) For guaranteeing freedom of navigation through international waterways in the area;

(b) For achieving a just settlement of the refugee problem;

(c) For guaranteeing the territorial inviolability and political independence of every State in the area, through measures including the establishment of demilitarized zones;

3. *Requests* the Secretary-General to designate a Special Representative to proceed to the Middle East to establish and maintain contacts with the States concerned in order to promote agreement and assist efforts to achieve a peaceful and accepted settlement in accordance with the provisions and principles in this resolution;

4. *Requests* the Secretary-General to report to the Security Council on the progress of the efforts of the Special Representative as soon as possible.

Adopted unanimously at the 1382nd meeting.

Appendix G

Security Council Resolution 338 (October 22, 1973)

The Security Council

1. *Calls upon* all parties to the present fighting to cease all firing and terminate all military activity immediately, no later than 12 hours after the moment of the adoption of this decision, in the positions they now occupy;

2. *Calls upon* the parties concerned to start immediately after the cease-fire the implementation of Security Council resolution 242 (1967) in all of its parts;

3. *Decides* that, immediately and concurrently with the cease-fire, negotiations start between the parties concerned under appropriate auspices aimed at establishing a just and durable peace in the Middle East.

Appendix H

U.S. Pledges to Israel Accompanying Sinai II Accord

I

Memorandum of Agreement Between the Governments of Israel and the United States

September 1, 1975

The United States recognizes that the Egypt-Israel Agreement initialed on September 1, 1975, (hereinafter referred to as the Agreement), entailing the withdrawal from vital areas in Sinai, constitutes an act of great significance on Israel's part in the pursuit of final peace. That Agreement has full United States support.

United States–Israeli Assurances

1. The United States Government will make every effort to be fully responsive, within the limits of its resources and Congressional authorization and appropriation, on an on-going and long-term basis to Israel's military equipment and other defense requirements, to its energy requirements and to its economic needs. The needs specified in paragraphs 2, 3 and 4 below shall be deemed eligible for inclusion within the annual total to be requested in FY76 and later fiscal years.

2. Israel's long-term military supply needs from the United States shall be the subject of periodic consultations between representatives of the United States and Israeli defense establishments, with agreement reached on specific items to be included in a separate United States-Israeli memorandum. To this end, a joint study by military experts will be undertaken within 3 weeks. In conducting this study, which will include Israel's

1976 needs, the United States will view Israel's requests sympathetically, including its request for advanced and sophisticated weapons.

3. Israel will make its own independent arrangements for oil supply to meet its requirements through normal procedures. In the event Israel is unable to secure its needs in this way, the United States Government, upon notification of this fact by the Government of Israel, will act as follows for five years, at the end of which period either side can terminate this arrangement on one-year's notice.

(a) If the oil Israel needs to meet all its normal requirements for domestic consumption is unavailable for purchase in circumstances where no quantitative restrictions exist on the ability of the United States to procure oil to meet its normal requirements, the United States Government will promptly make oil available for purchase by Israel to meet all of the aforementioned normal requirements of Israel. If Israel is unable to secure the necessary means to transport such oil to Israel, the United States Government will make every effort to help Israel secure the necessary means of transport.

(b) If the oil Israel needs to meet all of its normal requirements for domestic consumption is unavailable for purchase in circumstances where quantitative restrictions through embargo or otherwise also prevent the United States from procuring oil to meet its normal requirements, the United States Government will promptly make oil available for purchase by Israel in accordance with the International Energy Agency conservation and allocation formula as applied by the United States Government, in order to meet Israel's essential requirements. If Israel is unable to secure the necessary means to transport such oil to Israel, the United States Government will make every effort to help Israel secure the necessary means of transport.

Israeli and United States experts will meet annually or more frequently at the request of either party, to review Israel's continuing oil requirement.

4. In order to help Israel meet its energy needs, and as part of the overall annual figure in paragraph 1 above, the United States agrees:

(a) In determining the overall annual figure which will be requested from Congress, the United States Government will give special attention to Israel's oil import requirements and, for a period as determined by Article 3 above, will take into account in calculating that figure Israel's additional expenditures for the import of oil to replace that which would have ordinarily come from Abu Rodeis and Ras Sudar (4.5 million tons in 1975).

(b) To ask Congress to make available funds, the amount to be determined by mutual agreement, to the Government of Israel necessary for a project for the construction and stocking of the oil reserves to be stored in Israel, bringing storage reserve capacity and reserve stocks now standing at approximately six months, up to one-year's need at the time of the completion of the project. The project will be implemented within four years. The construction, operation and financing and other relevant questions of the project will be the subject of early and detailed talks between the two Governments.

5.   The United States Government will not expect Israel to begin to implement the Agreement before Egypt fulfils its undertaking under the January 1974 Disengagement Agreement to permit passage of all Israeli cargoes to and from Israeli ports through the Suez Canal.

6.   The United States Government agrees with Israel that the next agreement with Egypt should be a final peace agreement.

7.   In case of an Egyptian violation of any of the provisions of the Agreement, the United States Government is prepared to consult with Israel as to the significance of the violation and possible remedial action by the United States Government.

8.   The United States Government will vote against any Security Council resolution which in its judgment affects or alters adversely the Agreement.

9.   The United States Government will not join in and will seek to prevent efforts by others to bring about consideration of proposals which it and Israel agree are detrimental to the interests of Israel.

10.   In view of the long-standing United States commitment to the survival and security of Israel, the United States Government will view with particular gravity threats to Israel's security or sovereignty by a world power. In support of this objective, the United States Government will in the event of such threat consult promptly with the Government of Israel with respect to what support, diplomatic or otherwise, or assistance it can lend to Israel in accordance with its constitutional practices.

11.   The United States Government and the Government of Israel will, at the earliest possible time, and if possible, within two months after the signature of this document, conclude the contingency plan for a military supply operation to Israel in an emergency situation.

12.   It is the United States Government's position that Egyptian commitments under the Egypt-Israel Agreement, its implementation, validity and duration are not conditional upon any act or developments between the other Arab states and Israel. The United States Government regards the Agreement as standing on its own.

13.   The United States Government shares the Israeli position that under existing political circumstances negotiations with Jordan will be directed toward an overall peace settlement.

14. In accordance with the principle of freedom of navigation on the high seas and free and unimpeded passage through and over straits connecting international waters, the United States Government regards the Straits of Bab-el-Mandeb and the Strait of Gibraltar as international waterways. It will support Israel's right to free and unimpeded passage through such straits. Similarly, the United States Government recognizes Israel's right to freedom of flights over the Red Sea and such straits and will support diplomatically the exercise of that right.

15. In the event that the United Nations Emergency Force or any other United Nations organ is withdrawn without the prior agreement of both Parties to the Egypt-Israel Agreement and the United States before this Agreement is superseded by another agreement, it is the United States view that the Agreement shall remain binding in all its parts.

16. The United States and Israel agree that signature of the Protocol of the Egypt-Israel Agreement and its full entry into effect shall not take place before approval by the United States Congress of the United States role in connection with the surveillance and observation functions described in the Agreement and its Annex. The United States has informed the Government of Israel that it has obtained the Government of Egypt agreement to the above.

Yigal Allon
Deputy Prime Minister and
Minister of Foreign Affairs

For the Government of Israel

Henry A. Kissinger
Secretary of State

For the Government of
the United States

II

Memorandum of Agreement Between the Governments of Israel and the United States on the Geneva Peace Conference

1. The Geneva Peace Conference will be reconvened at a time coordinated between the United States and Israel.

2. The United States will continue to adhere to its present policy with respect to the Palestine Liberation Organization, whereby it will not recognize or negotiate with the Palestine Liberation Organization so long as the Palestine Liberation Organization does not recognize Israel's right to exist and does not accept Security Council Resolutions 242 and 338.

The United States Government will consult fully and seek to concert its position and strategy at the Geneva Peace Conference on this issue with the Government of Israel. Similarly, the United States will consult fully and seek to concert its position and strategy with Israel with regard to the participation of any other additional states. It is understood that the participation at a subsequent phase of the Conference of any possible additional state, group or organization will require the agreement of all the initial participants.

3. The United States will make every effort to ensure at the Conference that all the substantive negotiations will be on a bilateral basis.

4. The United States will oppose and, if necessary, vote against any initiative in the Security Council to alter adversely the terms of reference of the Geneva Peace Conference or to change Resolutions 242 and 338 in ways which are incompatible with their original purpose.

5. The United States will seek to ensure that the role of the cosponsors will be consistent with what was agreed in the Memorandum of Understanding between the United States Government and the Government of Israel of December 20, 1973.

6. The United States and Israel will concert action to assure that the Conference will be conducted in a manner consonant with the objectives of this document and with the declared purpose of the Conference, namely the advancement of a negotiated peace between Israel and each one of its neighbors.

Yigal Allon	Henry A. Kissinger
Deputy Prime Minister and	Secretary of State
Minister of Foreign Affairs	
For the Government of Israel	For the Government of the United States

III

Assurances from the United States to Israel

On the question of military and economic assistance to Israel, the following conveyed by the U.S. to Israel augments what the Memorandum of Agreement states.

The United States is resolved to continue to maintain Israel's defensive strength through the supply of advanced types of equipment, such as the F-16 aircraft. The United States Government agrees to an early meeting to undertake a joint study of high technology and sophisticated items, including the Pershing ground-to-ground missiles with conventional warheads, with the view to giving a positive response. The U.S. Administration will submit annually for approval by the U.S. Congress a request for military and economic assistance in order to help meet Israel's economic and military needs.

Appendix I

Excerpts from Camp David Frameworks for Peace (September 17, 1978)

Preamble

The search for peace in the Middle East must be guided by the following:

—The agreed basis for a peaceful settlement of the conflict between Israel and its neighbors is United Nations Security Council Resolution 242, in all its parts.

—After four wars during thirty years, despite intensive human efforts, the Middle East, which is the cradle of civilization and the birthplace of three great religions, does not yet enjoy the blessings of peace. The people of the Middle East yearn for peace so that the vast human and natural resources of the region can be turned to the pursuits of peace and so that this area can become a model for coexistence and cooperation among nations.

—The historic initiative of President Sadat in visiting Jerusalem and the reception accorded to him by the Parliament, government and people of Israel, and the reciprocal visit of Prime Minister Begin to Ismailia, the peace proposals made by both leaders, as well as the warm reception of these missions by the people of both countries, have created an unprecedented opportunity for peace which must not be lost if this generation and future generations are to be spared the tragedies of war.

—The provisions of the Charter of the United Nations and the other accepted norms of international law and legitimacy now provide accepted standards for the conduct of relations among the states.

—To achieve a relationship of peace, in the spirit of Article 2 of the United Nations Charter, future negotiations between Israel and any neighbor prepared to negotiate peace and security with it, are necessary for the purpose of carrying out all the provisions and principles of Resolutions 242 and 338.

—Peace requires respect for the sovereignty, territorial integrity and political independence of every state in the area and their right to live in peace within secure and recognized boundaries free from threats or acts of force. Progress toward that goal can accelerate movement toward a new era of reconciliation in the Middle East marked by cooperation in promoting economic development, in maintaining stability, and in assuring security.

—Security is enhanced by a relationship of peace and by cooperation between nations which enjoy normal relations. In addition, under the terms of peace treaties, the parties can, on the basis of reciprocity, agree to special security arrangements such as demilitarized zones, limited armaments areas, early warning stations, the presence of international forces, liaison, agreed measures for monitoring, and other arrangements that they agree are useful.

Framework

Taking these factors into account, the parties are determined to reach a just, comprehensive, and durable settlement of the Middle East conflict through the conclusion of peace treaties based on Security Council Resolutions 242 and 338 in all their parts. Their purpose is to achieve peace and good neighborly relations. They recognize that, for peace to endure, it must involve all those who have been most deeply affected by the conflict. They therefore agree that this framework as appropriate is intended by them to constitute a basis for peace not only between Egypt and Israel, but also between Israel and each of its other neighbors which is prepared to negotiate peace with Israel on this basis. With that objective in mind, they have agreed to proceed as follows:

A. West Bank and Gaza

1. Egypt, Israel, Jordan and the representatives of the Palestinian people should participate in negotiations on the resolution of the Palestinian problem in all its aspects. To achieve that objective, negotiations relating to the West Bank and Gaza should proceed in three stages:

(a) Egypt and Israel agree that, in order to ensure a peaceful and orderly transfer of authority, and taking into account the security concerns of all the parties, there should be transitional arrangements for the West Bank and Gaza for a period not exceeding five years. In order to provide full autonomy to the inhabitants, under these arrangements the Israeli military government and its civilian administration will be withdrawn as soon as a self-governing authority has been freely elected by the inhabitants of these areas to replace the existing military government. To negotiate the details of a transitional arrangement, the Government of Jordan will be invited to join the negotiations on the basis of this framework. These new arrangements should give due consideration both to the principle of self-government by the inhabitants of these territories and to the legitimate security concerns of the parties involved.

(b) Egypt, Israel, and Jordan will agree on the modalities for establishing the elected self-governing authority in the West Bank and Gaza. The delegations of Egypt and Jordan may include Palestinians from the West Bank and Gaza or other Palestinians as mutually agreed. The parties will negotiate an agreement which will define the powers and responsibilities of the self-governing authority to be exercised in the West Bank and Gaza. A withdrawal of Israeli armed forces will take place and there will be a redeployment of the remaining Israeli forces into specified security locations. The agreement will also include arrangements for assuring internal and external security and public order. A strong local police force will be established, which may include Jordanian citizens. In addition, Israeli and Jordanian forces will participate in joint patrols and in the manning of control posts to assure the security of the borders.

(c) When the self-governing authority (administrative council) in the West Bank and Gaza is established and inaugurated, the transitional period of five years will begin. As soon as possible, but not later than the third year after the beginning of the transitional period, negotiations will take place to determine the final status of the West Bank and Gaza and its relationship with its neighbors, and to conclude a peace treaty between Israel and Jordan by the end of the transitional period. These negotiations will be conducted among Egypt, Israel, Jordan, and the elected representatives of the inhabitants of the West Bank and Gaza. Two separate but related committees will be convened, one committee, consisting of representatives of the four parties which will negotiate and agree on the final status of the West Bank and Gaza, and its relationship with its neighbors, and the second committee, consisting of representatives of Israel and representatives of Jordan to be joined by the elected representatives of the inhabitants of the West Bank and Gaza, to negotiate the peace treaty between Israel and Jordan, taking into account the agreement reached on the final status of the West Bank and Gaza. The negotiations shall be based on all the provisions and principles of UN Security Council Resolution 242. The negotiations will resolve, among other matters, the location of the boundaries and the nature of the security arrangements. The solution from the negotiations must also recognize the legitimate rights of the Palestinian people and their just requirements. In this way, the Palestinians will participate in the determination of their own future through:

1) The negotiations among Egypt, Israel, Jordan and the representatives of the inhabitants of the West Bank and Gaza to agree on the final status of the West Bank and Gaza and other outstanding issues by the end of the transitional period.

2) Submitting their agreement to a vote by the elected representatives of the inhabitants of the West Bank and Gaza.

3) Providing for the elected representatives of the inhabitants of the West Bank and Gaza to decide how they shall govern themselves consistent with the provisions of their agreement.

4) Participating as stated above in the work of the committee negotiating the peace treaty between Israel and Jordan.

All necessary measures will be taken and provisions made to assure the security of Israel and its neighbors during the transitional period and beyond. To assist in providing such security, a strong local police force will be constituted by the self-governing authority. It will be composed of inhabitants of the West Bank and Gaza. The police will maintain continuing liaison on internal security matters with the designated Israeli, Jordanian, and Egyptian officers.

During the transitional period, representatives of Egypt, Israel, Jordan, and the self-governing authority will constitute a continuing committee to decide by agreement on the modalities of admission of persons displaced from the West Bank and Gaza in 1967, together with necessary measures to prevent disruption and disorder. Other matters of common concern may also be dealt with by this committee.

Egypt and Israel will work with each other and with other interested parties to establish agreed procedures for a prompt, just and permanent implementation of the resolution of the refugee problem.

B. Egypt-Israel

1. Egypt and Israel undertake not to resort to the threat or the use of force to settle disputes. Any disputes shall be settled by peaceful means in

accordance with the provisions of Article 33 of the Charter of the United Nations.

2. In order to achieve peace between them, the parties agree to negotiate in good faith with a goal of concluding within three months from the signing of this Framework a peace treaty between them, while inviting the other parties to the conflict to proceed simultaneously to negotiate and conclude similar peace treaties with a view to achieving a comprehensive peace in the area. The Framework for the Conclusion of a Peace Treaty between Egypt and Israel will govern the peace negotiations between them. The parties will agree on the modalities and the timetable for the implementation of their obligations under the treaty.

C. Associated Principles

1. Egypt and Israel state that the principles and provisions described below should apply to peace treaties between Israel and each of its neighbors—Egypt, Jordan, Syria, and Lebanon.

2. Signatories shall establish among themselves relationships normal to states at peace with one another. To this end, they should undertake to abide by all the provisions of the Charter of the United Nations. Steps to be taken in this respect include:

(a) full recognition;

(b) abolishing economic boycotts;

(c) guaranteeing that under their jurisdiction the citizens of the other parties shall enjoy the protection of the due process of the law.

3. Signatories should explore possibilities for economic development in the context of final peace treaties, with the objective of contributing to the atmosphere of peace, cooperation and friendship which is their common goal.

4. Claims Commissions may be established for the mutual settlement of all financial claims.

5. The United States shall be invited to participate in the talks on matters related to the modalities of the implementation of the agreements and working out the timetable for the carrying out of the obligations of the parties.

6. The United Nations Security Council shall be requested to endorse the peace treaties and ensure that their provisions shall not be violated. The permanent members of the Security Council shall be requested to underwrite the peace treaties and ensure respect for their provisions. They shall also be requested to conform their policies and actions with the undertakings contained in this Framework.

. . . The following matters are agreed between the parties:

(a) the full exercise of Egyptian sovereignty up to the internationally recognized border between Egypt and mandated Palestine;

(b) the withdrawal of Israeli armed forces from the Sinai;

(c) the use of airfields left by the Israelis near El Arish, Rafah, Ras en Naqb, and Sharm el Sheikh for civilian purposes only, including possible commercial use by all nations;

(d) the right of free passage by ships of Israel through the Gulf of Suez and the Suez Canal on the basis of the Constantinople Convention of 1888 applying to all nations; the Strait of Tiran and the Gulf of Aqaba are international waterways to be open to all nations for unimpeded and non-suspendable freedom of navigation and overflight;

(e) the construction of a highway between the Sinai and Jordan near Elat with guaranteed free and peaceful passage by Egypt and Jordan; and

(f) the stationing of military forces listed below.

Stationing of Forces

A. No more than one division (mechanized or infantry) of Egyptian armed forces will be stationed within an area lying approximately 50 kilometers (km) east of the Gulf of Suez and the Suez Canal.

B. Only United Nations forces and civil police equipped with light weapons to perform normal police functions will be stationed within an area lying west of the international border and the Gulf of Aqaba, varying in width from 20 km to 40 km.

C. In the area within 3 km east of the international border there will be Israeli limited military forces not to exceed four infantry battalions and United Nations observers.

D. Border patrol units, not to exceed three battalions, will supplement the civil police in maintaining order in the area not included above.

The exact demarcation of the above areas will be as decided during the peace negotiations.

Early warning stations may exist to ensure compliance with the terms of the agreement.

United Nations forces will be stationed: (a) in part of the area in the Sinai lying within about 20 km of the Mediterranean Sea and adjacent to the international border, and (b) in the Sharm el Sheikh area to ensure freedom of passage through the Strait of Tiran; and these forces will not be removed unless such removal is approved by the Security Council of the United Nations with a unanimous vote of the five permanent members.

After a peace treaty is signed, and after the interim withdrawal is complete, normal relations will be established between Egypt and Israel, including: full recognition, including diplomatic, economic and cultural relations; termination of economic boycotts and barriers to the free movement of goods and people; and mutual protection of citizens by the due process of law.

Appendix J

Egyptian-Israeli Peace Treaty (March 26, 1979)

The Government of the Arab Republic of Egypt and the Government of the State of Israel:

Preamble

Convinced of the urgent necessity of the establishment of a just, comprehensive and lasting peace in the Middle East in accordance with Security Council Resolutions 242 and 338;

Reaffirming their adherence to the "Framework for Peace in the Middle East Agreed at Camp David," dated September 17, 1978;

Noting that the aforementioned Framework as appropriate is intended to constitute a basis for peace not only between Egypt and Israel but also between Israel and each of its other Arab neighbors which is prepared to negotiate peace with it on this basis;

Desiring to bring to an end the state of war between them and to establish a peace in which every state in the area can live in security;

Convinced that the conclusion of a Treaty of Peace between Egypt and Israel is an important step in the search for comprehensive peace in the area and for the attainment of the settlement of the Arab-Israeli conflict in all its aspects;

Inviting the other Arab parties to this dispute to join the peace process with Israel guided by and based on the principles of the aforementioned Framework;

Desiring as well to develop friendly relations and cooperation between themselves in accordance with the United Nations Charter and the principles of international law governing international relations in times of peace;

Agree to the following provisions in the free exercise of their sovereignty, in order to implement the "Framework for the Conclusion of a Peace Treaty Between Egypt and Israel:"

Article I

1. The state of war between the Parties will be terminated and peace will be established between them upon the exchange of instruments of ratification of this Treaty.

2. Israel will withdraw all its armed forces and civilians from the Sinai behind the international boundary between Egypt and mandated Palestine, as provided in the annexed protocol (Annex I), and Egypt will resume the exercise of its full sovereignty over the Sinai.

3. Upon completion of the interim withdrawal provided for in Annex I, the Parties will establish normal and friendly relations, in accordance with Article III(3).

Article II

The permanent boundary between Egypt and Israel is the recognized international boundary between Egypt and the former mandated territory of Palestine, as shown on the map at Annex II, without prejudice to the issue of the status of the Gaza Strip. The Parties recognize this boundary as inviolable. Each will respect the territorial integrity of the other, including their territorial waters and airspace.

Article III

1. The Parties will apply between them the provisions of the Charter of the United Nations and the principles of international law governing relations among states in times of peace. In particular:

a. They recognize and will respect each other's sovereignty, territorial integrity and political independence;

b. They recognize and will respect each other's right to live in peace within their secure and recognized boundaries;

c. They will refrain from the threat or use of force, directly or indirectly, against each other and will settle all disputes between them by peaceful means.

2. Each Party undertakes to ensure that acts or threats of belligerency, hostility, or violence do not originate from and are not committed from within its territory, or by any forces subject to its control or by any other forces stationed on its territory, against the population, citizens or prop-

erty of the other Party. Each Party also undertakes to refrain from organizing, instigating, inciting, assisting or participating in acts or threats of belligerency, hostility, subversion or violence against the other Party, anywhere, and undertakes to ensure that perpetrators of such acts are brought to justice.

3. The Parties agree that the normal relationship established between them will include full recognition, diplomatic, economic and cultural relations, termination of economic boycotts and discriminatory barriers to the free movement of people and goods, and will guarantee the mutual enjoyment by citizens of the due process of law. The process by which they undertake to achieve such a relationship parallel to the implementation of other provisions of this Treaty is set out in the annexed protocol (Annex III).

Article IV

1. In order to provide maximum security for both Parties on the basis of reciprocity, agreed security arrangements will be established including limited force zones in Egyptian and Israeli territory, and United Nations forces and observers, described in detail as to nature and timing in Annex I, and other security arrangements the Parties may agree upon.

2. The Parties agree to the stationing of United Nations personnel in areas described in Annex I. The Parties agree not to request withdrawal of the United Nations personnel and that these personnel will not be removed unless such removal is approved by the Security Council of the United Nations, with the affirmative vote of the five Permanent Members, unless the Parties otherwise agree.

3. A Joint Commission will be established to facilitate the implementation of the Treaty, as provided for in Annex I.

4. The security arrangements provided for in paragraphs 1 and 2 of this Article may at the request of either party be reviewed and amended by mutual agreement of the Parties.

Article V

1. Ships of Israel, and cargoes destined for or coming from Israel, shall enjoy the right of free passage through the Suez Canal and its approaches through the Gulf of Suez and the Mediterranean Sea on the basis of the Constantinople Convention of 1888, applying to all nations. Israeli nationals, vessels and cargoes, as well as persons, vessels and cargoes destined for or coming from Israel, shall be accorded non-discriminatory treatment in all matters connected with usage of the canal.

2. The Parties consider the Strait of Tiran and the Gulf of Aqaba to be international waterways open to all nations for unimpeded and nonsuspendable freedom of navigation and overflight. The Parties will respect each other's right to navigation and overflight for access to either country through the Strait of Tiran and the Gulf of Aqaba.

Article VI

1. This Treaty does not affect and shall not be interpreted as affecting in any way the rights and obligations of the Parties under the Charter of the United Nations.

2. The Parties undertake to fulfill in good faith their obligations under this Treaty, without regard to action or inaction of any other party and independently of any instrument external to this Treaty.

3. They further undertake to take all the necessary measures for the application in their relations of the provisions of the multilateral conventions to which they are parties, including the submission of appropriate notification to the Secretary General of the United Nations and other depositaries of such conventions.

4. The Parties undertake not to enter into any obligations in conflict with this Treaty.

5. Subject to Article 103 of the United Nations Charter, in the event of a conflict between the obligations of the Parties under the present Treaty and any of their other obligations, the obligations under this Treaty will be binding and implemented.

Article VII

1. Disputes arising out of the application or interpretation of this Treaty shall be resolved by negotiations.

2. Any such disputes which cannot be settled by negotiations shall be resolved by conciliation or submitted to arbitration.

Article VIII

The Parties agree to establish a claims commission for the mutual settlement of all financial claims.

Article IX

1. This Treaty shall enter into force upon exchange of instruments of ratification.

2. This Treaty supersedes the Agreement between Egypt and Israel of September, 1975.

3. All protocols, annexes, and maps attached to this Treaty shall be regarded as an integral part hereof.

4. The Treaty shall be communicated to the Secretary General of the United Nations for registration in accordance with the provisions of Article 102 of the Charter of the United Nations.

Done at Washington, D.C. this 26th day of March, 1979, in triplicate in the English, Arabic, and Hebrew languages, each text being equally authentic. In case of any divergence of interpretation, the English text shall prevail.

For the Government of the Arab Republic of Egypt:
    A. Sadat

For the Government of Israel:
    M. Begin

Witnessed by:

    Jimmy Carter
    Jimmy Carter, President of
    the United States of America

Appendix K

Excerpts from U.S.-Israel Memorandum of Understanding (November 30, 1981)

Preamble

This Memorandum of Understanding reaffirms the common bonds of friendship between the United States and Israel and builds on the mutual security relationship that exists between the two nations. The Parties recognize the need to enhance strategic cooperation to deter all threats from the Soviet Union in the region. Noting the long-standing and fruitful cooperation for mutual security that has developed between the two countries, the Parties have decided to establish a framework for continued consultation and cooperation to enhance their national security by deterring such threats in the whole region.

The Parties have reached the following agreements in order to achieve the above aims:

Article I

United States-Israeli strategic cooperation, as set forth in this Memorandum, is designed against the threat to peace and security of the region caused by the Soviet Union or Soviet-controlled forces from outside the region introduced into the region. It has the following broad purposes:

A. To enable the Parties to act cooperatively and in a timely manner to deal with the above mentioned threat;

B. To provide each other with military assistance for operations of their forces in the area that may be required to cope with this threat;

C. The strategic cooperation between the Parties is not directed at any

State or group of States within the region. It is intended solely for defensive purposes against the above mentioned threat.

Article II

1. The fields in which strategic cooperation will be carried out to prevent the above mentioned threat from endangering the security of the region include:

A. Military cooperation between the Parties, as may be agreed by the Parties;

B. Joint military exercises, including naval and air exercises in the eastern Mediterranean Sea, as agreed upon by the Parties;

C. Cooperation for the establishment and maintenance of joint readiness activities, as agreed upon by the Parties;

D. Other areas within the basic scope and purpose of this agreement, as may be jointly agreed.